The Diversity Scorecard:
Evaluating the Impact of Diversity on Organizational Performance

The Diversity Scorecard:
Evaluating the Impact of Diversity
on Organizational Performance

Edward E. Hubbard, Ph.D.

ELSEVIER
BUTTERWORTH
HEINEMANN

An Imprint of Elsevier

Amsterdam Boston Heidelberg London New York Oxford Paris
San Diego San Francisco Singapore Sydney Tokyo

Elsevier Butterworth–Heinemann
200 Wheeler Road, Burlington, MA 01803, USA
Linacre House, Jordan Hill, Oxford OX2 8DP, UK

Recognizing the importance of preserving what has been written, Elsevier prints its books on acid-free paper whenever possible.

Library of Congress Cataloging-in-Publication Data

Hubbard, Edward E.
    The diversity scorecard / Edward E. Hubbard.
        p. cm.
    Includes bibliographical references and index.
    ISBN 0-7506-7457-1
    1. Diversity in the workplace—Measurement. I. Title.

    HF5549.5.M5H828 2003
    658.3′008—dc22

                                                                    2003055685

British Library Cataloguing-in-Publication Data
A catalogue record for this book is available from the British Library.

For information on all Butterworth–Heinemann publications
visit our website at www.bh.com

03 04 05 06 07 08 09 10 9 8 7 6 5 4 3 2 1

Printed in the United States of America

Contents

PART II   The Diversity Return-on-Investment (DROI) Process

C H A P T E R   3

C H A P T E R   4

C H A P T E R   5

C H A P T E R   6

Options, 115. Institutionalizing Your Scorecard System, 115. Final
Thoughts, 116. Reference, 117. Further Reading, 117.

PART III   Building a Diversity Scorecard

CHAPTER 7

CHAPTER 8

CHAPTER 9

CHAPTER 10

CHAPTER 11

PART IV   Implementation Issues

Foreword

Diversity has become one of the most important issues of the 21st century, commanding much attention in the popular press, conferences, magazines, and the executive suite. We are pleased to include Ed Hubbard's book, *The Diversity Scorecard*, in our *Improving Human Performance* series.

Recognizing the importance of having diverse work teams, executives are exploring ways to enhance diversity. In recent years, measuring the impact of diversity initiatives has become an important issue. Some professionals often argue that you cannot (or should not) measure the ROI on diversity. Others argue that it is possible (and necessary) to measure the ROI on the outcomes of diversity programs or initiatives. Ed is in the second group with this one-of-a-kind book.

While there are many approaches to diversity, executives usually address the issue from one of two perspectives. Some take the reactive approach—the defensive posture—arguing that diversity is necessary for compliance and to avoid discrimination complaints. Others take the proactive approach. They argue that a diverse group is more valuable to the organization and that the impact of diversity, in business terms, should drive decisions for investing more in this important process. Ed has devoted most of his career to taking the proactive approach, showing the impact and value of a diverse workforce.

Ed tackles the diversity measurement issue from all sides. He applies the ROI process, captured in several of our books on ROI, to the issue of diversity. This process generates six types of data: reaction, learning, application, impact, ROI, and intangible data. Ed also relates the measurement of diversity to the balanced scorecard process originally developed by Kaplan and Norton. This in-depth coverage essentially makes this a very important book on measurement—a diversity accountability handbook.

No other person is better suited to develop this book. Ed combines an ideal background for this challenging assignment. First, he has had a tremendous amount of organizational experience in human resources and diversity; he writes from experience. Next, Ed is a very successful diversity consultant, assisting all types of organizations to plan diversity initiatives, literally all over the world. Third, Ed has a passion for measurement and evaluation. He has become certified in the ROI methodology and has applied measurement concepts to all types of diversity initiatives. Fourth, Ed has much research and publication experience. His previous books are great additions to diversity, human resources, and management. Finally, Ed's education has prepared him well for this assignment. He has strong academic training along with important research skills. When considered in its entirety, Ed's background is the perfect backdrop from which to develop such an important and useful tool.

This new book should be a valuable reference for anyone interested in building a powerful team. Whether in management, human resources, or a special assignment dedicated to harnessing the ingenuity and innovation of people, this is the book to read. It's a great "go-to" book that shows, step by step, how to tackle many of the key issues of diversity measurement, showing the accountability of a variety of diversity initiatives. Embracing the differences along with the commonalities of our human capital makes our organizations stronger. Now there's a book showing how to measure the strength and success of diversity in the workplace. Please enjoy this new addition to the IHP series. As always, if you have any comments or concerns, let us know.

Jack Phillips

Preface

THE PURPOSE OF THIS BOOK

Senior leaders and diversity professionals are eager to see practical applications of the models, techniques, theories, strategies, and issues that constitute the diversity arena. In recent years, diversity practitioners have developed an intense desire to learn about diversity measurement strategies that create compelling evidence that highlights how diversity adds value to organizational performance and the bottom line. This book is intended to fill some of that need. Each chapter covers key aspects of a diversity measurement scorecard process and outlines a comprehensive return-on-investment system that helps identify diversity's contribution to the organization's bottom line in financial terms. It will provide step-by-step diversity scorecard processes that are proven to work in the real environment of the workplace.

This book addresses the question: How can diversity practitioners measure their contribution to the organization's strategy implementation and therefore be "at" the table, not "on" the table. Effective diversity measures serve at least two purposes: (1) they should help guide decision making throughout the organization, and (2) they serve as a basis for evaluating performance. The diversity measurement strategies utilized here address these two purposes in three ways.

First, these strategies encourage a clear, consistent, and shared view of how an organization can implement its strategy at each level in the organization. They won't guarantee that every employee will be able to articulate the entire value creation process and how diversity plays a role; however, these strategies should ensure that each employee has a clear understanding of his or her own role in the process. The approaches used will help build consensus around how different elements within the organization contribute to its value creation.

Second, the approach in this book forces diversity professionals and others who use it to concentrate on the vital few measures that really make a difference. Anyone can easily generate 50 or more measures of organizational performance across a variety of categories, but this exercise would be counterproductive because too many measures are difficult to track. A truly effective measurement system usually contains no more than 20 to 25 measures. These measures are spread across a balanced framework of strategic perspectives using lead and lag indicators that change as conditions require. Selecting the vital few measures is important; however, organizations will need a full complement of measures to select from to make informed choices about what vital few are needed to create a comprehensive picture of performance as conditions change.

Third, this approach lets the diversity practitioner express the vital few measures in terms that line managers and senior executives will understand and value. In diversity, conventional measures of cost control, such as hours of diversity training, time-to-fill rates, employee turnover numbers, and even employee satisfaction, will continue to lack credibility unless they are shown to influence key performance drivers in the organization.

How This Book Is Organized

The fundamental structure of this book reflects a basic process for implementing a diversity scorecard measurement system in your organization. It is divided into four critical parts to help build knowledge and basic skills as you proceed.

Part I provides an understanding of the need for diversity measurement. It provides an informational and statistical business case for diversity and addresses some critical measurement issues that help you gain a solid foothold to establish diversity's link to the organization's strategy. This information will be covered in Chapters 1 and 2.

Part II presents the diversity return-on-investment (DROI) model in a step-by-step process. An overview of the model is discussed in segments across three chapters. After an introduction to the model in Chapter 3, Chapter 4 outlines the model's planning and data collection processes. Chapter 5 explores the model's techniques for evaluating diversity's contribution to the bottom line, and Chapter 6 wraps up Part II of the book with methods and software tools to track and assess your progress. A detailed discussion of the entire DROI model can be found in the book *How to Calculate Diversity Return on Investment* by Dr. Edward Hubbard. At the conclusion, the reader has a clear understanding of the overall DROI process. Examples are used to explain key elements of the model and to enhance application strategies in the organization.

Part III provides the basic building blocks for assembling a diversity scorecard of the DROI process results to report diversity's contribution. Each diversity scorecard index perspective is explained in detail in Chapters 7 through 13, and critical measures and processes clarify its use. Chapter 14 wraps up Part III with steps to create a Diversity Scorecard and highlights sample Diversity Scorecards for the private (for-profit), public, and not-for-profit sectors.

Part IV examines some key implementation issues that must be addressed to embed diversity into the fabric of the organization. A discussion of strategies and tactics to address these issues is covered in Chapters 15 and 16. In addition, a list of resources and tools to support the development and implementation of the Diversity Scorecard are available in the Appendix.

Each major part of this book will help you gain a level of level of diversity measurement competence to ultimately compile a basic scorecard.

WHO SHOULD READ THIS BOOK

This book is written for anyone who wants to analyze, measure, demonstrate, and/or improve his or her diversity initiative's impact and report results using a scorecard methodology, such as the following:

- ☐ Senior executives and managers
- ☐ Senior vice presidents of diversity
- ☐ Diversity council members
- ☐ Workforce diversity directors and managers
- ☐ Global diversity executives
- ☐ Vice presidents of human resources
- ☐ EEO and affirmative action executives
- ☐ CEOs
- ☐ COOs
- ☐ Organization development specialists

This book is designed to help you learn how to implement a formal diversity scorecard measurement process to demonstrate diversity's return-on-investment impact in the least possible time. It will act as your coach and guide while providing implementation ideas to help carry out this process.

After working through the diversity scorecard process outlined in this book, you will be able to complete the following tasks:

- ☐ Link diversity measures to the organization's measures of performance.
- ☐ Build a business case for diversity measurement.
- ☐ Implement a multistep process to evaluate diversity's impact and contribution.
- ☐ Identify some basic diversity scorecard components.
- ☐ Construct a series of diversity scorecard indices that are linked to the organization's business drivers.
- ☐ Report the diversity metrics, demonstrating its contribution and return-on-investment.
- ☐ Plan how to track each diversity measure.
- ☐ Address critical implementation issues that help integrate the diversity scorecard into the fabric of the organization's normal mode of operation.

In addition, you will improve the accuracy of your diversity metrics by linking them to critical success factors, as well as learn how to select the right metrics that support organizational performance and success.

Acknowledgments

My first and deepest appreciation must go to my beautiful wife, best friend, and partner, Myra. Her love, caring, encouragement, and support provide the fuel and focus for my writing endeavors. This book is dedicated to you.

There are a number of people, whether they know it or not, who made the completion of this book possible. Some of them provided their scholarly works. Others provided personal encouragement and detailed conversations, which enriched my thinking.

First and foremost, I am deeply indebted to scholars Jack J. and Patti Phillips. Your seminal scholarly work in the human resource measurement field has set a tremendous standard for us to follow. In addition, your kindness, friendship, and generosity are greatly appreciated. I am also deeply indebted to other influential thinkers on measurement such as Jac Fitz-enz and the Saratoga Institute staff, Ron Stone, Donald Kirkpatrick, Wayne Casio, Lyle Spencer, Brian E. Becker, Mark A. Huselid, Dave Ulrich, and others too numerous to mention. Their thought-provoking research helps shape some of the major processes utilized in this return on investment approach.

No one writes a book about a scorecard without acknowledging Robert S. Kaplan and David P. Norton. Their phenomenal work in the area of strategy formulation, implementation, and measurement is the business scorecard standard. Your work has set a new model for performance excellence in organizations. This work benefited immensely from the stellar research work completed by scholars such as Paul R. Niven, Nils-Goran, Jan Roy, Magnus Wetter, Carl Thor, Mark Graham Brown, and others. Thank you all for sharing your knowledge so that others can learn and grow.

I am particularly indebted to several diversity professionals. I would like to express my deepest appreciation and gratitude to all of the members of the Diversity Collegium for your scholarly and thought-provoking exchanges regarding our diversity work. Your intense caring and hard work to take diversity to a higher level of understanding and application is crucial to our survival as a society. I would also like to thank Taylor Cox, John Fernandez, Alfred Schreiber, Edie Fraser, Samuel Betances, Laura Soder, Roosevelt Thomas, our clients, participants in the many Hubbard Diversity Measurement and Productivity Institute programs, and others too numerous to name.

I owe a special debt of gratitude to Joyce Alff, whose hard work, editorial comments, and suggestions helped clarify the message and refine the outcome. It was great working with you. I would also like to thank the Butterworth–Heinemann and Elsevier publishing staff for their mentoring and guidance throughout this project.

In any work like this, there are many people whose contributions deserve recognition that I may have overlooked. Please forgive me if I missed you in this list. Thank you all for your guidance and support.

Edward E. Hubbard

Petaluma, California

PART I

The Need for Diversity Measurement

CHAPTER 1

The Business Case for Diversity

A DIVERSITY MEASUREMENT CHALLENGE: HOW CAN WE ENSURE THAT DIVERSITY IS "AT" THE STRATEGIC BUSINESS TABLE, NOT "ON" THE TABLE?

Many diversity professionals and others interested in diversity have asked the following questions:

How will we be able to demonstrate that diversity contributes to the organization's bottom line?

How do we show senior executives and others that diversity is a strategic business partner that is aligned and linked to the strategic goals and objectives of the organization?

How can we measure the impact of diversity on organizational performance and an improved work environment?

How does the strategic diversity process help an organization excel in the domestic and global marketplace and provide favorable returns to stockholders and stakeholders?

If your organization is like most, you have probably found it challenging to answer these questions. Experience has shown that the diversity organization has its own brand of strategy and visions and has developed its own perspective regarding the value of its efforts to implement a diverse work environment; however, senior leaders and line management are skeptical, at best, of diversity's impact on the organization's success and their ability to demonstrate any financial or strategic contributions that a diverse workforce makes to the bottom line. In many firms, executives and others want to believe the cliché that views people as the organization's most important asset; however, they simply cannot understand how diversity realistically makes that vision a reality that results in a measurable difference in organizational performance.

Organizations typically define their diversity efforts in terms of race and gender, which get reflected in the elements they track regularly. This list is usually sorted by demographic group and might include items such as number recruited, employee turnover, cost per hire, number of minority personnel or women on the organization's board of directors, and employee attitudes. Now consider those diversity attributes that push beyond race and gender that you believe are crucial to implementing your organization's competitive strategy. In this list, you might include items such as penetrating diverse customer markets, retaining capable and committed diverse work teams that generate new, paradigm-shifting ideas in half the time of competitors, improving customer issue resolution processes, reducing cycle time, increasing market share and shareholder value, and the like.

How well do your existing diversity measures capture the strategic diversity drivers you identified in the second list? For most organizations, there will not be a very close match between the two lists. Even more important, in those firms where diversity professionals think there is a close match, the senior executives frequently do not agree that this second list actually describes how diversity creates value. In either case, a serious disconnect exists between what is measured and what is important to organizational performance.

These questions are fundamental because new economic realities are putting pressure on organizations to widen their traditional focus of diversity as the guardian of ethnic representation and social well-being to a broader, more strategic factor in business success. As a primary source of production and performance impact, our economy has shifted from physical to intellectual capital (which comes in all colors, backgrounds, genders, orientations, thinking styles, and so on). As a result, senior diversity managers are increasingly coming under fire to demonstrate exactly how they are helping the organization organize, utilize, and document this critically significant organizational asset to create performance and value.

The primary issue that diversity must deal with is difficult for some to imagine and believe (i.e., showing diversity's measurable impact on organizational strategy and the financial bottom line). The ability to utilize a diverse mixture of human and other resources to create a unique blend of strategy-focused solutions, by its very nature, creates an innovative competitive process that is difficult to copy—thus making it a competitive advantage (largely invisible to competitors).

Simply put, utilizing diversity as a strategic asset keeps an organization's competitive edge sharp for the long haul. This makes diversity a prime source of sustainable competitive potential. To realize this potential, however, diversity professionals must understand the organization's strategic plan for developing and sustaining this competitive advantage throughout the organization and its marketplace. In order to gain its benefits, this diversity must be utilized.

CAN A PERCEIVED INTANGIBLE ASSET LIKE DIVERSITY GENERATE TANGIBLE BENEFITS?

Yes, it can! Executives and other organizational personnel are beginning to recognize the importance and benefits of calculating the impact of perceived intangible human assets in today's marketplace. This has been challenging in the past for a number of reasons. As Becker, Huselid, and Ulrich (2001) point out, the accounting systems in use today evolved during a time when tangible capital, both financial and physical, constituted the principal source of profits. During this time, they state, those organizations that had the most access to money and equipment enjoyed a huge competitive advantage. With today's economic emphasis on knowledge and intangible assets, however, conventional accounting systems actually create dangerous informational distortions. As just one example, these systems encourage limited, short-term thinking with respect to managing intangibles. Why? Because expenditures in these areas are treated as expenses rather than investments in assets. In contrast to this view, investments in buildings and machinery are capitalized and depreciated over their useful lives.

Consider the following dilemma faced by executives and managers: Decide whether to invest $10 million in hard assets or $10 million in people. In practical terms, when an organization invests $10 million in a building or physical asset, this investment is depreciated over time and earnings are reduced gradually over a 20- to 30-year period. In contrast, a $10 million investment in people is expensed in its entirety (and therefore earnings are reduced by $10 million) during the current year. For executives and managers whose pay is tied to this year's earnings (as many are), the choice of which investment to make is clear.

As a result, organizations under financial pressure tend to invest in physical capital at the expense of human capital—even though the latter may very well generate more value. This kind of pressure can lead to poor decision-making behavior, such as using personnel layoffs, downsizing, and right-sizing to generate short-term cost savings. We know from past experience that after a layoff, the market may initially respond with a jump in share value; however, investors often eventually lose most, if not all, of these gains. This pattern is not surprising, given that people are a crucial source of competitive advantage rather than an expensive luxury that should be minimized.

The clear bottom line is this: If current accounting methods cannot give diversity professionals the measurement tools they need, then it is imperative that we, as diversity professionals, develop our own ways of demonstrating diversity's contribution to the organization's performance. Like any other discipline, diversity must be composed of both solid theory and applied sciences to gain credibility as a key contributor to organizational performance. At some point, the theory has to be put into practice and evaluated for its ability to add measurable value and understanding to real organizational issues.

We have evidence of a great deal of solid diversity theory, such as those put forth by R. Roosevelt Thomas (1991, 1996, 1999), Judith Rosner (1991), Marilyn Loden (1996), Taylor Cox (1993, 1997), and many others; however, notwithstanding the seminal diversity measurement work completed by Edward E. Hubbard (1997, 1999), the Hubbard Diversity Measurement and Productivity Institute's research, and a chapter on the subject by Lawrence M. Baytos (1995), there has been little scientific inquiry research and operational processes that measure the real financial impact of diversity.

The first step in building a diversity contribution process is to discard the accounting mentality that suggests diversity or human resource–based efforts are primarily cost centers in which cost minimization is the primary objective and measure of success. At the same time, it is important to take advantage of the opportunity to help define the standards for measuring diversity's impact. Investors and organizations such as the Swedish firm Skandia have made it clear that intangible assets are important. Skandia, for example, includes intellectual assets as a normal part of its profit and loss (P&L) reporting.

Edward E. Hubbard has pioneered efforts to create a wide variety of measures for the diversity field in his books *Measuring Diversity Results* (1997) and *How to Calculate Diversity Return on Investment* (1999). In addition to these books, Hubbard founded the Hubbard Diversity Measurement and Productivity (HDM&P) Institute. The HDM&P Institute is dedicated to creating applied sciences for measuring diversity performance and results to improve organizational performance. It is really up to diversity professionals to develop a new measurement system that creates real value for the organization. This will help position diversity as a legitimate strategic business partner.

A key ingredient of any organization's success is its ability to strategically utilize human capital and leverage performance-based measurement feedback as a competitive advantage. To sustain success, maintain high productivity levels, retain talented employees, create new systems, and keep its diverse customer base, an organization must know its strengths and weaknesses in order to improve its overall performance. It is critical to have the diversity tools and systems required to lead a measurement-managed diversity implementation strategy. These tools must channel the energies, abilities, and specific knowledge held by a diverse workforce throughout the organization toward achieving its long-term strategic goals and objectives.

DIVERSITY FACTS, FIGURES, AND FINANCIAL PERFORMANCE

Diversity professionals are increasingly challenged to take a more strategic perspective regarding their role in producing results for the organization. As diversity professionals respond to these challenges, measuring the impact of diversity and its contribution to the organization's performance will consistently emerge as a critical theme. This should really come as no surprise because over the last 5 to 7 years there has been an ever-increasing appreciation for the value of the softer people side or intangible assets of the organization's business and an associated trend toward strategic performance measurement systems, such as those of Robert Kaplan and David Norton's *The Balanced Scorecard* (1996).

During the past few years, several surveys of executives and human resource professionals have identified broad areas of diversity as one of the top priorities now and in the immediate future. Certainly, the growth of consulting firms, seminars, conferences, and publications are evidence of the interest and needs of organizations. The staying power of diversity as a corporate priority has been demonstrated by the high level of interest that carried through the recession periods of the 90s and the beginning of the 21st century. In fact, during the early part of the 90s, Towers Perrin reported in a survey that 96 percent of the responding companies had either maintained or increased their support for diversity management during the recession. The HDM&P Institute conducted a diversity measurement benchmarking survey in 2001 that reflected similar results. This survey found that 83 percent of the responding organizations planned to spend either the same amount or more on diversity in 2002.

WHAT DO WE MEAN BY DIVERSITY?

Diversity can be defined as a collective mixture characterized by differences and similarities that are applied in pursuit of organizational objectives (Thomas, 1996, 1999). *Diversity management* is the process of planning for, organizing, directing, and supporting these collective mixtures in a way that adds a measurable difference to organizational performance.

Diversity can be organized into four interdependent and sometimes overlapping aspects: Workforce Diversity, Behavioral Diversity, Structural Diversity, and Business and Global Diversity.

Workforce Diversity encompasses group and situational identities of the organization's employees (i.e., gender, race, ethnicity, religion, sexual orientation, physical ability, age, family status, economic background and status, and geographical background and status). It also includes changes in the labor market demographics.

Behavioral Diversity encompasses work styles, thinking styles, learning styles, communication styles, aspirations, beliefs/value system, as well as changes in employees' attitudes and expectations.

Structural Diversity encompasses interactions across functions, across organizational levels in the hierarchy, across divisions and between parent companies and subsidiaries, and across organizations engaged in strategic alliances and cooperative ventures. As organizations attempt to become more flexible, less layered, more team-based, and more multi- and cross-functional, measuring this type of diversity will require more attention.

Business and Global Diversity encompasses the expansion and segmentation of customer markets, the diversification of products and services offered, and the variety of operating environments in which organizations work and compete (i.e., legal and regulatory context, labor market realities, community and societal expectations/relationships, business cultures and norms). Increasing competitive pressures, globalization, rapid advances in product technologies, changing demographics in the customer bases both within domestic markets and across borders, and shifts in business/government relationships all signal a need to measure an organization's response and impact on business diversity.

Lawrence Bayos (1995) suggested that the 3 Ds have generated widespread corporate concern and interest in addressing diversity management issues, whether an organization has 100 or 100,000 employees. The 3 Ds are as follows:

☐ **Demographics.** Females, minorities, and foreign-born personnel are projected to produce 85 percent of the net new growth in the U.S. workforce, while white males are fast becoming a minority in the workforce. In 1960, nine out of ten consumers were white. Currently, it is estimated that only six out of ten are white. The changing demographics of the workplace are also the changing demographics of the marketplace. Organizations are looking at ways to align their organizations to the new realities of their customer bases.

☐ **Disappointment.** The traditional U.S. method for handling diversity was to bring women and people of color into the workforce under the banner of affirmative action. In doing so, it is often assumed that those individuals possess some deficiencies and may not have been hired if not for affirmative action. It was also assumed that they should be willing to assimilate their differences to better fit the norms of the majority group (usually white males) and thereby enhance their opportunities for recognition and advancement. In other words, to "make it," females and people of color would have to leave their needs and differences at the organization's front door. After a little more than two decades of affirmative action, it seems clear that the existing model has resulted in females and people of color being trapped in lower levels of the organizational pyramid. Turnover, discontent, and underutilization of talent are by-products of using the previous approaches for more than two decades.

☐ **Demands.** The demands for new approaches to diversity come from employees who have become less willing than their predecessors to assimilate their points of difference in hopes of gaining the elusive acceptance into the club. Furthermore, the intense pressure of industry and global competition to reengineer the organization requires that organizations tap the full potential of all their human assets.

DIVERSITY PROVIDES A BUSINESS ADVANTAGE

Organizations that want to thrive in today's global marketplace know that they have to focus well beyond adding technology, efficient production processes, and innovative products (Poole, 1997). In fact, it can be argued that none of these approaches will add significantly measurable improvements unless all employees have an environment that allows them to do their absolute personal best work. Forward-thinking organizations know that their competitive strength lies in focusing on their employees and their clients. For an organization to improve performance and results, it must be able to attract, motivate, and retain high-potential employees—including men and women from all backgrounds and walks of life.

In addition to attracting and retaining the best workforce, successful businesses must also attract and retain clients. The ability to retain clients can have a major impact on the organization's bottom line. For example, the lifetime revenue stream from a loyal pizza eater can be $8,000, a Cadillac owner $332,000, and a corporate purchaser of commercial aircraft literally billions of dollars (Haskett et al., 1994). A White House Office of Consumer Affairs study estimates that 90 percent of unhappy customers will not tell you they are unhappy with your service. Only 10 percent will complain. They also estimate that each unhappy person will tell nine other people about your poor service. They in turn will tell nine others. Therefore, 81 people will learn about your poor service.

If your business is a local coffee shop and 100 diverse customers (who order a $3 Café Mocha each week) were unhappy with your service, these potential $3–per-week coffee-drinking customers can potentially affect the success of your business in a major way, which may not be completely obvious until it is too late. For example, if these 100 unhappy customers tell nine others, 900 people will know about your poor service. If they choose not to come to your coffee shop for one day per week, then you have just potentially lost $1,263,600 in one year from only 100 customers!

Globalization and changing domestic markets reflect a changing buying public. It is no longer homogeneous. There is little doubt that an organization that is serious about diversity can gain an improved understanding of diverse customers' needs and therefore foster better customer service to an increasingly diverse market.

Some of the latest American workforce projections put forth by the U.S. Department of Labor indicate that only 15 percent of the new entrants to the workforce will be white males and nearly 85 percent will be women, minorities, and immigrants. "In 50 of America's 200 cities with populations over 100,000, the so-called minority is the majority. Workers 55 and older are the fastest growing segment of the workforce. By some estimates, one in 10 Americans is gay. And technology is enabling more and more people with disabilities to enter the workforce" (Capowski, 1996).

The global marketplace has opened up a wide range of possibilities for organizational performance and success. Many organizations are broadening their potential markets beyond U.S. borders to include China, India, the Pacific Rim, all parts of Europe, South Africa, and the like. These organizations realize that differences in language, culture, processes, and business practices must be acknowledged to successfully enter these markets. In addition, they must learn from these diverse experiences and incorporate the skills, beliefs, and/or practices into organizational processes to capitalize on diversity for a competitive advantage.

Poole (1997) highlights the following example: An American investment bank experienced problems when it launched an aggressive expansion plan into Europe. Their relocated American employees lacked credibility, were ignorant of local cultural norms and market conditions, and could not connect with their new clients. The investment bank responded to this problem by hiring Europeans who had attended North American business schools and assigning them in teams to the foreign offices. This strategy was enormously successful. The European operations were highly profitable and were staffed by a truly international group of professionals; however, the investment bank realized it still had a problem. If the French team, the German team, or the team in another country suddenly resigned, they would be right back where they were 10 years ago. The investment bank had not learned what the cultural differences really were or how they change the process of doing business. Cultural identity issues were never talked about openly. While they knew enough to use people's cultural strengths, they never internalized them or learned from them. Differences were valued, but they were not valued enough to be integrated into the organization's culture and business practices. In order to implement an effective diversity process, the investment bank needed to incorporate the extra steps to ensure that diversity was fully integrated into the organization's culture, skill sets, and functioning as a strategic capability issue.

Events such as mergers and acquisitions, changing customer marketplace demographics, and the like require organizations to work together. Organizations are also realizing that system flexibility, teamwork, measurement, and analysis is central to the drive for Six Sigma–level quality and innovation in products and services. Years of research have shown

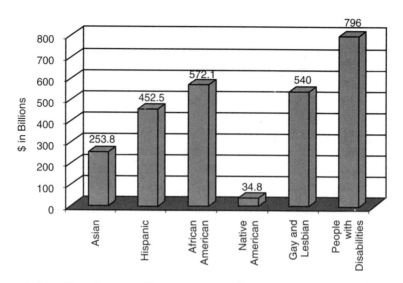

Figure 1-1. Minority spending power in the U.S. (Source: Multicultural Marketing, Selig Center for Economic Growth.)

that well-managed, heterogeneous groups will generally outperform homogeneous ones in problem solving, innovation, and creative solution building—exactly the capabilities that are critical to business success.

Organizations will have to be diverse because their customers are becoming more diverse, both abroad and in the United States. In the United States today, African Americans, Hispanics, Asian Americans, and Native Americans have an estimated combined spending power of more than $1.3 trillion. The shift to a service economy only increases the value of diverse employees, who may be better able to read and negotiate with such customers. Figure 1-1 shows the spending power of minorities in the United States.

FAILURE TO IMPLEMENT A DIVERSITY PROGRAM CAN BE COSTLY

If the lures of increased productivity, global marketing effectiveness, improved problem-solving performance, and enhanced creativity are not enough to initiate change in your organization's culture, the downside risks and impacts of turnover costs, poor training return-on-investment due to short tenure, poor overall brand image, failing community image as a good place to work for all employees, litigation charges, and the like is certainly worth considering. It can cost as much as $112,000 to recruit and train a full-time sales employee with a salary of $100,000 per year. Other examples of retention costs include the following (*Workplace News*, 1996):

☐ $116,340 for a chief engineer with 17 years of service, earning $77,560 annually

☐ $110,000 for a government services underwriter with 11 years of service, earning $110,000 annually

☐ $105,000 for a vice president for 15 years of service, earning $63,000 annually

☐ $104,000 for a middle manager with 38 years of service, earning $52,000 annually

☐ $52,065 for a store manager with 21 years of service, earning $34,710 annually

☐ $44,888 for a shift foreperson with 14 years of service, earning $51,300 annually

In addition to these costs, there are lost productivity costs and dissatisfied client costs. Time, effort, and money must be spent on recruitment and selection to replace the employee who is leaving the organization. Lost productivity will result from the downtime created by the person leaving and the new employee's training and learning curve. Employees who are leaving, particularly those who believe they have not been treated fairly, are not likely to be overly productive after they hand in their resignations. New employees have to learn the job, the organizational structure, the formal rules, the informal rules, the workplace culture, and so on. This takes time. These downtimes could even result in an organization's product or service being delivered late—resulting in extremely dissatisfied customers.

Typically, replacement costs are at least 1.5 times the yearly salary of employees. Replacement costs for women and people of color are higher because the time-to-fill rate can be longer if the organization has poor candidate source pools. These costs do not account for lost accumulated company knowledge or low morale where turnover is high. Add to this a whole host of legislation (e.g., Family and Medical Leave Act, Americans with Disabilities Act, Age Discrimination in Employment Act, Immigration Reform and Control Act of 1986), the cost of litigation with judgments exceeding $1 million, and the price of rebuilding a corporate image because of negative publicity, and some of the economic reasons for retaining employees become clear.

DIVERSITY LINKS TO PRODUCTIVITY AND PERFORMANCE

It is no secret that employees who are treated with respect and integrity and who are given an opportunity to have input into their work, on average, perform at higher levels. Employees figure out the level of effort they are required to put into their work. There is little doubt that satisfied employees are going to be better workers (i.e., their productivity will be higher than that of unsatisfied employees). In addition, fair employment practices allow organizations to more effectively attract, motivate, and retain the most qualified talent. Expectancy theory shows that treating employees fairly leads to higher levels of employee satisfaction and morale. An organization that has satisfied employees will find that it has low employee voluntary turnover (better known from an asset point of view as human capital depletion) and a highly productive workforce.

Research bears out the observation that employees who truly like their jobs and the organizations they work for tend to stay with the organization and have a positive impact on customer service and performance. One such body of research is the Service-Profit Chain developed by Haskett, Jones, Loveman, Sasser, and Schlesinger (1994). They established a causal pathway relationship that demonstrated that factors such as improving an organization's environment and an employee's satisfaction had a direct impact on customer satisfaction, retention, and loyalty, which generated a corresponding increase in organizational revenues and profits. In further research, Rucci, Quinn, and Kirn (1998) applied this Service-Profit Chain approach to organizational issues at Sears, Inc. and found that for every 5 percentage point improvement made in employee satisfaction, a 1.3 percentage point improvement in customer satisfaction and loyalty resulted, which drove a .5 percentage point improvement in store revenues. In one year, this accounted for an additional $200 million in revenue.

Employee satisfaction has a tremendous influence on employee commitment, which is reflected in key performance variables such as retention and productivity.

RETENTION

Employees will often cast their vote of dissatisfaction and level of commitment by using the Law of Two Feet (i.e., they go somewhere else).

When this happens, it is usually already too late to recapture their commitment. Employees who are leaving, particularly those who believe they have not been treated fairly, are not likely to be overly productive after they hand in their resignations.

It has been estimated that when an exempt (salaried) employee leaves an organization, it costs the organization 1.5 times the salary of the person who must be replaced. At the nonexempt (hourly) level, the impact is equivalent to 6 months of salary and benefits. It should also be noted that these figures only represent the costs needed to get a new person in the door! Costs incurred—such as learning curve costs, acculturation costs, formal and informal rules coaching, building customer and co-worker relationships, and network building costs equal to at least 90 percent of the departing employee—can represent a tremendous drain on the bottom line. These downtimes could even result in an organization's products and services being late—resulting in dissatisfied customers. This merely points out that it is critical that an organization manages employee retention and tracks who is leaving, for what reason, and at what cost.

When highly productive employees leave the organization, it can be disastrous. In many cases, high-performing employees are not allowed to work to their full potential because the workplace environment does not take employee differences and similarities into consideration as a competitive advantage. Dissatisfied employees will begin to look for work elsewhere. Under intense competition for the most qualified talent, an organization's ability to attract and retain high-caliber talent will depend in part on its reputation as an employer and whether employees are allowed to do their absolute personal best work. The consulting firm Deloitte & Touche, for example, found that it attracted more prospective employees after implementing diversity initiatives. Both men and women stated that they wanted to work for a firm that is progressive and growing.

Conversely, a study conducted at a different workplace noted that women who do manage to get through the glass ceiling "feel so unsatisfied and undervalued that they leave early—and in proportionately greater numbers than their male counterparts." A study of 500 organizations found that nearly 40 percent of private-sector workers regularly think about quitting their jobs (Davis, 1996). Another workforce study showed that dissatisfied employees were three times more likely than satisfied employees to indicate their intent to leave the organization (Haskett et al., 1994). When these things occur, organizations jeopardize their ability to meet strategic business objectives.

PRODUCTIVITY

Another result of poor employee satisfaction is its impact on productivity. Drew Davis (1996) noted in a study of 500 organizations that downsized because they thought downsizing would reduce costs, increase productivity, and encourage people to work smarter, that these organizations experienced varying results. The fear of downsizing, eroding trust, disillusionment, and frustration about dwindling promotion opportunities and job security caused employees to be demotivated and bitter. This had a devastating hidden effect on the organization's bottom line. Seventy-five percent of the 500 organizations found that employee morale had collapsed, and two-thirds of these organizations showed no increase in efficiency.

Productivity relates not only to direct effort but also to discretionary effort. This relates to the extra effort that employees give to their work. In today's workplaces, discretionary effort can make the difference between getting and not getting a client and between keeping and losing a client. Many organizations can replicate their competitors' technology, but they cannot replicate their workforces. In an information- and intellectual capital–based society, competitive organizational capability will come through people—people who are valued regardless of their backgrounds and who are given the opportunity to be innovative and fully productive. Demotivated, nonvalued employees will rarely expend the extra effort that may be required to win over customers and gain a competitive advantage.

Diverse work teams have been found to possess the potential to achieve higher levels of performance than homogeneous teams. Diverse groups of people bring a broad range of skills, knowledge, abilities, and perspectives to organizational challenges. Research has shown that diverse teams frequently develop more ideas and potential solutions to problems than homogeneous teams. Capowski (1996) described studies of four organizations: AT&T, Harris Bank, Northrup Grumman, and GE Power Systems. They found that the performance of the diverse work teams generated more ideas that evolved into new products and services than the performance of homogeneous teams. The latter group does not have as many perspectives to bring to the table as a diverse work team. The synergy that can be created by a homogeneous group of people is limited because they are so similar. With the proper training, diverse work teams can make the most of their varied perspectives and outperform homogeneous teams; however, homogeneous teams do come to the table with a common frame of reference, and they know how to communicate effectively with each other. Members of a diverse team are unlikely to have that knowledge and often must be trained in specific processes and techniques that effectively utilize their varied perspectives. To ensure effectiveness, team members must understand their differences, the communication process, group dynamics, and ways to integrate their many ideas into cohesive solutions. Diversity can "breed tension, conflict, misunderstandings, and frustration unless an organization develops a culture that supports, honors, and values differences" (Van Eron, 1995).

In the following examples, Addison Reid (1994) illustrates the impact of diversity on the bottom line of two organizations:

> **Example One.** A Spanish speaker in the decision-making loop could have saved General Motors the expense of trying to market the Chevy Nova in Mexico. Nova is Spanish for "it doesn't go."
>
> **Example Two.** If Gerber baby foods had known the local customs, it would have been saved the expense of recalling and relabeling jars and apologizing to its clients in one African country for suggesting that they were cannibals. In that country, it is customary for a label to picture the product, not the intended client. Gerber, in its attempt to address diversity, had simply changed the white baby on the label of their baby food jars to a black baby.

In both cases, this lack of diversity awareness and diversity utilization cost the organizations millions of dollars in lost revenue and damage to its brand image—not to mention its major impact on productivity costs.

THE LINK BETWEEN THE LACK OF DIVERSITY PROGRAMS AND ABSENTEEISM

Productivity is directly affected by the cost of absenteeism and hostile work environments. Satisfied employees are absent less often than unsatisfied employees, are late less often, are less apt to leave early, and are less apt to use expensive short-term and long-term disability benefits. Employees witnessing and/or experiencing hostile work environments and harassment are often away more often and are less productive. Imperial Oil of Canada estimates that harassment costs them close to $8 million annually in absenteeism, employee turnover, and loss of productivity. This does not include legal fees (Poole, 1997). This is a high price to pay for something that can be prevented.

If employees are staying with the organization and working well, customers are more apt to be happy and satisfied. While employee turnover costs money and time for recruiting, hiring, and training replacements, it also affects customer satisfaction. The employee who left, for example, may have been in contact with the organization's customers, and the customers will now have to deal with someone new who does not understand their needs. The customer, more than likely, may have been satisfied with the employee who just left. This employee may have been their primary contact with the organization for the past five or so years. He or she knew the customer's special needs. Now the customer will have to deal with the new employee or choose to go somewhere else. An even more frightening scenario is that the customers follow the employee who is leaving your organization (who knows all of the company's secrets) to your competitor, taking their business with them.

One study showed that low employee turnover was found to be linked closely to high customer satisfaction. The study found that when an employee who had direct contact with a customer left, their customer satisfaction level dropped sharply from 75 percent to 55 percent (Haskett et al., 1994). Another study by Abt Associates concluded that there was an average monthly cost of $36,000 in sales for replacing a sales representative with five to eight years of experience with an employee who had less than one year of experience. Conservative estimates of replacing a broker at a securities firm concluded that it takes nearly five years for a broker to rebuild relationships with customers that can return $1 million per year in commissions to the brokerage house, which amounts to a cumulative loss of at least $2.5 million in commission (Haskett et al., 1994).

Customers who know that their needs are going to be met are usually satisfied customers; however, as Janet Lapp (1996) points out, cynicism has developed among customers about what to expect from organizations. Many customers have low expectations about the ability of organizations to do what they say they will do or to be different from their competitors in a meaningful way. In order to be successful, organizations should be looking for ways to build strong, solid reputations for delivery and working to sustain the loyalty of their customers. Lapp points out that the "CEO of Starbucks believes that the quality of his workforce is the company's only sustainable, competitive advantage. He believes that workers need to feel pride in and to have a stake in the outcome of their efforts on the job." In essence, they must feel valued and included in the work climate and the decisions that affect their lives.

DIVERSITY'S CONTRIBUTION TO THE BOTTOM LINE

Satisfied customers tend to be loyal customers; not many satisfied customers go to the competition. One way of ensuring that customers are satisfied is to have a workforce that clearly reflects the organization's marketplace. This has become clear in the banking industry. Most banks, for example, offer about the same rates; it is the people who make the difference—the customer service difference (Martinez, 1995). We know from past experience that satisfied and loyal customers often become life-long customers bringing repeat business. Not only will this repeat business boost revenues, but satisfied and loyal customers will also make referrals. Referrals are one of the best ways to increase an organization's customer base and, in turn, its profitability. This includes direct referrals as well as pass-along referrals, where the customer brags about your organization and customers show up without any intervention (e.g., marketing, sales efforts) on your part. Satisfied customers also make excellent references when your business calls for them in a bidding situation. Good references can make the difference between being an unsuccessful bidder and winning the contract! Conversely, a dissatisfied customer can severely damage your organization's reputation and can affect future sales and profits.

In general, whenever an organization experiences customer-base growth, it translates into a better bottom line, increasing sales and profits. One study by Reicheld and Sasser (1990) found that a 5 percent increase in customer loyalty can produce profit increases that range from 25 to 85 percent. Organizations can determine customer loyalty by tracking customer retention, the number of services used by each customer, and the level of customer satisfaction. The strategies derived from this information helped explain why one of the organizations studied had achieved a return on assets in recent years more than double that of its competitors (Haskett et al., 1994).

Organizations that have included diversity in their organizational goals realize the importance of investing in their employees and servicing the varying needs of their customers. Increases in profits give organizations an opportunity to spend more time and money to make certain the workplace meets the needs of all workers while providing a fair return to shareholders.

Organizations that do not have an effective diversity process or no process at all will also incur costs, including high turnover, low morale, ineffective products or services, unproductive teams, inability to attract and retain employees, and legal and other expenses. Some well-known discrimination and bias cases that illustrate this impact on the bottom line include the following:

- [ ] Coca-Cola ($192.5M) Race
- [ ] State Farm ($250M) Gender
- [ ] Home Depot ($110M) Gender
- [ ] Lucky Stores ($107M) Gender
- [ ] Publix ($82M) Gender
- [ ] Texaco ($176M) Race
- [ ] Shoneys ($132M) Race
- [ ] Denny's ($54M) Race

Poorly implemented diversity processes can damage an organization's reputation with current and future (potential) employees as well as current and future customers and investors. An effective process, on the other hand, will increase the organization's goodwill and reputation (Poole, 1997). By effectively measuring and tracking the costs and benefits of diversity, organizations truly understand that diversity is a bottom-line business issue that is critical to organizational performance and results.

BUILDING CENTERS OF DIVERSITY EXCELLENCE

Doing diversity work as a strategic partner is some of the most important work we can do. It is critical to the myriad of customers served and vital to the people utilized inside the organization that diversity supports. Learning to serve as a strategic partner within the organizational structure is not just a way for diversity practitioners to justify their existence or defend their turf. It has implications for the very survival of the diversity department and of the organization as a whole. If the diversity function cannot show that it adds value, it risks being on the table for reduction, or worse—dismantling. With the right diversity mindset and measurement tools, implementing diversity-strategic business objectives can mean the critical difference between an organization that is just keeping pace with the competition or one that is making major strides ahead. In essence, it requires creating centers of diversity excellence using behavioral and technical measurement capability, demonstrating commitment, and building communities of practice to sustain it over time.

In order for an organization to take full advantage of the potential wealth in its diversity mixtures, it must completely embrace the level of diversity required to meet critical organizational challenges head on.

This occurs when organizations foster a climate and culture that values differences and maximizes the potential of employees through utilization—in other words, when the organization and the individuals within it operate in a mature fashion.

According to Dr. R. Roosevelt Thomas (1999), diversity-maturity requires both an individual and organizational set of behaviors that drive success. He states that diversity-mature individuals do the following:

- ☐ Accept personal responsibility for enhancing their own and their organization's effectiveness.
- ☐ Demonstrates contextual knowledge (i.e., they know themselves and their organizations and they understand key diversity concepts and definitions).
- ☐ Are clear about requirements and base include/exclude decisions about differences on how they impact the ability to meet these requirements.
- ☐ Understand that diversity is accompanied by complexity and tension and are prepared to cope with these in pursuit of greater diversity effectiveness.
- ☐ Are willing to challenge conventional wisdom.
- ☐ Engage in continuous learning.

Diversity-mature individuals see themselves, not others, as responsible for addressing diversity effectively. They understand the impact of organizational culture on diversity-related practices, but they do not use it as an excuse for inaction and indifference. Thomas points out that individuals aiming for greater diversity effectiveness would do well to ask themselves the following personal diversity questions:

- ☐ Am I comfortable working with people from all demographic groups?
- ☐ Is there a group or groups that I struggle to accept? If so, how have I attempted to overcome my biases?
- ☐ How will my comfort or lack of comfort with people different from me affect my ability to advance within this workplace?
- ☐ Do I enjoy diversity? If so, what kind? If so, how much?

Diversity professionals are not exempt from these issues and must answer these questions for themselves. Diversity-mature individuals know that when people with different backgrounds, perspectives, and objectives express themselves openly, there will be tension. This tension is not inherently positive or negative, good or bad; it simply is. Tension that promotes healthy competition can be good. Tension that immobilizes a unit is clearly not. The difficulty is that many individuals, like organizations, are so uncomfortable with tension that they focus on eliminating it rather than managing it. They place more importance on harmony than on achieving objectives.

Diversity-mature individuals learn to function in the face of tension. They know it is not personal but rather part and parcel of the dynamics of diversity. Tension and conflict are not the same. Tension becomes conflict when it is responded to ineptly. Diversity conflict arises when people ask unproductive questions, such as, "What's wrong with you that you aren't more like me?" (Thomas, 1999). Diversity-mature individuals have challenged conventional wisdom and made mindset changes along the way that equip them to respond effectively to these challenges.

By adjusting to this new mindset and accepting personal responsibility for action, diversity practitioners can develop new competencies to fulfill their strategic roles. The new economic paradigm of diversity as a financial contributor requires diversity professionals to do different things and help the organization deal with the dynamic tension that comes with managing a diverse workforce. This means more than just understanding the organization's articulated strategy; it means that diversity professionals must become strategic business partners who comprehend exactly what capabilities, environments, and other factors are needed to drive successful strategy implementation in their organizations and the ways in which diversity affects these components.

To create this center of diversity excellence, diversity-mature individuals must be able to let go of hindering concepts, such as only people with good interpersonal skills can be successful in managing diversity. Good interpersonal skills help, but they are not the sole arbiters of success. Diversity-mature individuals are highly capable of unlearning when needed. Diversity effectiveness requires a willingness and ability to monitor both yourself and the environment, to challenge yourself regularly, and to devise specific ways to work with new concepts so that they eventually become second nature (Thomas, 1999).

To create excellence in performance (utilizing diversity), diversity professionals must possess core diversity skills, which are implemented from a strategic framework. These skills, among others, include the following:

☐ *Ability to identify diversity mixtures and their related tensions.* Because unidentified mixtures cannot be addressed, this is a critical skill. On the surface this skill seems simple and straightforward, yet according to Thomas (1999), many people fail to master it. There is a natural tendency to focus on the diversity mixture that is of most interest to them and to ignore the others. People often overemphasize one diversity dimension such as race or gender at the expense of identifying a critical mixture that may have the most impact on organizational performance.

☐ *Ability to analyze mixtures and related tensions.* Not all mixtures need to be addressed, only those that interfere with achieving the goal. How key is the mixture? How disruptive are the tensions? Is any action needed? If action is taken, will it significantly enhance meeting the organizational objectives?

☐ *Ability to select an appropriate response.* If action is needed, what should the action be? In *Redefining Diversity* (1996), Thomas suggests responses from a framework that identifies at least eight choices, including increase/decrease, deny, assimilate, suppress, isolate, tolerate, build future relationships or foster mutual adaptation. Diversity professionals who are skilled in using these responses can quickly sort through the possible options and select the most effective one.

To be effective, diversity professionals must demonstrate a kind of diversity maturity that allows them to internalize key diversity concepts and use them to guide their actions along with integrating the core skills.

Similarly, to be effective at diversity measurement, individuals aiming for greater diversity measurement effectiveness would do well to ask themselves some critical personal questions:

☐ Am I comfortable with working with metrics and evaluating data from all demographic groups?

☐ Are there concepts around measuring diversity, especially beyond race and gender, that I struggle to accept? If so, how have I attempted to overcome my biases?

☐ How will my comfort or lack of comfort with metrics affect my ability to utilize them within this workplace?

☐ Do I enjoy diversity measurement? If so, what kind? If so, how much?

☐ Do I need to hire someone to conduct this portion of our strategic diversity impact analysis or simply support our efforts as a reviewer?

☐ Do I really want to do the real work required to rigorously apply diversity measures and following the diversity return-on-investment (DROI) process through to its conclusion?

Answers to these questions will help identify any baseline resistance to the diversity measurement process. Sometimes biases toward diversity measurement can come from within our profession and impede setting standards of excellence.

To sustain diversity professionals' momentum for excellence and measurement, communities of practice are required. What is a diversity measurement community of practice? It is a group of people who share a concern, set of problems, or a passion for identifying the impact of diversity using measurement processes and who deepen their knowledge and expertise in this area by learning about diversity measurement and interacting on an ongoing basis. They find it useful to compare designs regularly and to discuss the intricacies of their area of interest in diversity measurement. Currently, the Hubbard Diversity Measurement and Productivity Institute (HDM&P) operates a community of practice focused on diversity measurement called the Diversity Return on Investment (DROI) Forum.

As communities of practice, these people do not necessarily work together every day, but they meet as strategic business partners because they find value in their interactions. As they spend time together, they typically share information, insight, and advice. They help each other solve problems. They discuss their diversity measurement situations, their aspirations, and their needs. They ponder issues, explore ideas, and act as sounding boards. They may create tools, standards, generic designs, manuals, and other documents. However they accumulate knowledge, they become informally bound by the value they find in learning about diversity measurement together. This value is not merely instrumental for their work. It also accrues in personal satisfaction of knowing colleagues who understand each other's perspectives and of belonging to a group of people who enjoy the diversity measurement work. Over time, they develop a unique perspective on the topic as well as a body of common knowledge, practices, and approaches. They may even develop a common sense of identity (Wenger, McDermott, Snyder, 2002). They become a diversity measurement community of practice.

FINAL THOUGHTS

An effective, measurable business case for diversity must be built on a solid framework of both concept and science through the work of competent, credible diversity professionals using clear standards of excellence linked to business performance. They must view diversity as an integral part of the organizational system. By integrating the ideas under-lying diversity with specific measurement strategies and organizational systems theory, diversity professionals can help the organization exam-ine and utilize its diverse resources more dynamically. It is, of course, impossible to predict future events and results; however, we can make better decisions for the future by using tools such as the diversity score-card to guide us and to test alternatives as a basis for discussing how the future might look.

REFERENCES

Addison Reid, Barbara. "Mentorships Ensure Equal Opportunity." *Personnel Journal*, November 1994, 122–123.

Baytos, Lawrence M. *Designing & Implementing Successful Diversity Programs*. Englewood Cliffs, NJ: Prentice Hall, 1995.

Becker, Brian E., Mark A. Huselid, and Dave Ulrich. *The HR Scorecard: Linking People, Strategy, and Performance*. Boston: Harvard Business School Press, 2001.

Capowski, Genevieve. "Managing Diversity." *Management Review*, 85: 13–19.

Cox, Taylor, Jr. *Cultural Diversity in Organizations*. San Francisco: Berrett-Koehler, 1993.

Cox, Taylor, Jr., and Ruby L. Beale. *Developing Competency to Manage Diversity*. San Francisco: Berrett-Koehler, 1997.

Davis, Drew. "Beyond Casual Fridays: Are Managers Tuned in to Workplace Culture?" *Canadian HR Reporter*, May 6, 1996, 17.

Haskett, James L., Thomas O. Jones, Gary W. Loveman, Earl W. Sasser, Jr., and Leonard A. Schlesinger. "Putting the Service-Profit Chain to Work." *Harvard Business Review*, March/April 1994, 164–174.

Haskett, James L., Earl W. Sasser, Jr., and Leonard A. Schlesinger. *The Service Profit Chain*. New York: The Free Press, 1997.

Hubbard, Edward E. *Measuring Diversity Results*. Petaluma, CA: Global Insights, 1997.

Hubbard, Edward E. *How to Calculate Diversity Return on Investment*. Petaluma, CA: Global Insights, 1999.

IBM and Towers Perrin. *Priorities for Competitive Advantage*. New York: IBM and Towers Perrin, 1991.

Kaplan, Robert S., and David P. Norton. *The Balanced Scorecard*. Boston: Harvard Business School Press, 1996.

Lapp, Janet. *Plant Your Feet Firmly in Mid-Air*. Albany, NY: Delmar, 1996.

Loden, Marilyn. *Implementing Diversity*. Chicago: Irwin, 1996.

Loden, Marilyn, and Judith Rosener. *Workforce America*. Homewood, IL: Business One Irwin, 1991.

Martinez, Michelle Neely. "Equality Effort: Sharpens Bank's Edge." *HR Magazine*, January 1995, 38–43.

Poole, Phebe-Jane. *Diversity: A Business Advantage*. Ajax, Ontario: Poole Publishing, 1997.

Reichheld, Frederick F., and Earl W. Sasser, Jr. "Zero Defections: Quality Comes to Services." *Harvard Business Review*, October 1990.

Rucci, Anthony J., Steven P. Kirn, and Richard T. Quinn. "The Employee-Customer-Profit Chain at Sears." *Harvard Business Review*, 76(1):1998, 90.

Thomas, R. Roosevelt, Jr. *Beyond Race and Gender*. New York: AMACOM, 1991.

Thomas, R. Roosevelt, Jr. *Redefining Diversity*. New York: AMACOM, 1996.

Thomas, R. Roosevelt, Jr. *Building a House for Diversity*. New York: AMACOM, 1999.

See "No More Business as Usual," *Working Woman*, Special Advertising Section: Strength Through Diversity for Bottom-line Success: A Call to Manage Diversity. MacDonald Communications Corporation, March 1999.

Von Eron, Ann M. "Ways to Assess Diversity Success." *HR Magazine*, August 1995, 51–60.

Wenger, Etienne, Richard McDermott, and William M. Snyder. *Cultivating Communities of Practice*. Boston: Harvard Business School Press, 2002.

CHAPTER 2

Introduction to Diversity Measurement

IT'S ALL SUBJECTIVE ... OR IS IT?

There seems to be a myth operating within business and governmental communities that suggests that the outcomes or results created by a diversity change process defy measurement or can only be measured in the long term. In a sense, this myth suggests that creating an effective diversity-mature work environment is something of a complex and mysterious art form. Allegedly, the real value of diversity work can only be judged by those who perform it, those who are truly committed to its purpose or value it as important. Even then, the assessment of the results is saddled with subjectivity.

Some diversity specialists perceive that an inherent conflict exists between what is good for business and what is good for people. Some others believe, like truth, that the real reward is in the work itself. The words used to describe the results often include terms such as working better, appreciating differences, understanding each other better, less conflict, getting along, working as a team, and other similar non-measurement-specific words. Although these are admirable aims in themselves, they are not enough, especially when organizations are looking for strategies to deal with increased competition, options for reducing cost, adding value, adding dollars, and increasing productivity to affect the bottom line.

These notions seem to imply that quantifiable and quality-based measures cannot be applied to the diversity implementation process or a diverse work culture. Some people even believe that diversity is not a business-focused activity, but simply another form of affirmative action regulatory compliance, even though demographics, which are irrefutable, have been set in motion that show diversity is not only a business and customer issue but also a global competitive issue!

Whether the subjective position is valid is a key question to be sure; however, just the fact that it exists and that some diversity professionals and other businesspeople support it creates major problems. It sets managing and leveraging diversity apart from the rest of the organization. While peers in other organizational areas are focusing on metrics that reflect their contribution, such as sales, reduced costs, profits, income and expenses, and so on, those implementing the diversity process may limit its contribution to increased awareness, improved feelings, and increased satisfaction among groups. It is a real missed opportunity.

Some line managers quickly make judgments about diversity being a soft, non-business-oriented endeavor that contributes little to bottom-line performance. In addition, these managers may also assume that those involved in diversity neither understand nor are interested in measuring diversity's contribution to the organization. As a result, diversity is not taken seriously. Fewer managers support it in actual practice by sending their workforce to be trained or structuring their workforce to leverage diversity mixtures through teaming or implementing multicultural marketing strategies that penetrate key ethnic customer markets, and so on. We know from current organizational practice that diversity initiatives result in fewer follow-throughs than other business initiatives. Many diversity professionals resent this second-hand treatment, yet it is inevitable given the lack of a common connection and language that is fundamental to business.

There is no escaping numbers. Without them the line departments would have little idea of their performance. Also, it would be impossible to report back to stakeholders and stockholders. This being the case, how does the diversity department or professional exist in this climate? Some surveys of human resource professionals in general show that although they knew the number of employees in the company, "[a] majority of major corporation human resource professionals couldn't state the dollar volume of sales for their company, didn't know the profit level, and had little idea of the rate of return on corporate dollars invested" (Fitz-enz, 1995).

These issues are all part of the daily lives of line managers. The conclusion is somewhat obvious: If diversity professionals want to be effective communicators, they must build rapport with their audiences. The most direct way to do this is by recognizing their audience's values and using their language to communicate—the language of numbers.

REASONS FOR LACK OF QUANTIFICATION IN DIVERSITY

There are several reasons why quantification in diversity is lacking. Probably the most prevalent is that diversity professionals simply do not know how to objectively measure diversity activities.

The focus on diverse workforce management and development is still relatively new, and there are many methods to implement diversity and the process of diverse workforce development. Many diversity professionals are still trying to understand all of the implications of diverse workforce trends in the national and global arena. Because there are few predecessors, it is not surprising that many diversity professionals still rely on subjective measures.

Some practitioners in the diversity field have human resources backgrounds and have had the opportunity to study human resource development in college. Unfortunately, statistical courses are not always a part of many human resource development curricula. Even when they are, they tend to be either financial or behavioral science methods. Statistical procedures have seldom been adapted to the creation of input-output ratios for measuring diversity processes or the results of a human resources function. The reason for this is fairly simple: Many of the academic processes have never really been applied to the problem. Little formal training in diversity metrics existed before the founding of the HDM&P Institute.

The second reason behind the subjectivity myth is the values conflict. Some believe that objective measurement is simply inappropriate for diversity work. In their eyes, diversity work is a function devoted to stimulating and supporting human development, and they see no reason to evaluate outcomes in other than humanitarian terms. This one-sided approach is prevalent in many occupations. Some managers believe the sole mission of training is to transfer technical information about work from one person's brain into the brains of the workers. This is the technical competency model of human development. They see no real responsibility to teach workers to think, evaluate, or form values. Some architects, for example, believe their job is to create a container within which some kind of activity can be efficiently carried out. They overlook the fact that human beings interact with the space and can be depressed or stimulated by it. These perspectives ignore the holistic philosophies of systemic organizational views.

For those whose value system conflicts with the notion of measuring diversity, there is little hope for change—unless they experience a significant emotional event like losing their diversity position, funding, and/or support because it is thought that very little value is derived from their diversity work. Even then, some people still may not get it. Until they expand their outlook to include supporting the strategic purpose of the organization, there will be the perception that management should just see this as a good thing or the right thing to do.

Another very common reason why diversity departments or diversity activities are not measured is that some diversity professionals fear measurement. Perhaps this notion is born out of a fear of knowing; however, if you don't know, you can almost guarantee that nothing will ever improve. But what if you're making terrific progress and don't know it? What if several areas were doing a great job in utilizing the diversity mixtures of their work groups but are beginning to slip back into old, less effective habits? Key opportunities for adjustment and reinforcement would be missed. The implications of this can be mind boggling. This brings us to the fourth and last reason for the subjectivity myth.

Some members of top management have bought the myth of subjectivity—but not for long! Perhaps this is because for a long time there has been little interest in human resources issues. The early captains of industry simply never asked the question. As time progressed, the tradition of nonmeasurability went unchallenged. Few CEOs have taken more than a cursory tour in the human resources or diversity department during their careers. It was often just a quick stop along the way to the executive suite. Just about the time they were beginning to sink their teeth into what could be accomplished and what may need to be changed, they were off to another developmental assignment. Many of these budding executives, knowing the assignment would be a brief 12 to 18 months, looked for quick projects with a lot of visibility. Very few embarked on major, fundamental projects that would touch all facets of human resource issues.

Today this attitude is changing. Rotational developmental assignments in diversity are being given to high-potential movers and shakers as part of their development. Certainly all of the glass ceilings have not been shattered, but they are beginning to break in organizations that are serious about understanding and utilizing diversity as a key competitive strategy. Part of the diversity professional's hesitation is in the challenges of quantification.

CHALLENGES OF QUANTIFICATION

GTE (now part of Verizon) has been a leader in efforts to develop measures of intangible assets such as human capital. The firm has recognized both the limitations of traditional accounting measures for intangible assets and the potential represented by a more balanced performance measurement system. According to Lawrence R. Whitman, deputy CFO at GTE, "[a] direct link between human capital and corporate financial results is not readily apparent in traditional accounting practices. Right now, we are only beginning to understand the potential of this tool, but it's the measurement process that's important.... Once we are able to measure intangible assets more accurately, I think investors and finance professionals will begin to look at human capital metrics as another indicator of a company's value" (Becker, Huselid, Ulrich, 2001).

Certainly, at a gut level, people may have an inclination that having diverse human capital in a diverse and/or global marketplace may be beneficial, but how is it really? When we speak of measurement as a strategic resource for diversity professionals and others, what do we really mean? For example, many firms identify one or two people-related measures, such as employee satisfaction, in a balanced set of measures of organizational performance. Line managers, even diversity managers, might be held accountable for these measures, which could be incorporated into an executive bonus plan. These measures capture the quantity, or level, of a particular attribute—in this case, employee satisfaction—but how much is there? Does it change over time? How does it compare with the employee satisfaction experienced at other organizations or across strategic business units (SBUs)? Most of us would simply *assume* that more employee satisfaction is a good thing for the organization because organizations often have very little real *evidence* supporting this link between employee satisfaction and organizational performance. Such organizations emphasize the level of the attribute, rather than the *relationship* between the attribute and some strategic outcome, such as performance drivers or the organization's performance.

Good measurement requires an understanding of and expertise in measuring both levels and relationships. Too many diversity professionals succumb to pressures to demonstrate diversity's link to performance by merely relying on *levels* of diversity outcomes as substitutes for measures of *relationship*. In other words, they cannot show the direct causal links between diversity outcomes and the organization's performance, so they select several plausible diversity or human resource measures as candidates for strategic drivers, then simply assert their connection to the organization's performance.

This inability to demonstrate these relationships is sometimes obscured by diagrams that vaguely suggest cause and effect, as shown in the following diagram:

People $\rightarrow$ Customers $\rightarrow$ Profits

This diagram shows a common example of what might be called a superficial strategy map. A firm might include one or two measures under each of these three categories and do a good job of measuring the levels of those attributes. But what does doing well on those measures really mean? The arrows imply that better performance on the People dimension improves performance on the Customer dimension, which in turn will improve Profits. But the real story of value creation in any firm is much more complicated, so the story is incomplete (Becker, Huselid, Ulrich, 2001). It provides only the most superficial guide to decision making or performance evaluation. It is only marginally better than traditional measures that make no effort to incorporate a larger strategic role for diversity. Boxes and arrows give the illusion of measurement and understanding, but because the *relationship* measures are so limited, such diagrams and the thinking behind them can actually undermine the confidence and credibility the organization has for diversity processes.

Even though relationship measurement is the most compelling assessment challenge facing diversity professionals today, attribute measures should form the foundation of a measurement system. Why? Because evidence of a strong relationship between A and B is worthless if the measures of A and B themselves are worthless. But words such as "worthless" or "useful" or "appropriate" are not precise enough for a discussion about the elements of good measurement. In fact, there are well-defined principles outlining effective measurement practice. Understanding those principles lets the diversity professional take that essential step forward in developing a strategically focused diversity measurement system. Let's briefly explore a few of these principles.

THE DEFINITION OF MEASUREMENT

Measurement is defined as the assignment of numbers to properties (or characteristics) of objects based on a set of rules. Because we are often interested in the quantities related to a diversity outcome, numerical representation is important; however, we are not interested in just any quantities—we want the quantities to have meaning. For example, if we conduct a diverse workforce climate survey and ask the question: "*My* manager/supervisor knows how to work with a diverse workforce," knowing that the average score is 3.5 on a 5-point scale is numerical does not have much inherent meaning. Is scoring 3.5 good or bad? Or consider an employee turnover rate of 15 percent. Percentage points have more inherent meaning than 5-point scales, but simply observing the number does not reveal much about whether 15 percent is a problem.

To add meaning to these levels, we need to add context. This is the appeal of a benchmark. If we find our 3.5 on a 5-point scale is considerably better than our industry peers' ratings, we can begin to attach some significance to that measure; however, we might observe that our 3.5 is considerably below our historical level on this measure. We are doing better than our peers but not maintaining our historical performance. Of course, in both cases we have made interpretations about the relative value only (i.e., we are better or worse than some standard). In neither case do we have any measure of managerial value. In other words, what difference does it make whether we have a 3.0 or 4.0 value on a 5-point diverse workforce climate survey? To have managerial value, the measure must be expressed in numerical units that have inherent performance significance (such as a dollar impact). Barring that, we have to be able to translate the measure into performance-relevant units.

Let's take a look at another example: Suppose you want to demonstrate the dollar impact cost (recruitment and retention costs, lower productivity) associated with each additional percentage point in your organization's diverse workforce turnover numbers. To get managerial value out of this exercise, you would have to link diversity measures to performance drivers in other parts of the organization and ultimately to the organization's overall performance. Remember the finding from Sears in the previous chapter, where Sears put the Service-Profit Chain to work. The key people measures in the Sears measurement model reflect employees' attitudes toward their jobs and the organization overall. Sears could have benchmarked those attitudes against similar levels at other companies or perhaps against Sears' own historical norms. From this, the organization might have identified a gap, but then it would have to ask, so what? Unlike most companies, Sears had an answer to this question because it could translate changes in those attitude measures into changes in the organization's performance. Therefore, the people numbers had a business meaning.

Measuring relationships gives meaning to the levels and to potential changes in those levels; however, those relationships are very likely to be organization specific. Therefore, the more these (the impact of one measure on another) relationships are unique to your organization, the less useful it will be for your organization to benchmark on these levels with other organizations. Benchmarking on measurement levels assumes that the relationships among these levels are the same in all firms, and thus they have the same meaning in all organizations. That is the same as saying that the strategy implementation process is a commodity. For this reason, benchmarking on diversity strategic measures can be misguided at best and counterproductive at worst.

In addition, to fully understand another measurement principle, it is helpful to examine the differences between measures versus concepts or visions. To effectively measure diversity, our focus should be on the structure and value-creating elements of the diversity measurement system. These elements show up as diversity deliverables and the organization's key performance drivers that the deliverables influence. We can think of these properties as abstract concepts but also as observable measures. First, an organization or top management team can identify key links in the value-creation chain by taking what might be called a conceptual or vision perspective. For example, the simple relationship between employee attitudes and the organization's performance serves as the foundation of the Sears measurement model discussed earlier. Sears refined its model further with brief vision statements about the important attributes of each element in its model. The Sears top management team felt that Sears must be a *compelling* place to work, a *compelling* place to shop, and a *compelling* place to invest (the three C's).

This kind of concept or vision, commonly referred to as *constructs*, is the property of the organization's strategy implementation process; however, constructs are so abstract that they provide very little guidance for decision making or performance evaluation. For example, identifying superior cross-selling performance in ethnic markets as a key performance driver may get you closer to an effective assessment beyond the vision stage, but it is still too conceptual to be operational. What does it mean? How will we know it if we see it? Will two different managers both know it when they see it? In short, how do we measure it?

Compelling and easy-to-grasp constructs are important because they help you capture and communicate the essence of powerful ideas. Nevertheless, they are not measures. Rather, they constitute the foundation on which you *build* your measures. Clarifying a construct is the first step in understanding your organization's value-creation story, but you must then know how to move beyond the construct to the level of measure.

One way to detect a good measure is to see how accurately it reflects its underlying construct. Earlier, we said that a measure of the relationship between A and B is worthless. A or B would be worthless if they did not reflect the constructs behind them. For example, if Sears measured the construct "compelling place to work" simply by assessing the level of employee satisfaction with pay, the measure would not have very much relevance. Why? Because it omits key dimensions, such as understanding business strategy or relationships with supervisors, of the underlying idea that it is designed to tap (Becker, Huselid, Ulrich, 2001).

One way to avoid this kind of mistake is to use multiple measures that reflect different dimensions of the same construct. In Sears' case, managers used a 70-item survey that they then distilled to 10 items along two dimensions: employee attitudes about the job and employee attitudes about the company (see Figure 2-1).

This approach gave the organization an explicit way to assess how well it was realizing its vision of being a compelling place to work.

Another problem that can arise when choosing metrics is that of contamination. This means the measure does not correspond to its underlying construct. Often, this can happen for at least two reasons: (1) the

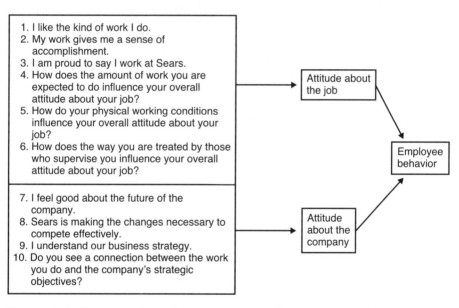

Figure 2-1. Survey of employee attitudes. Responses to these 10 questions on a 70-question employee survey had a higher impact on employee behavior (and, therefore, on customer satisfaction) than the measures that were devised initially: personal growth *and* empowerment teams. *(Source:* The HR Scorecard: Linking People, Strategy, and Performance, *2001.)*

measure does not fully capture all of the properties of the construct, or (2) the measure is capturing something beyond the construct. This is an all-too-common error. Remember the example discussed previously identifying superior cross-selling performance in ethnic markets as a key performance driver? How should the organization measure this construct? It might use total sales at all divisions, under the assumption that employees and divisions with more cross-selling skills in ethnic markets would have higher total sales. But total sales would also include sales other than those derived from cross-selling and those other than from ethnic markets by employees. The other data in each case would contaminate the metric. What about assessing total number of different products sold per customer or new sales to existing customers in ethnic markets? In either case, the organization would still have to develop a measure that tapped into the important attribute of the performance driver in question without blurring the picture with unrelated influences.

These sorts of measurement errors severely reduce the value you can derive from your diversity measurement system. If you use deficient measures, it is very likely that the organization will begin to ignore—or worse, misrepresent—the diversity link to the performance driver. For example, if a key driver is positive customer buying experience, you might use time with customer as a measure. Market research shows that customers appreciate it when sales staffs do not pressure them to make a quick purchase. On the other hand, if this is the *only* measure of the customer's buying experience, salespeople might be tempted to needlessly drag out their encounters with customers. It is still true that what gets measured, gets managed. Simply put, we cannot measure A and hope for B (Becker, Huselid, Ulrich, 2001).

OUTCOME MEASURES OR PERFORMANCE DRIVERS?

In a balanced scorecard, outcome measures are combined with measures that describe resources spent or activities performed. We are interested in how the measures will help us track the outcomes of one diversity initiative and how it drives the performance of a key aspect of the organization's business. By focusing on performance drivers, we emphasize that we want to measure those factors that will determine or influence future outcomes.

Goals and measures can be placed in a traditional input-output model to illustrate how goals and measures may be placed along a causal

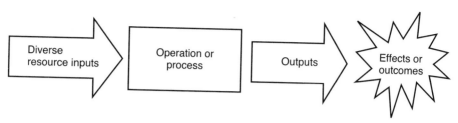

Figure 2-2. Traditional input-output model.

chain, from resource input to effects created by the outputs (or results) (see Figure 2-2).

Effect means the action of one thing on another or some kind of outcome. A higher reported profit, reduced turnover of people of color, improved brand image, or reduced cycle time are examples. Several of these effects will in turn influence the organization's future operations, thus becoming another input for the operation of a subsequent period. This relationship is clearest in the case of internal outcomes: New diversity learning regarding multicultural marketing leads to improved marketing processes and techniques, which leads to a greater volume of customers from multicultural markets.

In general, it is better to measure at the right of the above figure. Only when we see the effects do we know whether an intelligently planned use of diverse resource inputs and/or a well-managed operation was actually successful. There are also reasons to manage measures at the left of the figure. Sometimes these act as surrogate measures of conditions closer to the actual effects. For example, we might believe that our new multiethnic customers will be loyal, but we do not know that for sure. We may believe that rapid delivery means satisfied customers, but we do not know the exact nature of the relationship, or at least we would need a certain period of observation to learn how the two are connected. Because of this relationship, we may refer to the measures on the left of the figure as performance drivers. By understanding them, and taking care to manage them well, we can improve performance in a way that over time will result in better outcomes and effects (Olve, Roy, Wetter, 2000).

Good scorecards will combine outcome measures, of which profits is one, with performance drivers. Often it is difficult to draw the line between the two. They are interrelated in a chain of ends and means; for people in charge of logistics, delivery time is an outcome, but for purposes of customer relations, it may be considered as one of several performance drivers that can improve customer loyalty. What is important is that we measure thoroughly enough and use a credible diversity measurement process to identify the specific measures that highlight diversity links to bottom-line organizational performance.

BUILDING A SOLID DIVERSITY MEASUREMENT STRATEGY

A diversity measurement process is not an end in itself. It has value only if the result it produces provides meaningful input into subsequent decisions you want to make and/or contributes to a more effective analysis of the organization's performance. Therefore, as you think about the choice and form of a particular measure, stop and think carefully about what you would do with the results. Imagine receiving your first report summarizing this measure. What key decisions will these results tell you that you need to consider? Will another manager or executive, particularly one outside of the diversity organization, consider recommendations based on this measure to be persuasive? Would these results provide a compelling foundation for a resource-allocation decision in your organization?

Answers to questions such as these will help you formulate a solid diversity measurement strategy built with metrics that matter. Ideally, you will develop a measurement system that lets you answer questions such as, how much will we have to change "x" in order to achieve our target change in "y"? For example, if you increase the level of diversity leadership competency in the first-level managers by 25 percent, how much will that change employee satisfaction scores that we know are linked to improved customer retention and sales? Or, if you reduce turnover among key technical staff in research and development (R&D) using improved sourcing techniques with key demographic groups by 10 percent, how long before that action begins to improve the new-product-development cycle time? A measurement system that can provide this kind of specificity is not easy to develop and may be beyond the reach of some organizations, but diversity measurement quality is a continuum, not an absolute. As with most decisions, developing a strategic diversity measurement system involves tradeoffs. To make the correct tradeoff, you need to choose the point along the measurement-quality continuum that you think your organization can reasonably achieve, yet not compromise the measurement system's integrity and credibility by selecting easy measures that have no real performance and value impact.

Even if you are unable to link new-product-cycle time reduction to customer satisfaction, and ultimately profitability, establishing just the

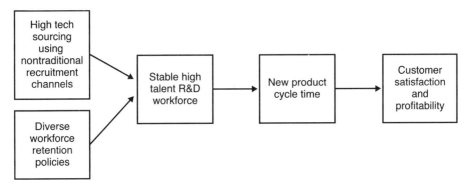

Figure 2-3. Links between diversity and R&D cycle time.

first few links shown in Figure 2-3 between diversity and the R&D cycle time would say a lot about diversity's strategic influence.

By establishing the first few links shown, diversity professionals could begin to talk about diversity deliverables that make the difference in the organization's business.

Thinking strategically about measurement means understanding whether the measurement system you are building will provide you with the kinds of information that will help you manage the diversity function in a strategic fashion. Understanding the value-creation process and developing construct-valid measures of that process form a top-down approach. A diversity measurement system that only utilizes available measures without analyzing their performance and value-creation impact is a bottom-up approach that will be a waste of time in most cases. Ultimately, these bottom-up measures can undermine diversity's strategic capability. To be effective, a strategic diversity measurement approach is rooted in a process that links a clear line of sight to the organization's goals, objectives, and performance drivers.

FINAL THOUGHTS

This chapter has briefly outlined some of the issues in measurement and described some of the challenges that must be addressed to be effective. In the next series of chapters, the diversity return-on-investment (DROI) process and the application of measurement are explored to help you move beyond the limits of best available measurement approaches. It is designed to help you demonstrate diversity's link to performance and bottom-line results in financial terms that highlight diversity's value.

REFERENCES

Becker, Brian E., Mark A. Huselid, and Dave Ulrich. *The HR Scorecard: Linking People, Strategy, and Performance*. Boston: Harvard Business School Press, 2001.

Fitz-enz, Jac. *How To Measure Human Resources Management*. New York: McGraw-Hill, 1984.

Fitz-enz, Jac. *How To Measure Human Resources Management*, 2nd ed. New York: McGraw-Hill, 1995.

Olve, Nils-Goran, Jan Roy, and Magnus Wetter. *Performance Drivers: A Practical Guide to Using the Balanced Scorecard*. Chichester, UK: John Wiley & Sons, 2000.

PART II

The Diversity Return-on-Investment (DROI) Process

CHAPTER 3

Introduction to the Diversity ROI Process

Interest in diversity and the return-on-investment associated with it is increasing. Several issues are driving this increased interest and its application to a wide range of diversity-related issues. Pressures from senior managers and clients to show the return on their diversity investment is probably the most influential driver. Competitive economic pressures are causing intense scrutiny of all expenditures, including all diversity costs. In addition, diversity professionals know they must begin to show how diversity is linked to the bottom line in hard numbers. In short, they must calculate and report their diversity ROI.

DROI: A Systematic Approach to Measurement

Calculating DROI requires asking key questions and performing key tasks along the way. To achieve a successful result, measuring DROI requires a systematic approach that takes into account both costs and benefits. The Hubbard Diversity ROI Analysis Model, as shown in Figure 3-1, provides a step-by-step approach that keeps the process manageable so users can tackle one issue at a time (Hubbard, 1999).

The model also emphasizes that this logical, systematic process flows from one step to another. Applying the model provides consistency from one DROI calculation to another. In essence, it suggests that the major aspects of diversity measurement you need to address include the following:

☐ Initial analysis and planning
☐ Collecting and analyzing data

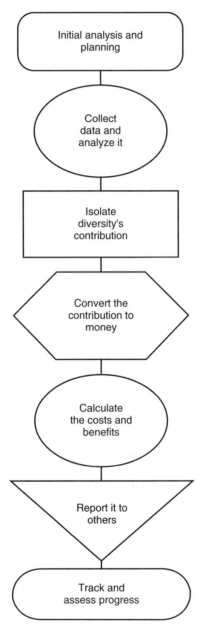

Figure 3-1. Hubbard Diversity ROI Analysis Model.

- ☐ Isolating diversity's contribution
- ☐ Converting the contribution to money
- ☐ Calculating the costs and benefits
- ☐ Reporting data
- ☐ Tracking and assessing progress

Step 1: Initial Analysis and Planning

Creating a DROI-based scorecard requires that you clearly identify what you want to know as a result of implementing a diversity measurement study. This should be based on, at bare minimum, the identification of business problems or opportunities related to the organization's key business strategy. You should also be prepared to list a series of research questions you would like answered or hypotheses you would like to test. These questions may include things such as "In what racial categories do we have the most turnover?", "What diverse customer markets are not utilizing our products or services?", and "How can we improve the idea- and solution-generation (creative) process using current cross-functional teams to improve operational performance?"

While planning ways to address these research questions and ideas, it may be helpful to begin with the end in mind. That is, think of what will appear on your research report that will ultimately become an outcome that drives your scorecard, creates placeholders for them, and then generates the questions or hypotheses that must be answered in order for data to show up on the report as results. The final step in this phase is to summarize the questions you would like answered and formulate diversity measurement study objectives that will guide your work. Once this is done, you are ready to consider the appropriate data collection methods and develop your data collection plan.

Step 2: Collecting and Analyzing Data

Data collection is central to the DROI process. In some situations, post-DROI study data are collected and compared to prestudy situations, control group differences, and expectations. Both hard data (representing output, quality, cost, time, and frequency) and soft data (including work habits, work climate, and attitudes) are collected. Data are collected using a variety of methods, including but not limited to the following:

- ☐ Follow-up surveys
- ☐ Post-study interviews

☐ Focus groups
☐ Short-term pilot project assignments
☐ Action plans
☐ Performance contracts (agreements to produce certain levels of results)
☐ Performance monitoring (reports and other literature reviews)

The important challenge in the data collection phase is to select the method or methods appropriate for the organizational setting and within the time and budget constraints of the organization. During this phase, you will identify the data collection processes and specific metrics to use, create the appropriate evaluation instruments, and apply an organizational change methodology such as the Hubbard Diversity 9-S Framework, which includes Shared Vision, Shared Values, Standards, Strategy, Structure, Systems, Style, Skills, and Staff (Hubbard, 1999).

Step 3: Isolating Diversity's Contribution

An often-overlooked issue in most diversity assessments or evaluation studies is the process of isolating the effects of diversity. In this step of the process, specific strategies are explored that determine the amount of output performance directly related to the diversity initiative. This step is essential because many factors will influence performance data after the diversity initiative. The result is increased accuracy and credibility of the DROI calculation. The following strategies have been utilized by organizations to tackle this important issue:

☐ Control groups
☐ Trend lines
☐ Forecasting model
☐ Participant estimates
☐ Supervisor of participant estimates
☐ Senior management estimates
☐ Expert estimates
☐ Subordinate's estimates (those who work for the participants)
☐ Identifying other influencing factors
☐ Customer inputs

Collectively, these strategies provide a comprehensive set of tools to tackle the important and critical issue of isolating the effects of diversity initiatives. Calculating and isolating DROI will require an analysis of operational and other business processes to isolate the specific areas where diversity can be applied to improve business performance. One tool to analyze operational processes is the S-I-P-O-C Chain. This analysis tool allows you to break down operational processes and view them in terms of the way business is done from *supplier* to *input* to *process* to *output* to *customer*. Once all contributing factors have been identified and their contributions calculated, you would be ready to convert the contribution to money.

Step 4: Converting the Contribution to Money

To calculate the DROI, data collected in a DROI evaluation study are converted to monetary values and are compared to the diversity initiative costs. This requires a value to be placed on each unit of data connected with the initiative. There are at least 10 different strategies available to convert data to monetary values. The specific strategy selected usually depends on the type of data and the initiative under analysis (Phillips, 2001):

1. **Output data** are converted to profit contribution or cost saving. In this strategy, output increases are converted to monetary value based on their unit contribution to profit or the unit of cost reduction.
2. The **cost of quality** is calculated and quality improvements are directly converted to cost savings.
3. For diversity initiatives where employee time is saved, the **participant's wages and benefits** are used for the value of time. Because a variety of programs focus on improving the time required to complete projects, processes, or daily activities, the value of time becomes an important and critical issue.
4. **Historical costs** are used when they are available for a specific variable. In this case, organizational cost data are utilized to establish the specific value of an improvement.
5. When available, **internal and external experts** may be used to estimate a value for an improvement. In this situation, the credibility of the estimate hinges on the expertise and reputation of the individual.
6. **External databases** are sometimes available to estimate the value or cost of data items. Research, government, and industry databases can provide important information for these values.

The difficulty lies in finding a specific database related to the diversity initiative under analysis.

7. **Participants** estimate the value of the data item. For this approach to be effective, participants must be capable of providing a value for the improvement.

8. **Supervisors of participants** provide estimates when they are both willing and capable of assigning values to the improvement. This approach is especially useful when participants are not fully capable of providing this input or in situations where supervisors need to confirm or adjust the participant's estimate.

9. **Senior management** may provide estimates on the values of an improvement. This approach is particularly helpful to establish values for performance measures that are very important to senior management.

10. **Diversity staff** estimates may be used to determine the value of an output data item. In these cases, it is essential for the estimates to be provided on an unbiased basis.

Step 4 in the Hubbard DROI Analysis Model is very important and is absolutely necessary for determining the monetary benefits from a diversity initiative. The process is challenging, particularly with soft data, but it can be methodologically accomplished using one or more of these strategies.

Step 5: Calculating the Costs and Benefits

CALCULATING THE DIVERSITY INITIATIVE COSTS

To successfully calculate DROI, both cost and benefits must be tracked and calculated in the process. The first part of the equation in a cost/benefit analysis is the diversity initiative costs. Tabulating the costs involves monitoring or developing all of the related costs of the diversity initiative targeted for the DROI calculation. Among the cost components that should be included are the following:

- ☐ The cost to design and develop the diversity initiative, possibly pro-rated over the expected life of the initiative
- ☐ The cost of any materials and external staff resources utilized
- ☐ The costs of any facilities, travel, lodging, and so on
- ☐ Salaries, plus employee benefits of the employees involved
- ☐ Administrative and overhead costs allocated in some way

CALCULATING THE DROI

The DROI is calculated using the initiative's benefits and costs. The benefit/cost ratio (BCR) is the initiative benefits divided by cost. In formula form it is:

$$\text{BCR} = \text{Diversity Initiative Benefits} \div \text{Diversity Initiative Costs}$$

Sometimes the ratio is stated as a cost-to-benefit ratio, although the formula is the same as BCR. The DROI calculation uses the net benefits of the diversity initiative divided by the initiative costs. The net benefits are the diversity initiative benefits minus the costs. As a formula, it is stated as:

$$\text{DROI\%} = (\text{Net Diversity Initiative Benefits} \div \text{Initiative Costs}) \times 100$$

In other words, the DROI formula is calculated as:

$$\frac{\text{Diversity Benefits} - \text{Initiative Costs}}{\text{Initiative Costs}} \times 100$$

This is the same basic formula used in evaluating other investments where the ROI is traditionally reported as earnings divided by investment. The DROI from some diversity initiatives is often high. DROI figures above 450 percent are not uncommon (Hubbard, 1999).

IDENTIFYING INTANGIBLE BENEFITS

In addition to tangible, monetary benefits, most diversity initiatives will have intangible, nonmonetary benefits. The DROI calculation is based on converting both hard and soft data to monetary values. Intangible benefits include items such as the following:

- ☐ Increased job satisfaction
- ☐ Increased organizational commitment
- ☐ Improved teamwork
- ☐ Reduced conflict

During data analysis, every attempt is made to convert all data to monetary values. All hard data such as output, quality, and time are converted to monetary values. The conversion of soft data is attempted for each data item; however, if the process used for conversion is too subjective or inaccurate, the resulting values can lose credibility in the process. This data should be listed as an intangible benefit with the appropriate explanation. For some diversity initiatives, intangible, nonmonetary benefits are extremely valuable, often carrying as much influence as the hard data items.

Step 6: Reporting Data

Next, it is critical that you have an organized communications plan to let others know the progress and challenges being addressed by diversity initiatives. During the development cycle of the communications plan, it is important to identify communication vehicles to use, how and when the report will be created, when it will be delivered, and how to evaluate its implementation.

Step 7: Tracking and Assessing Progress

Finally, in order to maintain any gains made or benefits from lessons learned during the process, you must make plans to track and assess the effectiveness of your diversity initiatives over time.

THE ROLE OF DIVERSITY IN CREATING ROI

Building an effective diversity measurement scorecard system requires a firm understanding of the role diversity plays in creating a return-on-investment for the organization. As stated previously, a diversity scorecard lets you do two important things: (1) manage diversity as a strategic asset and (2) demonstrate diversity's contribution and link it to your organization's strategic business and financial success. Although each organization will describe its scorecard in its own way, a well-thought-out scorecard should get you thinking about four major themes:

1. The key diversity deliverables that will leverage diversity's role in the organization's overall strategy
2. Developing a high-performance work environment that utilizes diversity as an asset
3. The extent to which that environment is aligned with the organization's strategy
4. The efficiency with which those deliverables are generated

IDENTIFYING DIVERSITY DELIVERABLES

To build an effective diversity scorecard for any organization, we must understand the organization's strategy implementation process in detail, along with its strategic business goals, objectives, and key performance drivers. This means understanding diversity's role in supporting these elements as part of a strategy map. For example, the organization could have profitability goals focusing on *revenue growth* and *productivity improvement*. We could describe diversity's role in this process in the following way:

☐ *Revenue growth* ultimately derives from increased customer satisfaction in all market segments, which in turn is boosted by product innovation and reliable delivery schedules, among other things.

☐ *Product innovation* strongly depends on the presence of talented staff with significant experiences. Through competency-based, diversity-friendly selection methods and retention programs, diversity contributes to a *stable, high-talent staffing deliverable* that helps the organization meet its objectives.

☐ *Reliable delivery schedules* in part hinge on the maintenance of optimal staffing levels. Even if turnover is low, the organization must fill vacancies quickly. By reducing the recruiting cycle time through more diverse candidate sources, diversity supports an *optimal staffing level deliverable*, which can reduce overall costs that adds to the DROI impact.

Productivity improvement has links to maintaining optimal production and process schedules, which in turn depend on maintaining appropriate staffing levels. Again, diversity assistance in driving recruiting cycle time drives staffing levels that help keep production downtime resulting from personnel issues to a minimum (Becker, Huselid, Ulrich, 2001).

DEVELOPING A HIGH-PERFORMANCE WORK ENVIRONMENT

Once the diversity deliverables have been clearly identified, we can begin to identify and measure the primary environmental components that help generate these deliverables. This high-performance work environment system is specifically designed to help drive the organization's strategy implementation process using diversity deliverables. This could involve, for example, designing and implementing a valid diversity leadership competency model that is linked to major elements in the high-performance work environment system and providing regular 360-degree multirater feedback to these leaders regarding their use and level of competence in applying these diversity management skills. As with any element of the diversity scorecard, these data can be presented in a variety of ways.

ALIGNMENT WITH STRATEGY

The next component in the diversity scorecard encourages you to gauge alignment of the diversity measurement system with the organization's strategy implementation process. To transform a generic high-performance work system into a strategic asset, you need to focus that system directly on the diverse workforce talent aspects of those drivers. The focus must be on the diversity deliverables required to create value in the organization, which in turn highlight specific elements of the diversity system that reinforce one another in order to produce those deliverables. Therefore, specific alignment measures will be linked directly to specific deliverables in the scorecard. Connecting them in this way highlights the cause-and-effect relationships needed to support diversity's contribution to the organization's performance.

To select the appropriate alignment measures, focus on those elements of your diversity measurement system that make a definable and significant contribution to a particular diversity deliverable. These can differ for each organization. Identifying these measures requires that you combine a professional understanding of diversity with a thorough knowledge of the value-creation process in your organization. Remember that these alignment measures will follow directly from a top-down approach. Based on a larger strategy map that you will create in the diversity scorecard process, you will identify your diversity deliverables, which in turn will point to certain elements of the DROI system that require alignment. Therefore, no standard alignment measures can be provided as examples. Instead, each organization must develop a standard process by which it develops its own set of alignment measures, both internal and external.

DIVERSITY EFFICIENCY: CORE VERSUS STRATEGIC MEASURES

There are a wide variety of benchmarks and standards by which you can measure diversity's efficiency. Some of these measures include the following:

- [ ] Absenteeism rate by job category and job performance by group
- [ ] Number of stress-related illnesses by group
- [ ] Turnover costs
- [ ] Number of recruiting advertising programs in place by demographic group
- [ ] Average employee tenure by performance level by group
- [ ] Number of incidents of injury by group
- [ ] Time to fill an open position by group
- [ ] Offer-to-acceptance rate by group (diversity hit rate)
- [ ] Average time for dispute resolution by group
- [ ] Cost per grievance by group
- [ ] Cost per trainee-hour
- [ ] Lost time due to accidents by group

All of these measures encourage cost savings and are diversity operational measures. For the most part, they only position diversity as a commodity and serve as generic benchmarks. The key is to identify those measures that help create strategic value for the organization. Of course, these will differ for each organization because each organization's strategic value will be unique. It is important to select the measures you include in your diversity scorecard carefully. Otherwise, it is possible to become overwhelmed by all of the potential metric choices. Benchmarking is fine for diversity commodity activities, but it has no significant influence on your organization's ability to implement its strategy.

Therefore, an approach to creating your measurement strategy is to divide your key efficiency metrics into two categories: core and strategic. *Core efficiency measures* represent significant diversity expenditures, but they make no real direct contribution to the organization's strategy implementation. *Strategic efficiency measures* assess the efficiency of diversity activities and processes designed to produce diversity deliverables. To make the distinction between these two types of measures, you must trace the links between the specific measure and its connection with the diversity value chain. An example might be reducing the minority recruiting cycle time. Because this is one of the first steps in helping the organization achieve the strategic objective of stable staffing levels (a key performance driver), it is an enabler and essential to a key performance driver that adds value. Separating the two helps you evaluate the net benefits of strategic deliverables and guides resource-allocation decisions.

FINAL THOUGHTS

The implementation of your DROI study and your diversity scorecard is critical to the success of the organization and the credibility and survival of the diversity profession. In order to be taken seriously, diversity professionals must become adept at measuring and reporting the right diversity results that tie diversity to the organization's bottom-line objectives. By using a systematic, logical, planned approach, the DROI process and the diversity scorecard instrument, diversity represents one of the organization's best investments in improved performance.

REFERENCES

Becker, Brian E., Mark A. Huselid, and Dave Ulrich. *The HR Scorecard: Linking People, Strategy, and Performance*. Boston: Harvard Business School Press, 2001.

Hubbard, Edward E. *How to Calculate Diversity Return on Investment*. Petaluma, CA: Global Insights, 1999.

Phillips, Jack J., Ron D. Stone, and Patricia P. Phillips. *The Human Resources Scorecard*. Boston: Butterworth–Heinemann, 2001.

FURTHER READING

Casio, Wayne F. *Costing Human Resources: The Financial Impact of Behavior in Organizations*, 4th ed. Australia: South-Western College Publishing, 2000.

Phillips, Jack J. *Accountability in Human Resources Management*. Boston: Butterworth–Heinemann, 1996.

CHAPTER 4

Planning and Collecting Data

Creating an effective diversity scorecard requires that you have a detailed understanding of the diversity return-on-investment (DROI) study process and how it works. It begins with some initial planning and continues with the implementation of a comprehensive data collection process. The initial planning and analysis step is critical for generating a successful evaluation and/or DROI study. Many practitioners trying to generate a diversity scorecard find out after the fact that they should have spent more time planning the strategic linkage and alignment of the diversity initiatives that will drive their scorecard outcomes. Initial analysis and planning creates several advantages and involves several key issues we will explore. The first issue is outlining what the diversity evaluation or DROI study will involve and ways to determine the success of the study in advance, in specific detail. In addition, we will focus on techniques for collecting data during and after a diversity initiative. You will be introduced to a range of approaches and methods for gathering data that will help you better understand the processes that link to creating the measures that support your diversity scorecard.

DIVERSITY EVALUATION: PROJECT REQUIREMENTS

It is important to include as much detail as possible when specifying the requirements of a DROI evaluation study. Many projects run into difficulty, misunderstandings, and differences in expected outcomes because the requirements are not planned and well documented. These issues are often outlined in a diversity project proposal or detailed in the project's scope documentation. Regardless of the way it is developed, the following items should be included to achieve the best chance for success.

More important, the diversity professional and the evaluation project's sponsor (the client) need to reach agreement about these key issues to create partnership and accountability for the end result.

OBJECTIVES OF THE DIVERSITY EVALUATION PROJECT

When it comes to evaluation projects, there are two sets of objectives. First, there are the objectives for the evaluation project itself, indicating specifically what will be accomplished and delivered through the evaluation process. The other set of objectives is called the initiative objectives and focuses on the goals of the actual diversity initiative that will ultimately add value to the organization. This section focuses on the objectives of the diversity evaluation project.

Every diversity evaluation project should have a major project objective, and in most cases, multiple objectives. The objectives should be as specific as possible and focused directly on the diversity evaluation. Sample project objectives may include the following:

- ☐ Determine if the diversity initiative is accomplishing its objectives.
- ☐ Identify the strengths and weaknesses in the diversity initiative.
- ☐ Determine the benefit/cost ratio of the diversity initiative.
- ☐ Identify who benefited the most and least from the diversity initiative.
- ☐ Gather data to assist in pursuing future initiatives.

As the list illustrates, the objectives are broad in scope, outlining from an overall perspective what is to be accomplished. The details of timing, specifications, and specific deliverables come later. The broad diversity evaluation project objectives are critical because they focus the project quickly. They define the basic parameters of the project and are often the beginning points of a discussion with those involved in the project (Phillips, Stone, Phillips, 2001).

Scope

The scope of the diversity evaluation project needs to be clearly defined. The scope can pinpoint key parameters addressed by the project. The following list shows typical scope issues that should be defined in the project:

- ☐ Target group for the evaluation
- ☐ Location of the target group

☐ Timeframe for the evaluation
☐ Technology necessary to conduct the evaluation
☐ Access to stakeholders
☐ Functional area for coverage
☐ Product line for coverage
☐ Type of diversity process/activity being evaluated
☐ Constraints on data collection

Perhaps the project is limited to certain employee or demographic groups, a functional area of the business, a specific location, a unique type of system, or a precise timeframe. Sometimes there is a constraint on the type of data collected or access to certain individuals, such as particular diverse customers. Whatever the scope involves, it needs to be clearly defined in this section.

Timing

Timing is critical in showing specifically when the diversity activities will occur. This means not only the timing of the delivery of the final DROI study report but also the timing of particular steps and events, including when data are needed, analyzed, and reported and when presentations are made. The following list shows typical scheduled activities:

☐ Diversity initiatives and/or solutions developed
☐ Implementation started
☐ Implementation completed
☐ Start of the DROI evaluation project
☐ Data collection design complete
☐ Evaluation design complete
☐ Data collection begins
☐ Data collection completed
☐ Specific data collection issues (e.g., pilot testing, executive interviews)
☐ Data analysis complete
☐ Preliminary results available
☐ Report developed
☐ Presentation to management

Deliverables

This section describes exactly what your project sponsor or client will receive when the evaluation project is completed in terms of reports, documents, systems, processes, manuals, forms, flowcharts, or rights to new technology. Whatever the specific deliverables, they are clearly defined in this section. Most projects will have a final report, but they often go much further, delivering process tools and suggested methodologies for improving the diversity process or initiative evaluated.

Methodology

If a specific methodology is to be used for the DROI study, it should be defined. A reference should be made to the appropriateness of the methodology, as well as its reliability, validity, previous success, and how the methodology will accomplish what is needed for the evaluation project to be successful.

Steps

The specific steps that will occur should be defined, showing key milestones. This provides a step-by-step understanding and tracking of the diversity evaluation project such that at any given time the project sponsor or client and the diversity staff can see not only where progress is made but also where the evaluation project is going next.

Resources

This section will define the specific resources required to implement the evaluation. This could include access to individuals, vendors, technology, equipment, facilities, competitors, or customers. All resources that may be needed should be listed, along with details regarding the timing and circumstances under which the resources will be needed.

Cost

The cost section details the specific costs tied to the different steps of the evaluation process. There is often reluctance to detail costs; however, it is important to understand the different steps of the process and their relative costs. When calculating the DROI for a diversity initiative, all costs are considered. This includes not only development and implementation costs but also the costs of evaluating the program. We will discuss this in detail in a later chapter.

Levels of Objectives

Eventually, a diversity initiative or intervention should lead to some level of impact on the business of the organization. In some situations, the diversity initiative is aimed at softer issues, such as employee satisfaction, diverse customer group satisfaction, and diverse workgroup conflict reduction. In other situations, diversity initiatives are aimed at more tangible issues, such as cost reductions, productivity, and the number of voluntary turnovers, all sorted by demographic group. Whatever the case, diversity initiatives and interventions should have multiple levels of objectives. These levels of objectives, ranging from qualitative to quantitative, define precisely what will occur as a particular diversity initiative is implemented in the organization. Table 4-1 highlights the different levels of objectives. These objectives are so critical that they need special attention in their development and use.

Table 4-1. Multiple Levels of Objectives for Diversity Initiatives

Level 1: Reaction and Satisfaction	Defines a specific level of satisfaction and reaction to the diversity initiative as it is revealed and communicated to the stakeholders involved.
Level 2: Learning	Defines specific skills and knowledge requirements as the stakeholders learn new skills and acquire new knowledge through the diversity initiative.
Level 3: Application and Implementation	Defines key issues around the implementation of a diversity initiative in the workplace.
Level 4: Business Impact	Defines the specific business measures that will change or improve as a result of the implementation of diversity initiatives.
Level 5: Diversity Return-on-Investment (DROI)	Defines the specific return-on-investment from the implementation of the diversity initiative, comparing costs to benefits.
Level 6: Intangibles	Defines specific types of items that may surface and will be recorded as "intangibles or softer evidence" of the diversity initiative's impact.

Source: Edward E. Hubbard, *Measuring Diversity Results*, 1997.

Satisfaction and Reaction

For any diversity initiative to succeed, it is important that a wide range of stakeholders respond positively to the initiative. Ideally, the stakeholders should be satisfied with the program or initiative because it offered the best possible solution to the organization's needs and was performed in a way that provided opportunities for "win-win" outcomes. Stakeholders are those who are directly involved in implementing or using the diversity program or intervention. This includes employees involved in implementing the diversity initiative or the supervisors or team leaders responsible for the redesigned or changed process. Stakeholders could also be managers who must support or assist the process in some way. Finally, the stakeholders could involve the teams and task forces involved in the diversity intervention.

It is important to routinely obtain this type of information so that feedback can be used to make some adjustments, keep the diversity initiative on track, and perhaps even redesign certain parts of a process to make it more diversity-friendly. Many diversity practitioners do not often develop specific objectives at this level or put data collection mechanisms in place to ensure appropriate feedback for making the needed adjustments.

Learning Objectives

Many diversity programs and initiatives will involve learning objectives. Learning objectives are critical to the measurement process because they define the desired competence or performance necessary to make the diversity program or initiative successful. Learning objectives provide a focus for those involved, clearly indicating what they must learn.

The best learning objectives describe the observable and measurable behaviors that are necessary for success with the diversity initiative. They are often outcome based, clearly worded, and specific. They specify what the particular stakeholder must do as a result of implementing the diversity initiative. Learning objectives often have three components:

1. *Performance.* What the participant or stakeholder will be able to do as the diversity initiative or program is implemented
2. *Conditions.* Under which the participant or stakeholder will perform the various tasks and processes
3. *Criteria.* The degree or level of proficiency necessary to perform a new task, process, or procedure that is part of a diversity solution

The three types of learning objectives are often defined as follows:

☐ *Awareness.* Familiarity with terms, concepts, and processes
☐ *Knowledge.* General understanding of concepts, processes, or procedures
☐ *Performance.* Ability to demonstrate skills at least on a basic level

Application and Implementation Objectives

As a diversity solution is actually implemented in the workplace, the application and implementation objectives clearly define what is expected and often what *level of performance* is expected. Application objectives are similar to learning objectives but reflect actual implementation of the new diversity initiative or program. They also involve particular milestones, indicating specifically when intervals of the process are implemented. Application objectives are critical because they describe the expected outcomes in the interim (i.e, between the actual learning of new diversity tasks and procedures and the actual impact that will result). Application or implementation objectives describe how things should be performed or the state of the workplace after the diversity initiative is implemented. They provide a basis for the evaluation of on-the-job changes and performance. The emphasis is on what has occurred on the job as a result of the diversity initiative or process.

The best application objectives identify behaviors that are observable and measurable or action steps in a process that can easily be observed or measured. They specify what the various stakeholders will change or have changed as a result of the diversity initiative. As with learning objectives, application or implementation objectives may have three components:

1. *Performance.* Describes what the stakeholders have changed or have accomplished in a specific time frame after the implementation of the diversity initiative.
2. *Conditions.* Specifies the circumstances under which the stakeholders have performed or are performing the tasks or implementing the diversity initiative.
3. *Criteria.* Indicates the degree or level of proficiency under which the diversity initiative is implemented, the task is being performed, or the steps are completed.

There are two types of basic application objectives: (1) knowledge-based (when the general use or implementation of concepts, processes, and procedures is important) and (2) behavior-based (when the diversity target group is able to demonstrate the actual use of skills, accomplishments of particular tasks, or completion of particular milestones). Here are just a few of the typical questions that are key to application and implementation objectives:

- ☐ What new or improved knowledge will be applied on the job?
- ☐ What is the frequency of the skill application?
- ☐ What specific new task will be performed?
- ☐ What new steps will be implemented?
- ☐ What action items will be implemented?
- ☐ What new procedure will be implemented or changed?
- ☐ What new guidelines will be implemented?
- ☐ What new processes will be implemented?
- ☐ Which meetings need to be held?
- ☐ Which tasks, steps, or procedures will be discontinued?

Application objectives have always been included to some degree in diversity initiatives but have not been as specific as they need to be. To be effective, they must clearly define the workplace environment when the diversity initiative is successfully implemented.

Impact Objectives

Every diversity initiative should result in improving an organization's impact. Organizational impact represents the key business measures that should be improved as the application or implementation objectives are achieved. The impact objectives are critical to measuring business or organizational performance because they define the ultimate expected outcome from the diversity initiative. They describe the business or organizational unit of performance that should be connected to the diversity solution. Above all, they place emphasis on achieving bottom-line results, which stakeholders and client groups demand.

The best impact objectives contain measures that are linked to the solution from the diversity initiative. They describe measures that are easily collected and are well known to the organization. They are results based, are clearly worded, and specify what the stakeholders have ultimately accomplished in their unit as a result of the diversity initiative. Diversity impact objectives include items such as reduced turnover, improved diverse customer market penetration, increased ideas converted to production, improved cycle time, and so on.

Diversity Return-on-Investment (DROI)

A fifth level of objectives for diversity initiatives is the actual expected return-on-investment. These objectives define the expected payoff from the diversity initiative and compare the input resources, the costs of the diversity initiative, with the value of the ultimate outcome—the monetary benefits. This is typically expressed as a desired return-on-investment percentage that compares the annual monetary benefits minus the cost, divided by the actual costs, and multiplied by 100. A 0 percent DROI indicates a break-even diversity solution. A 50 percent DROI indicates that the cost of the initiative is recaptured and an additional 50 percent earnings are achieved.

For many diversity interventions, the DROI amount is often larger than what might be expected from the ROI of other expenditures, such as the purchase of a new company, a new building, or major equipment; but the two are related. In many organizations the DROI objective is set slightly higher than the ROI expected from other interventions because of the relative newness of applying ROI concepts to diversity initiatives and processes. For example, if the expected ROI from the purchase of a new company is 20 percent, the DROI from a diversity initiative might be closer to 25 to 35 percent. The important point is that the DROI objective target should be established upfront through discussions with stakeholders and the client.

Importance of Specific Objectives

Developing specific objectives at different levels for a diversity initiative is critical to the success of the effort. First, objectives provide direction to the diversity staff directly involved in the process to help keep them on track. Objectives define exactly what is expected at different timeframes from different departments or individuals and involve different types of data. Also, objectives guide the support staff and key stakeholders so that they fully understand the ultimate goal and impact of the diversity initiative. Furthermore, objectives provide important information and motivation for the stakeholders. In most diversity initiatives, the stakeholders are actively involved and will influence the results of the initiative. Specific objectives provide goals and motivation for the stakeholders so they will clearly see the gains that should be achieved. More important, objectives provide important information for key client groups so they can clearly understand what the outcome or environment will look like when the diversity initiative is complete. Finally, from an evaluation perspective, the objectives provide a basis for measuring success.

ALIGNING AND LINKING YOUR EVALUATION STRATEGY WITH BUSINESS NEEDS

A distinct link exists between evaluation objectives and original business needs driving a diversity intervention. In this chapter, we introduced the six levels of evaluation and showed how they are critical to providing an overall assessment of the impact of a diversity initiative. The earlier material in this chapter showed the importance of setting objectives around a diversity initiative. The objectives define the specific improvements sought. This section highlights additional connections to the original needs assessment. Figure 4-1 shows the connection between the diversity initiative evaluation levels and a business needs assessment.

This figure, based on a model by Phillips, Stone, Phillips (2001), shows the important linkage from the initial problem or opportunity that created the business need to the evaluation and measurement. Level 5 defines

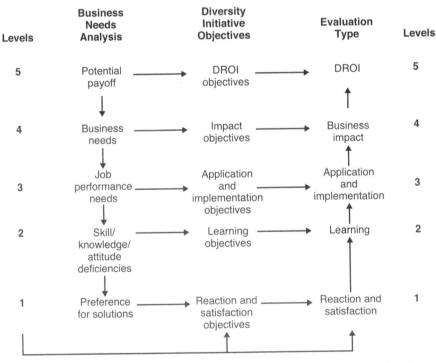

Figure 4-1. Linkage between diversity initiative evaluation levels and business needs assessment. (Source: Adapted from Phillips, J., R. Stone, P. Phillips. The Human Resources Scorecard, 2000, p. 52.)

the potential payoff and examines the possibility for a DROI before the project is even pursued. Level 4 analysis focuses directly on the business needs that precipitated a diversity initiative. At Level 3, the specific diversity issues in the workplace focus on job performance in detail. At Level 2, the specific knowledge, skill, or attitude deficiencies related to diversity and diversity processes are uncovered as learning needs are identified. Finally, the preferences for the structure of the solution define the Level 1 needs. This connection is critical and important to understanding all of the elements that must go into an effective diversity intervention solution.

An example will help illustrate this linkage and alignment. Figure 4-2 shows an example of linking a business needs assessment with the diversity evaluation of an initiative involving a reduction in absenteeism. As the figure shows, the first step is to see if the problem is great enough at Level 5; however, this sometimes causes a validation of the business problem using Level 4 data. The following four benchmarks are used to gauge the current absenteeism problem (Hubbard, 1999):

1. Absenteeism is higher than it used to be.
2. Absenteeism is higher than at other locations within the company.
3. Absenteeism is higher than at other facilities in the local area.
4. Absenteeism is higher than the general manager desires.

With the confirmation in Level 4 that a problem exists, a potential payoff is estimated. This involves estimating the cost of absenteeism and estimating the actual potential reduction that can come from the diversity intervention. This develops a profile of potential payoff to see if the problem is worth solving.

At Level 3, the causes of excessive absenteeism are explored using a variety of techniques. One issue that is uncovered is that a "business-based flexibility" work life policy covering flextime arrangements is not currently available to employees and managers. A pareto analysis revealed that the primary reported reasons for unexpected absences were due to daycare and elder-care responsibilities and the lack of flexibility in each business unit to adjust to employee family requirements. A learning component at Level 2 is also uncovered because the team leaders need to understand how and when to administer the business-based flexibility policies. Finally, the specific way in which the diversity initiative should be implemented is explored in terms of preferences at Level 1. In this case, supervisors preferred to attend a half-day meeting to learn how the policies should be implemented and leave with a job aid that helps them with the process as they apply it.

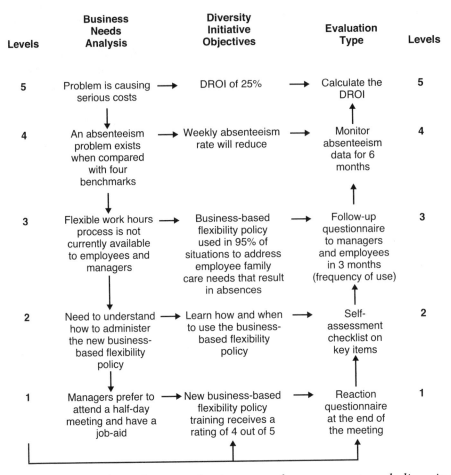

Levels	Business Needs Analysis	Diversity Initiative Objectives	Evaluation Type	Levels
5	Problem is causing serious costs	DROI of 25%	Calculate the DROI	5
4	An absenteeism problem exists when compared with four benchmarks	Weekly absenteeism rate will reduce	Monitor absenteeism data for 6 months	4
3	Flexible work hours process is not currently available to employees and managers	Business-based flexibility policy used in 95% of situations to address employee family care needs that result in absences	Follow-up questionnaire to managers and employees in 3 months (frequency of use)	3
2	Need to understand how to administer the new business-based flexibility policy	Learn how and when to use the business-based flexibility policy	Self-assessment checklist on key items	2
1	Managers prefer to attend a half-day meeting and have a job-aid	New business-based flexibility policy training receives a rating of 4 out of 5	Reaction questionnaire at the end of the meeting	1

Figure 4-2. Linkage between business needs assessment and diversity evaluation involving reduction of absenteeism.

These five levels provide an overall profile for determining if the problem is worth solving to begin with, as well as aligning problems with key measures and data necessary to develop the diversity initiative's objectives. The diversity initiative's objectives for each level are shown in the figure as well, as are the evaluation methods needed to verify that the appropriate changes occurred. This process is important to the development and implementation of a diversity business solution. Many diversity initiatives are involved in developing the actual solution and implementing the solution, as is the case in this particular example. When this occurs, the above linkage connects the needs to actual business objectives and then to evaluation.

The solution to the problem or opportunity is an important part of this linkage. Some diversity initiatives may be involved in uncovering needs with the initial analysis to determine the actual causes of the problem and then recommend solutions. It is up to the client or business unit to then implement the solution, or implementation becomes part of another diversity initiative. In both cases, the solutions are ultimately developed. If this has not been accomplished, multiple levels of analysis may be necessary for the intervention. Although other resources and references exist that focus more specifically on the performance analysis to uncover different levels of needs, a brief summary is presented here.

Payoff Needs

The first part of the process is to determine if the problem is worth solving or if the opportunity is large enough to warrant serious consideration. In some cases, this is obvious when serious problems are affecting the organization's operations and strategy. Still, others may not be so obvious. At Level 5, it is important not only to identify needed business improvement measures at Level 4 but also to convert them into monetary values so the actual improvement can be converted to financial measures.

The second part of the process is to develop an approximate cost for the entire diversity initiative. This could come from a detailed proposal or may be a rough estimate. At this stage it is only an estimate because the projected cost of the project is compared to the potential benefits to roughly determine if a payoff would result from addressing the issue. This step may be omitted in some situations when the problem must be solved regardless of the cost or if it becomes obvious that it is a high-payoff activity. Still other projects may be initiated when the potential payoff is not expected to be developed. For example, as an organization strives to be a technology leader, it may be difficult to place a value on that goal.

Business Needs

In conjunction with Level 5, actual business data are examined to determine which measures need to improve. This includes an examination of organizational records and involves examining all types of hard and soft data. Usually one of the data items and its performance trigger the diversity initiative or intervention (e.g., market share may not be as much as it should be, costs may be excessive, quality may be deteriorating, or productivity may not be as high as it should be). These key issues come directly from the data in the organization and are often found in the operating reports or records.

The supporting data may come not only from the operating reports but also from annual reports, marketing data, industry data, major planning documents, or other important information sources that clearly indicate operating performance in terms of operation or strategy.

Job Performance Needs

The Level 3 analysis involves job performance or workplace needs. The task is to determine the cause of the problem as determined at Level 4 (i.e., what is causing the business measure not to be at the desired level or to be inhibited in some way?). These needs can vary considerably and may include, among others, dealing with the following:

- ☐ Ineffective or inappropriate behavior
- ☐ Prejudice and stereotypes
- ☐ Dysfunctional work climate
- ☐ Ineffective systems
- ☐ Institutionalized bias in management practices
- ☐ Improper process flow
- ☐ Ethnocentrism
- ☐ Ineffective procedures
- ☐ Intergroup conflict
- ☐ Unsupported culture
- ☐ Inappropriate technology
- ☐ Unsupportive environment

These and other types of workplace needs will have to be uncovered using a variety of problem-solving or analysis techniques. This may involve the use of data collection techniques such as surveys, questionnaires, focus groups, or interviews. It may involve a variety of Six Sigma–based problem-solving or analysis techniques such as root-cause analysis, fishbone diagrams, and other analysis techniques. Whatever method is used, the key is to determine all the causes of the problem so solutions can be developed. Often, multiple solutions are appropriate.

Learning Needs

Most problem analysis from Level 3 uncovers specific learning needs. It may be that learning inefficiencies, in terms of knowledge and skills, contribute to the problem if they are not the major cause of it. In other situations, the actual solution applied may need a particular learning component as participants learn how to implement a new process, procedure, or system. The extent of learning required will determine whether formalized training is needed or if more informal, on-the-job methods can be used to build the necessary skills and knowledge. The learning would typically involve acquisition of knowledge or development of skills necessary to improve the situation. In some cases, perceptions or attitudes may need to be altered to make the process successful in the future.

Preferences

The final level is to consider the preference for the solution. This involves determining the way in which those involved in the process prefer to have it changed or implemented. It may involve implementation preferences and/or learning preferences. Learning preferences may involve decisions, such as when learning is expected and in what amounts, how it is presented, and the overall timeframe. Implementation preferences may involve issues such as timing, support, expectation, and other key factors. The important point is to try to determine the specific preferences to the extent possible so that a complete profile of the solution can be adjusted accordingly. Once all avenues of the planning process are addressed, it is time to begin your data collection effort.

COLLECTING DATA DURING A DIVERSITY INITIATIVE

Data collection is the most crucial step of the evaluation process because without data, there is no evidence of the diversity initiative's impact and therefore no need for an evaluation. During the data collection process, it is necessary to determine the participant's reactions and satisfaction to the diversity initiative (Level 1), their level of learning from the intervention (Level 2), the amount of application and implementation that happened as a consequence of the diversity initiative (Level 3), the resulting business impact (Level 4), and whether the initiative generated benefits and a return-on-investment (Levels 5 and 6). It is necessary to collect data from at least Levels 1 to 4 because of the chain of impact that must exist for a diversity initiative to be successful. To reap the chain of impact, a key business problem that can be addressed by diversity must be identified. Participants in the diversity initiative related to this business problem should experience a positive reaction to the initiative and its potential applications, and they should acquire new knowledge or skills to perform at an improved level as a result of the initiative. As application and/or implementation opportunities arise, changes in on-the-job behavior should result in a positive impact on the organization. The only way to know if the chain of impact has occurred up to this point is to collect data at all four levels. The diversity initiative will also generate benefits that are either quantitative or qualitative in the forms of benefit-to-cost impacts, dollar return-on-investment impact, and/or anecdotal information. If this is the case, all six levels of evaluation will be involved, as shown in Table 4-2.

Measuring Reaction and Satisfaction

Collecting reaction and satisfaction data during implementation of a diversity initiative is the first operational phase of the DROI process. Participant feedback data are powerful for making adjustments and measuring success. A variety of methods are available to capture reaction and satisfaction data at appropriate times during the implementation process. We will examine some of the more common approaches for collecting these data and highlight several key issues about use of the information.

Why Measure Reaction and Satisfaction?

It would be difficult to imagine a diversity initiative being implemented without collecting feedback from those involved in the process, or at least from the client. Client feedback is critical to understand how well the process is working or to gauge its success after it has been completed. It is always included in every diversity initiative because of its crucial

Table 4-2. Levels of Evaluation

Level of Data Analysis	Type of Data
1	Reaction/Satisfaction and planned action(s)
2	Learning
3	Application/Implementation
4	Business impact
5	Diversity Return-on-Investment (DROI)
6	Anecdotal

importance; however, the advantage of collecting this type of data goes beyond just client satisfaction and includes many other key issues, making it one of the most important data collection efforts. The advantages may include the following:

- ☐ Measuring diverse customer service impact
- ☐ Determining if the initiative is on target
- ☐ Making adjustment and changes
- ☐ Collecting participant reactions
- ☐ Evaluating expected involvement
- ☐ Comparing with data from other programs

Measuring Diverse Customer Service Impact

Customer service is a critical element for organizational success in today's economy; therefore, it is important to measure customers' reactions. Both internal organizational customers and diverse customers in new emerging ethnic markets have a variety of needs that must be fulfilled. Without continuous improvement feedback evidenced by customer satisfaction data, you will not know if your internal or external diversity initiatives and interventions are successful. It is also important to consider the different types of customers that may be involved in your initiative. First, there are those directly involved in the initiative. They are the key stakeholders who are directly affected by the diversity initiative and often have to change processes or procedures and make other adjustments related to the initiative. In addition, they often have to learn new skills, tasks, and behaviors to make the initiative successful. These participants are critical to the success of the initiative, and their feedback is vital to making adjustments and changes in the initiative (or interventions) as it unfolds and is implemented. For example, a new advertising campaign to attract minorities might have a reaction-focused feedback tool to use during an on-campus focus group session, or during a test market product release, or in a specific locale to determine diverse consumer reaction to a new advertisement or product. The organization would use this feedback to adjust the product offering to meet its target objectives.

The second set of customers is those who support from the sidelines (i.e., those who are not directly involved but have some interest in the diversity initiative). For example, this group might include specific store owners who will carry the new product or service shown in the advertisement for these ethnic consumers. Their perception of the success of the diversity initiative or its potential success is important feedback.

As a group, store owners are always in a strong position to influence the outcome of the campaign.

The third set of stakeholders is perhaps the most important group because it includes individuals such as the client or financial sponsor who pays for the diversity initiative or influences its budget approval, allocates resources, and ultimately lives with the success or failure of the diversity initiative. This important group must be completely satisfied with the diversity initiative as a solution. Their level of satisfaction must be determined early, and adjustments must be made. In short, customer satisfaction is key to success and must be obtained in a variety of different ways to focus on the success.

Determining if the Initiative Is on Target

Diversity initiatives can go off in the wrong direction, sometimes very quickly. You may discover that the particular initiative is the wrong or incomplete solution for the business challenge it was designed to address. There are times when the diversity initiative will be mismatched from the beginning, so it is essential to obtain feedback early in the process so adjustments can be made. This helps avoid misunderstandings, miscommunications, and more important, misappropriations, as an improperly designed initiative is altered or changed quickly before more serious problems are created.

Making Adjustments and Changes

It is critical to obtain feedback throughout the duration of a diversity initiative to make refinements and adjustments. There must be an important linkage between obtaining feedback and making changes and reporting changes back to the groups who provide the information. Customers, for example, will want to know if you used the feedback that they supplied to improve the product or service. This survey-feedback-action loop is vital to the success of any diversity initiative.

Collecting Participant Reactions

Many of the individuals involved in the diversity initiative, particularly the affected populations or participants, appreciate the opportunity to provide feedback. In too many situations, their input is ignored and their complaints disregarded. This happens often when assumptions are made that this population is just like all others. For example, some advertisers will assume that just because an advertisement worked well for the Caucasian majority market, all that is needed to sell to minorities is to replace the images of Caucasians with those of a minority. What they may forget is that the culture, background, specific situation, and other aspects of the advertisement do not match what a person from that culture would do or how they would respond. Employee Resource or Affinity Groups can be a great source of information and feedback if they are utilized properly. These groups appreciate it when they are asked for input and, more important, when action is taken as a result of their input. Other stakeholders and even clients appreciate the opportunity to provide feedback, not only early in the process but also throughout the process.

Expected Involvement

For some, collecting this type of feedback data is expected as the norm. In fact, if you did not collect it, your evaluation process would be suspect. Every diversity initiative should collect some form of reaction and satisfaction-level data. Unfortunately, some diversity evaluators stop here and use only reaction and satisfaction-level data to measure the success of the diversity change process. As this book will certainly illustrate, reaction and satisfaction-level feedback is only one part of the evaluation puzzle and represents only one of the six types of data that can be collected. Nonetheless, its importance in the diversity evaluation process cannot be underestimated.

Comparing with Data from Other Programs

Some organizations collect reaction and satisfaction-level data from several sources using standard questions, and the data are then compared with data from other diversity initiatives so norms and standards can be developed. This is particularly helpful at the end of a diversity initiative rollout when client satisfaction is assessed. These satisfaction data can be used not only to compare the success of the initiative but also to relate to the overall success of the initiative and even correlate with other successful measures. Data collection must be deliberately pursued in a systematic, logical, and rational way.

Areas of Feedback for Reaction and Satisfaction Data

Many topics are critical targets for feedback because so many issues and processes are involved in a typical diversity initiative implementation.

Feedback is needed in almost every major issue, step, or process to make sure things are moving forward properly. The following list shows the typical major areas of reaction and satisfaction feedback for many initiatives (Phillips, Stone, Phillips, 2001):

- ☐ Appropriateness of objectives
- ☐ Appropriateness of plans
- ☐ Appropriateness of schedule
- ☐ Progress made with plans
- ☐ Relevance of initiative
- ☐ Support for initiative
- ☐ Resources for initiative
- ☐ Integration of initiative with other systems
- ☐ Initiative leadership
- ☐ Initiative staffing
- ☐ Initiative coordination
- ☐ Initiative communication
- ☐ Motivation of initiative participants
- ☐ Cooperation of initiative participants
- ☐ Capability of initiative participants
- ☐ Likelihood of initiative success
- ☐ Barriers to project success
- ☐ Enablers to initiative success
- ☐ Continuing administration of the initiative

This list shows the key success factors in a diversity initiative, beginning with the issues that reflect the initial planning of the initiative. Different stakeholders react to the appropriateness of the initiative planning schedule and objectives and the progress made with those planning tools. The relevance of the initiative is critical for participants because if the initiative is perceived as irrelevant, more than likely it will not succeed in the workplace. The support for the initiative—including resources and how the initiative is integrated with other systems—represents an important area for feedback. Participants must see that the initiative has the necessary commitment. Several issues are important to management and the organization sponsoring the initiative, including initiative leadership, staffing levels, coordination, and communication. Also, it is important to gather feedback on how well the initiative implementation team is working to address such issues as motivation, cooperation, and capability. A dysfunctional team can spell disaster quickly. Finally, the issues that inhibit or enhance success are important, along with input on the likelihood of success. For a particular initiative, there can be other issues, and each can have specific parts. Each step, element, task, or part of the initiative represents an opportunity for feedback. The challenge is to sort out those things that are most important so participants can be provided valuable input.

Measuring Skill and Knowledge Changes

It may seem unnecessary to measure learning in a diversity initiative. After all, when application and implementation are measured, the actual progress made in the workplace is measured. Ultimately, when business impact variables are monitored, the success of the initiative becomes quite clear; however, it is sometimes critical to understand the extent to which learning has occurred, particularly in initiatives where a significant amount of job changes, procedure changes, new tools, new processes, and new technologies occur. The extent to which participants in the diversity initiative learn their job, the new procedure change, or new process can often make or break the success of the diversity initiative.

Three key areas determine why it is important to measure learning in a diversity initiative. Each of them on their own would be enough to justify why learning is measured. Taken together, they represent a powerful thrust and present strategic evidence for the amount of skill, knowledge, or change that occurred during the diversity initiative.

Measuring Knowledge, Expertise, and Competencies Is Important

Working in today's world requires the use of a wide range of competencies, skills, and behaviors. Having and/or acquiring core competencies and capabilities in a variety of technical, process, cultural, and interpersonal areas is a chief determinant of success in a multicultural world. Many diversity initiatives will test the use and application of this knowledge, expertise, and competency. Therefore, measuring whether participants in a diversity initiative actually acquired the intellectual knowledge base to function effectively in a diverse work environment is crucial.

Diversity initiatives often require employees to learn new approaches, develop expertise in processes, and understand cultural systems that are different from what they are used to. Many of these diversity interventions ask that employees increase their competence in cultural awareness and cross-cultural interaction skills in areas where this new learning runs counter to their current cultural/behavioral software programming. Learning represents a large part of a diversity initiative because many employees do not automatically use effective skills when interacting with others who are different from themselves and with systems that operate using new cultural norms. Gone are the homogeneous organizational environments where the employee mixtures are generally flat and the complexion somewhat predictable at each level. Instead, there are complex, diverse environments, complex human and other processes, and tools that must be used in intelligent ways to reap the benefits of a diverse workforce and society. Employees must learn in a variety of ways to gain the skills and competencies necessary to utilize the rich diversity reflected in all aspects of their environment and what they do. Also, diverse work team leaders and managers often reinforce, coach, and mentor employees in their use of newly learned skills to ensure that learning is transferred to the job and that the diversity initiative is implemented as planned (Hubbard, 1999).

Finding Out What Went Wrong When a Problem Occurs

If you want to find out what went wrong during the rollout of a diversity initiative and/or what needs to be changed, it is critical to measure learning. It is helpful to answer the following questions:

- [ ] What went wrong?
- [ ] What areas need adjustment?
- [ ] What needs to be altered completely?
- [ ] What portion of the initiative that required learning was learned?
- [ ] What portion of the initiative that required learning was not learned?

When learning is measured, it is easy to track down whether learning or something else was the problem. Without the learning component, diversity professionals will not know why employees are not performing the way they should or which part of the diversity initiative is not being managed properly. These critical issues make learning an important consideration in diversity measurement strategy. Competency and skill-based learning helps build strategic diversity capability that can be used as a competitive advantage.

COLLECTING DATA AFTER A DIVERSITY INITIATIVE

Measuring Application and Implementation

Measuring the actual application and implementation of skills and knowledge is critical because these steps play a pivotal role in the overall success or failure of a diversity initiative. If learned skills and knowledge are not applied effectively, there will be no change in the business function—and no benefit from the diversity initiative.

Why Measure Application and Implementation?

In addition to the obvious reasons for measuring application and implementation, there are several specific reasons why this is one of the most important measures to track in the diversity evaluation process:

The Value of the Information. The value of the information increases as progress is made through the chain of impact from Level 1 to Level 5. Thus, information concerning application and implementation at Level 3 is more valuable to the client or business unit than reaction/satisfaction (Level 1) and learning (Level 2). This is not meant to discount the importance of these two levels but to emphasize that measuring the extent to which the diversity initiative is implemented often provides critical data about not only the project's success but also the factors that can contribute to greater success as the diversity initiative is fully integrated within the organization (Phillips, Stone, Phillips, 2001).

A Key Transition Issue. The two previous measures, reaction/satisfaction and learning, occur during the diversity initiative when there is more attention and focus directly on the diversity initiative. Level 3, measuring application and implementation, occurs after the diversity intervention has been implemented and measures the success of the application and implementation. Essentially, this measure explains the degree to which the diversity initiative is handed off to those who are charged with its ultimate success. This is a key transition process and is the first measure that follows the process after the initiative has been fully implemented. This in itself makes it a critical issue, where various measures of success are identified and enhancements to additional success are pinpointed.

The Key Focus of Many Diversity Interventions. Because many diversity interventions focus directly on application and implementation, the diversity initiative's sponsor often speaks in these terms and is concerned about these measures of success. Many major diversity interventions designed to transform an organization and build a stronger team and customer focus will have key issues around Level 3, application and implementation. The sponsor will be interested in knowing the extent to which all of the key stakeholders are adjusting to and implementing the desired new (inclusive) behaviors, processes, and procedures. This interest is at the core of application and implementation.

Problems, Obstacles, and Barriers. When a diversity initiative goes astray, the first question is, "What happened?" More important, when an initiative appears not to be adding value, the first question should be, "What can we do to change the direction of the intervention?" In either scenario, it is critical to have information that identifies barriers to success, problems encountered in implementation, and obstacles to the actual application of the process. At Level 3, measuring application and implementation, these problems are addressed, identified, and examined for solutions. In many cases, the key stakeholders directly involved in the process provide important input into the recommendations for making changes or for using a different approach in the future.

Enablers and Enhancers. When there is success, the obvious question is, "How can we repeat this or even improve on this in the future?" The answer to this question is also found at Level 3. Identifying the factors that contribute directly to the success of the diversity initiative is critical because those same items can be used to replicate the process to produce specific results in the future and to enhance results. When key stakeholders identify those issues, it helps make the project successful and provides an important case history of what is necessary for success.

Rewards Those Who Are Most Effective. Measuring application and implementation allows the client, the business unit, and the diversity staff to reward those who are doing the best job of applying the processes and implementing the diversity initiative. Measures taken at this level present clear evidence of various efforts and roles, providing an excellent basis for performance review or special recognition. This often has a reinforcing value for keeping the project on track and communicating a strong message for future improvements (Phillips, Stone, Phillips, 2001).

Measuring Business Impact

Measuring and tracking business performance measures helps bring the diversity evaluation process full circle to connect with the initial business needs analysis. Some diversity staff members—and clients—regard business impact data as the most important type because of their connection to business unit success. Also, less-than-desired results in business measures are what translate into a business need that ultimately initiates diversity intervention.

Why Measure Business Impact?

Although there are several obvious reasons for measuring impact, four particular issues support the rationale for collecting business impact data related to a diversity initiative:

Higher-level Data. Following the assumption that higher-level data create more value for the client, the business impact measures in a five-level framework offer more valuable data. They are the data considered to be the consequence of the application and implementation of a diversity initiative. They often represent the bottom-line measures that are positively influenced when a program is successful.

A *Business Driver for Diversity Initiatives.* For most diversity initiatives, the business impact data represent the initial drivers for the diversity initiative. It is the problem of deterioration or less-than-desired performance, or the opportunity for improvement of a business measure, that often leads to a diversity initiative. If the business needs defined by business measures are the drivers for a project, then the key measure for evaluating the project is the business impact. The extent to which measures actually have changed is the key determinant of the success of the project.

Payoff with Clients. Business impact data often reflect key payoff measures from the perspective of the client (internal and/or external). These are the measures often desired by the client and that the client wants to see changed or improved. They often represent hard, indisputable facts that reflect performance critical to the business and operating unit level of the organization.

Easy to Measure. One unique feature about business impact data is that they are often very easy to measure. Hard and soft data measures at this level often reflect key measures that are found in plentiful numbers throughout an organization. It is not unusual for an organization to have hundreds or even thousands of measures reflecting specific business impact items. The challenge is to connect the diversity initiative objectives to the appropriate business measures. This is more easily accomplished at the beginning of the diversity initiative because of the availability and ease with which many of the data items can be located.

REVIEWING HISTORICAL DATA

Another alternative for identifying diversity measurement areas is reviewing historical data. Data are available in every organization to measure performance. Monitoring performance data enables you to measure diversity results in terms of output, quality, costs, and time. In determining the use of data in the diversity scorecard study area, the first consideration should include examining exiting databases and reports. In most organizations, performance data suitable for measuring improvements from a diversity initiative are available. If not, additional record-keeping systems will have to be developed for data collection, measurement, and analysis.

At this point, as with many other points in the process, the question of economics enters. Is it economical to develop the record-keeping system necessary to evaluate a diversity initiative? If the costs are greater than the expected return for the entire program, then it is meaningless to develop them.

Using Current Measures

When using current measures, be sure they are appropriate to the area you want to study. Performance measures should be thoroughly researched to identify those that are related to the proposed objectives of the diversity initiative. Frequently, an organization will have several performance measures related to the same item. For example, if the diversity organization works with the operations department to improve the efficiency of a production unit's work teams, it might start by analyzing diverse work styles. The impact of this could be measured in a variety of ways:

- ☐ The number of units produced per hour
- ☐ The number of on-schedule production units
- ☐ The percentage of utilization of the new work style
- ☐ The percentage of work group downtime resulting from conflict
- ☐ The labor cost per unit of production

☐ The overtime required per piece of production
☐ The total unit cost

Each of these factors, in its own way, measures the efficiency of the production unit. All related measures should be reviewed to determine those most relevant to the diversity initiative.

Converting Current Measures to Usable Ones

Occasionally, existing performance measures are integrated with other data, and it may be difficult to isolate them from unrelated data. In this situation, all existing related measures should be extracted and retabulated to be more appropriate for comparison in the evaluation.

At times, conversion factors may be necessary. For example, the average number of new recruits per month may be presented regularly in the performance measures for the staffing department. In addition, the cost of generating new recruits per recruiter is also presented. In the evaluation of the impact of a diversity initiative, however, the average cost of a diverse hire is needed. This will require at least two existing performance records to develop the data necessary for comparison (the average number and the cost data).

Developing a Data Collection Plan for Performance Data

A data collection plan defines when, by whom, and where the data are collected. This plan should contain provisions for the evaluator to secure copies of performance reports in a timely manner so that the items can be recorded and are available for analysis.

Developing New Measures

In some cases, data are not available for the information needed to measure the effectiveness of a diversity initiative's impact. The diversity organization must work with the appropriate department to develop record-keeping systems, if this is economically feasible. In one organization, a new employee orientation program was implemented on a companywide basis for new hires from diverse backgrounds. Several feedback measures were planned, including early turnover (known as survival and loss rates), which represents the percentage of people of color who left the company in the first six months of their employment. At the time of the initiative's inception, this measure was not available.

Table 4-3. Typical Questions when Creating New Measures

Which department will develop the measurement system?
Who will record and monitor the data?
Where will the information be recorded?
How often will you collect data?

When the initiative was implemented, the organization had to begin collecting early turnover figures for comparison (Hubbard, 1999).

These questions, as shown in Table 4-3, usually involve other departments or a management decision that extends beyond the scope of the diversity organization. Possibly the administration division, the HR Department, or the Information Technology Department will be instrumental in helping determine if new measures are needed and, if so, how they will be collected.

An effective diversity scorecard must be built on a comprehensive planning and data collection model that incorporates appropriate evaluation objectives and critical factual information. By utilizing these techniques to plan and collect data, your diversity evaluation study will begin on a solid foundation that positions your diversity scorecard for success.

FINAL THOUGHTS

Planning and data collection activities help establish the essential core elements for a successful evaluation and/or DROI study process. They are the building blocks for creating a strategic analysis framework that is in alignment with the organization's mission. In addition, it creates a set of guidelines for designing an effective information gathering system to understand the required scope, timing, and deliverables of the project. These steps are critical for accurately assessing diversity's impact on the organization's behavior and performance.

In the next chapter, we will add to these steps by examining the tools and processes needed to evaluate and calculate diversity's contribution to the bottom line.

REFERENCES

Hubbard, Edward E. *How to Calculate Diversity Return on Investment*. Petaluma, CA: Global Insights, 1999.

Phillips, Jack J., Ron D. Stone, and Patricia P. Phillips. *The Human Resources Scorecard*. Boston: Butterworth–Heinemann, 2001.

CHAPTER 5

Evaluating Diversity's Contribution

Once you have implemented your plans and collected data related to your diversity evaluation study, you are ready to evaluate the extent to which the diversity initiative made a contribution to the organization. This evaluation will encompass the remaining stages of the Hubbard Diversity ROI Process: isolating diversity's contribution, converting the contribution to money, calculating cost and benefits, calculating diversity's return-on-investment, identifying intangible effects, and reporting the contribution to others. Tools and techniques to track and assess your progress over time will be covered in a later chapter.

ISOLATING DIVERSITY'S CONTRIBUTION

This step will help you select a method to isolate diversity's contribution to the organization's goals and objectives. Imagine the following situation: While reviewing the results of a diversity initiative, along with other key indicators, a significant increase in work unit productivity is noted for the same period. This situation seems to have been repeated over several periods since the diversity initiative has been put in place. The two events appear to be linked. A key manager asks, "How much of this improvement was caused by the diversity initiative?" Often, when this potentially embarrassing question is asked, it is rarely answered with any degree of accuracy and credibility. Although the change in productivity may be linked to the diversity initiative, other nondiversity factors probably contributed to the improvement as well.

Preliminary Issues

Although there are at least 10 different approaches available to isolate the effects of diversity (e.g., control groups, trend-line analysis, forecasting, path analysis), we will focus on the use of only one of them: participant estimates. This strategy is utilized in leading organizations as they attempt to measure the return-on-investment in areas such as diversity, training and development, and the like. Other strategies are outlined in the book *How to Calculate Diversity Return on Investment,* by Dr. Edward E. Hubbard.

The cause-and-effect relationship between diversity and performance can be confusing and difficult to prove, but it can be accomplished with an acceptable degree of accuracy. But is proof the only reason we measure diversity results and performance? The answer is a resounding "NO!"

Diversity and the Double-Standard Subterfuge

Diversity is often held to a double standard when it comes to measurement. Disciplines such as marketing and finance, for example, are not asked to prove that inflation will be a particular number. The compensation and benefits department is not asked to prove that actuarial tables are accurate predictors of exactly when a person will die, yet they base many insurance and retirement benefits on them. Or what about executive retreats with the top management team? Has anyone asked for proof that spending thousands of dollars to host executives (and often their families) for a weekend of golf, relaxation, and a little business has yielded a specific dollar return-on-investment? I am not suggesting that these activities are not important, only that the same yardstick should apply in all places.

It's not about proof, it's about compelling evidence that a significant cost/benefit relationship exists. Calculating diversity ROI should help an organization achieve the following:

- ☐ Assess progress, urgency, and impact.
- ☐ Increase awareness, skill, and productivity.
- ☐ Improve structures, processes, and systems.
- ☐ Discontinue or expand initiatives.
- ☐ Approve diversity initiatives/projects (if pilots).
- ☐ Build a database on diversity performance and results.
- ☐ Enhance management and others' understanding and support.
- ☐ Improve measurement skills of the diversity staff.
- ☐ Achieve corporate, business unit, governmental, nonprofit, individual, and community goals.

The challenge is to develop one or more specific strategies to isolate the effects of diversity early in the process, usually as part of an evaluation plan. Upfront attention ensures the appropriate strategies will be used with minimum costs and time commitments.

Diversity Value Chain Impact

Before presenting the strategies, it may be helpful to consider the chain of impact implied at different stages in the diversity value chain process. Measurable results achieved from a diversity initiative or intervention should be derived from the application of diversity skills and knowledge on the job over a specified period after the diversity initiative has been implemented. This on-the-job application of diversity illustrates the notion that it is critical to link diversity to performance, as shown in Figure 5-1.

Continuing with this diversity value chain logic, successful application of the diversity initiative on the job should stem from participants in the diversity initiative learning and applying diversity knowledge and technologies in a formalized situation to meet a specific organizational goal or objective. Therefore, for an improvement in business results to be realized, this diversity value chain impact implies that measurable on-the-job applications of diversity knowledge and skills are utilized (i.e., tasks such as multicultural marketing, minority recruitment, bilingual customer service transactions, and so on are performed). Without this preliminary evidence, it is difficult to isolate the effects of diversity. In other words, if there is no specific learning or application of diversity strategies and technologies on the job, it is virtually impossible to conclude that the diversity initiative or intervention caused any performance improvements.

In addition, it is vital that measurements are taken throughout the entire diversity value chain. Although this requirement is a prerequisite to isolating the effects of diversity, it does not prove that a direct connection

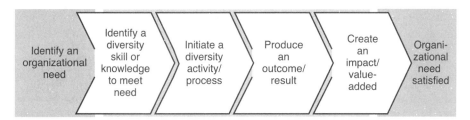

Figure 5-1. Linking diversity to performance.

existed, nor does it pinpoint how much of the improvement was caused by the diversity initiative. It merely shows that without improvements at each stage of the diversity value chain, it is difficult to make a connection between the ultimate outcome and the diversity initiative.

Identifying Other Factors: A First Step

As a first step in isolating diversity's impact on performance, all of the key factors that may have contributed to the performance improvement should be identified. This step communicates to interested parties that other factors may have influenced the results, underscoring that the diversity initiative is not the sole source of improvement. Consequently, the credit for improvement is shared with several possible variables and sources, an approach that is likely to gain the respect of those reviewing the results.

Several potential sources can be used to identify the major influencing variables. For example, if the diversity initiative is designed on request, the client may be able to identify factors that will influence the output variable. Clients will usually be aware of other initiatives or programs that may impact the output.

Participants in the diversity initiative are usually aware of other influences that may have caused performance improvement. After all, the impact of their collective efforts is being monitored and measured. In many situations, they witness previous movements in the performance measures and pinpoint the reasons for changes.

Organization analysts and diversity practitioners who conduct the needs analysis are another source for identifying variables that have an impact on results. The needs analysis will usually uncover these influencing variables. Diversity practitioners must analyze these variables while addressing organizational performance issues.

In some situations, supervisors who are involved in or affected by the performance improvement project using diversity may be able to identify variables that influence the performance improvement. This is particularly useful when the primary diversity initiative participants are nonexempt employees who may not be fully aware of the variables that can influence all of the systemic performance elements.

Finally, middle and top management may be able to identify other influences based on their experience and knowledge of the situation. Perhaps they have monitored, examined, and analyzed the variables previously. The authority level of these individuals often increases the credibility of the data.

Taking time to focus attention on variables that may have influenced performance brings additional accuracy and credibility to the process. It also moves beyond the scenarios where results are presented with no mention of other influences, a situation that often destroys the credibility of a diversity impact report. It also provides a foundation for some of the strategies described in this book by identifying the variables that must be isolated to show the effects of diversity. Keep in mind that halting the process after this step would leave many unknowns about the actual diversity impact and might leave a negative impression with management and others because the study may identify variables that management did not previously consider. Therefore, you should go beyond this initial step and use one or more of the strategies that isolate the impact of diversity.

Participant Estimates of Diversity's Impact

An easily implemented method to isolate the impact of diversity is to obtain information directly from the employees involved in the diversity initiative. The effectiveness of this approach rests on the assumption that employees involved in the diversity initiative are capable of determining or estimating how much of a performance improvement is related to the diversity initiative. Because their actions have produced the improvement, participants may have accurate input on the issue. They should know how much of a change was caused by applying the diversity approaches they learned. Although an estimate, this value will usually have considerable credibility with management because these employees are at the center of the change or improvement. In addition, these employees are paid decent salaries to make decisions and forecast the impact of events in other aspects of the business, so why not diversity?

Let's look at an example of participant estimations for a particular diversity initiative, as shown in Table 5-1 (Hubbard, 1999).

Figure 5-2 gives some typical questions that must be answered when participant estimates are considered.

Participants who do not provide information on these questions are excluded from the analysis. Also, erroneous, incomplete, and extreme information should be discarded before the analysis. To be conservative, the confidence percentage can be factored into the values. The confidence percentage is actually a reflection of the error in the estimate. Therefore, an 80 percent confidence level equates to a potential error range of ±20 percent. With this approach, the level of confidence is multiplied

Table 5-1. Example of Participants' Estimation

Factors that Influenced Improvement	Percentage of Improvement Caused by	Confidence Expressed as a Percentage
1. Diversity Multicultural Marketing Program	50%	70%
2. Change in Procedures	10%	80%
3. Adjustment in Standards	10%	50%
4. Revision to Incentive Plan	20%	90%
5. Increased Management Attention	10%	50%
6. Other_____	___%	___%
Total	100%	

Typical Questions to Answer

1. What percentage of this improvement can be attributed to the application of diversity skills/knowledge/techniques gained in a diversity-training program, from the employee's background and experience, etc.?
2. What is the basis for this estimate?
3. What confidence do you have in this estimate, expressed as a percent?
4. What other factors contributed to this improvement in performance?
5. What other individuals or groups could estimate this percentage or determine the amount?

Figure 5-2. Typical questions.

by the estimate using the lower side of the range. In the example, the following process steps explain how this calculation is applied:

1. The participant allocates 50 percent of the improvement to the diversity multicultural marketing program but is only 70 percent confident about this estimate.
2. The confidence percentage is multiplied by the estimate to develop a usable diversity impact factor value of 35 percent.
3. The adjusted percentage is then multiplied by the actual amount of the improvement (post-initiative minus pre-initiative value) to isolate the portion attributed to diversity.

4. The adjusted improvement is now ready for conversion to monetary values and, ultimately, to be used in the diversity return-on-investment calculation.

Perhaps an illustration of this process can reveal its effectiveness and acceptability. In a large global organization, the impact of a diversity leadership and mentoring program for new managers was being assessed. Because the decision to calculate the impact of this diversity training was made after the program had been conducted, the control group method was not feasible as a method to isolate the effect of diversity. Also, before the program was implemented, no specified Level 4 (Kirkpatrick Model—business results level) data were identified that were linked to the training program. Consequently, it was difficult to use trend-line analysis.

Participants' estimates proved to be the most useful way to estimate the impact. In a detailed follow-up questionnaire, participants were asked a variety of questions regarding the job applications of what was learned from the program. As part of the program, the individuals were asked to develop action plans and implement them, although no specific follow-up plan was needed. Figure 5-3 shows a series of impact questions that were provided with estimations of the diversity impact.

Diversity Impact Questions

1. How have you and your job changed as a result of attending this program? (skills and knowledge application)
2. What is the impact of these changes in your work unit? (specific measures)
3. What is the annual value of this change or improvement in your work unit? (Although this is difficult, please make every effort to estimate this value.)
4. What is the basis for the estimate provided above? (Please indicate the assumptions you made and the specific calculations you performed to arrive at the value.)
5. What confidence do you place in the above estimate? (100% = certainty, 0% = no confidence)
6. Recognizing that many factors influence output results in addition to this diversity training initiative, please estimate the percent of the improvement that is directly related to this program. (It may be helpful to first identify all the other factors and then provide an estimate of the diversity factor.)

Figure 5-3. Diversity impact questions. (Adapted from Phillips, Stone, Phillips, 2001.)

Although these questions are challenging, when set up properly and presented to participants appropriately, they can be very effective for collecting diversity impact data. Table 5-2 shows a sample of the calculations from these questions for this particular diversity training program (Hubbard, 1999).

Table 5-2. Sample of Input from Participants in a Diversity Leadership and Mentoring Skills Program for New Managers

Participant	Annual Improvement Value	Basis for Value	Confidence	Isolation Factor	Adjusted Value
11	$36,000	Improvement in efficiency of group. $3,000/month × 12 (group estimate)	85%	50%	$15,300
42	$90,000	Turnover Reduction. Two turnover statistics per year. Base salary × 1.5 = $45,000	90%	40%	32,400
74	$24,000	Improvement in customer response time. (8 hours to 6 hours). Estimated value: $2,000/month	60%	55%	$7,920
55	$2,000	5% in my effectiveness ($40,000 × 5%)	75%	50%	$750
96	$10,000	Absenteeism Reduction (50 absences per year × $200)	85%	75%	$6,375
117	$8,090	Team project completed 10 days ahead of schedule. Annual salaries $210,500 = $809 per day × 10 days	90%	45%	$3,276
118	$159,000	Under budget for the year by this amount	100%	30%	$47,700

Although this is an estimate, this approach does have considerable accuracy and credibility. Five adjustments are effectively utilized with this approach to reflect a conservative approach:

1. The individuals who do not respond to the questionnaire or provide usable data on the questionnaire are assumed to have no improvements. This is probably an overstatement because some individuals will have improvements but not report them on the questionnaire.
2. Extreme data and incomplete, unrealistic, and unsupported claims are omitted from the analysis, although they may be included in the intangible benefits.
3. Because only annualized values are used, it is assumed that there are no benefits from the program after the first year of implementation. In reality, a diversity leadership and mentoring program should expect to add value perhaps for several years after training has been conducted and implemented.
4. The confidence level, expressed as a percentage, is multiplied by the improvement value to reduce the amount of the improvement by the potential error.
5. The improvement amount is adjusted by the amount directly related to the diversity initiative, expressed as a percentage.

When presented to senior management, the results of this diversity impact study were perceived to be an understatement of the diversity initiative's success. The data and the process were considered to be credible and accurate.

As an added enhancement to this method, management may be asked to review and approve the estimates from participants. In this way management can actually confirm the estimates, which enhances their credibility.

The process does have some disadvantages, though. It is an estimate and, consequently, it does not have the accuracy desired by some managers. Also, the input data may be unreliable because some participants are incapable of providing these types of estimates. They may not be aware of exactly which factors contributed to the results.

Several advantages also make this strategy attractive. It is a simple process, easily understood by most diversity practitioners and others who review evaluation data. It is inexpensive, takes very little time and analysis, and therefore it results in an efficient addition to the evaluation process. Estimates originate from a credible source—the individuals who actually produced the improvement.

The advantages seem to outweigh the disadvantages. Isolating the effects of diversity may never be totally precise; however, this estimate may be accurate enough for most clients and management groups. The process is appropriate when the participants are managers, supervisors, team leaders, sales associates, engineers, and other professional and technical employees.

Considerations When Selecting Isolation Strategies

In this section, we only examined the use of one out of at least 10 strategies for isolating diversity's contribution. Even with this number, selecting the most appropriate strategies for the specific diversity initiative is difficult. Some strategies are simple and inexpensive, whereas others are more time consuming and costly. When attempting to make the selection decision, several factors should be considered (Phillips, Stone, Phillips, 2001):

☐ Feasibility of the strategy
☐ Accuracy provided with the strategy
☐ Credibility of the strategy with the target audience
☐ Specific costs to implement the strategy
☐ The amount of disruption in normal work activities as the strategy is implemented
☐ Participant, staff, and management time needed with the particular strategy

Multiple strategies or multiple sources for data input should be considered because two sources are usually better than one. When multiple sources are utilized, a conservative method is recommended to combine the inputs. A conservative approach builds acceptance. The target audience should always be provided with explanations of the process and the various subjective factors involved.

Multiple sources allow an organization to experiment with different strategies and build confidence with a particular strategy. For example, if management is concerned about the accuracy of the participant's estimates, a combination of control group arrangement and participant's estimates could be attempted to check the accuracy of the estimation process.

Many DROI Initiatives Will Generate Large Returns

It is not unusual for the ROI in diversity initiatives to be extremely large. Even when a portion of the improvement is allocated to other factors, the numbers are still impressive in many situations. The audience should understand that, although every effort was made to isolate the diversity impact, it is still an imprecise figure that may contain a certain amount of errors, similar to some other estimated business calculations such as inflation, actuarial table estimates, and so on. It represents the best estimate of the impact given the constraints, conditions, and resources available. Chances are the diversity isolation strategies are more accurate than other types of analysis regularly utilized in other functions within the organization.

Too often results are reported and linked to diversity without any attempt to isolate the portion of the results that can be attributed to diversity. If the diversity practice is to continue to improve its professional image as well as to meet its responsibility for obtaining results, this issue must be addressed early in the process.

CONVERT THE CONTRIBUTION TO MONETARY VALUE

In many evaluation impact studies, the examination usually stops with the tabulation of business results. In those situations, the initiative is considered successful if it produced improvements such as turnover reduction, improved customer satisfaction, reduced absenteeism, or the like. Although these results are important, it is more insightful to compare the value of the results to the cost of the initiative. This allows the initiative to be primed to calculate its return-on-investment.

Identifying the Hard and Soft Data Contained in the Diversity Contribution

After collecting diversity performance data, it is helpful to divide the data into hard and soft categories. Hard data are the traditional measures of organizational performance. They are objective, easy to measure, and easy to convert to monetary values. Hard data are often very common measures, they achieve high credibility with management, and they are available in every type of organization. Hard data represent the output, quality, cost, and time of work-related processes.

Almost every department or unit will have hard data performance measures. For example, a cross-functional team in a government office approving applications for work visas will have these four measures among its overall performance measurement: the number of applications processed (Output), cost per applications processed (Cost), the number of errors made in processing applications (Quality), and the time it takes to process and approve an application (Time). Ideally, diversity initiatives in this example can be linked to one or more hard data measures.

Because many diversity initiatives are more heavily related to soft skills, soft data are often reviewed in diversity measurement studies. Soft data are usually subjective, behaviorally oriented, sometimes difficult to measure, and almost always difficult to convert to monetary values. When compared to hard data, soft data are usually seen as less credible as a performance measure.

Measures such as employee turnover, absenteeism, and grievances appear as soft data items, not because they are difficult to measure, but because it is difficult to accurately convert them to monetary values.

Basic Steps to Convert Data

Before describing some specific strategies to convert either hard or soft data to monetary values, the basic steps used to convert data in each strategy are highlighted here. These steps should be followed for each data conversion process (Phillips, 1997).

1. *Focus on the unit of measure.* First, identify a unit of improvement. For output data, the unit of measure is the item produced, service provided, or sale consummated. Time measures are varied and include items such as the time to complete a project, cycle time, or customer response time. The unit is usually expressed as minutes, hours, or days. Quality is a common measure, and the unit may be one error, reject, defect, or rework item. Soft data measures are varied, and the unit of improvement may include items such as a grievance, an absence, an employee turnover statistic, or a one-point change in the customer satisfaction index.
2. *Determine the value of each unit.* Place a value (V) on the unit identified in the first step. For measures of production, quality, cost, and time, the process is relatively easy. Most organizations have records or reports reflecting the value of items, such as one unit of production or the cost of a defect. Soft data are more difficult to convert to a value because the cost of one absence, one grievance, or a one-point change in the diversity attitude survey is often difficult to pinpoint. The array of strategies offered in this chapter will include a variety of techniques to make this conversion. When more than

one value is available, either the most credible or the lowest value should be used.

3. *Calculate the change in performance data.* Calculate the change in output data after the effects of the diversity initiative have been isolated from other influences. The change (ΔP) is the performance improvement, measured as hard or soft data, that is directly attributable to the diversity initiative. The value may represent the performance improvement for individuals, a team, a group, or several groups of participants or an organization.

4. *Determine an annual amount for the change.* Annualize the ΔP value to develop a total change in the performance data for one year. This procedure has become a standard approach with many organizations that wish to capture the total benefits of the diversity initiative. Although the benefits may not be realized at the same level for an entire year, some diversity initiatives will continue to produce benefits beyond one year. Therefore, using one year of benefits is considered a conservative approach.

5. *Calculate the total value of the improvement.* Develop the total value of improvement by multiplying the annual performance change (ΔP) by the unit value (V) for the complete performance group in question. For example, if one group of participants for a diversity initiative is being evaluated, the total value will include the total improvement for all participants in the group. This value for annual diversity initiative benefits is then compared to the cost of the diversity initiative, usually through the diversity return-on-investment (DROI) calculation.

Strategies for Converting Data to Monetary Values

An example taken from a cross-functional team-building initiative at a manufacturing plant describes the five-step process of converting data to monetary values. This initiative was developed and implemented after a needs assessment revealed that a lack of teamwork was causing an excessive number of grievances. This diversity initiative was designed to reduce the number of grievances filed at Step 2. This is the step in which the grievance is recorded in writing and becomes a measurable soft data item. Therefore, the actual number of grievances resolved at Step 2 in the grievance process was selected as an output measure. Table 5-3 illustrates the steps taken to assign a monetary value to the data. The total monetary impact of this diversity initiative was $546,000.

Table 5-3. An Example of the Steps to Convert Data to Monetary Values
*Setting: Cross-functional Team-building Initiative in a
Manufacturing Plant*

Steps	Description
1	*Focus on a Unit of Improvement* One grievance reaching Step 2 in the four-step grievance resolution process
2	*Determine a Value of Each Unit* Using internal experts—the labor relations staff and the diversity staff—the cost of an average grievance was estimated to be $6,500 when considering time and direct costs. (V = $6,500)
3	*Calculate the Change in Performance Data* Six months after the initiative was completed, total grievances per month reaching Step 2 declined by 10. Seven of the 10 grievance reductions were related to the diversity initiative as determined by supervisors (*Isolating the Effects of Diversity*)
4	*Determine an Annual Amount for the Change* Using the six-month value, seven per month, yields an annual improvement of 84(ΔP).
5	*Calculate the Annual Value of the Improvement* Annual Value $= \Delta$P$\times$ V $= 84 \times \$6,500$ $= \$546,000$

Several strategies are available to convert data to monetary values. Some of the strategies are appropriate for a specific type of data category, while other strategies can be used with virtually any type of data.

CALCULATING DIVERSITY RETURN-ON-INVESTMENT (DROI)

For some time now, diversity practitioners and researchers have tried to calculate the actual return-on-investment in diversity. If diversity is considered an investment—not an expense—then it is appropriate to place the diversity investment in the same funding process as other investments, such as the investment in equipment and facilities. Although these other investments are quite different, management often views them in the same way. Thus, it is critical to the success of the diversity field to develop specific values that reflect the DROI (Hubbard, 1999).

To illustrate this calculation, assume that a work-life and family training program had initial costs of $50,000. The program will have a useful life of three years, with negligible residual value at that time. During the three-year period, the program produces a net savings of $30,000, or $10,000 per year ($30,000 ÷ 3). The average investment is $25,000 ($50,000 ÷ 2) because the average book value is essentially half the costs. The average return is:

$$\text{Average ROI} = \frac{\text{annual savings}}{\text{average investment}}$$

$$= \frac{\$10,000}{\$25,000}$$

$$= 40\%$$

Finance and accounting personnel may take issue with calculations involving the ROI for efforts such as diversity initiatives. Nevertheless, the expression is fairly common and conveys an adequate meaning of financial evaluation.

ROI may be calculated before a diversity program to estimate the potential cost effectiveness or after a program has been conducted to measure the results achieved. The methods of calculation are the same; however, the estimated return before a program is usually calculated for a proposal to implement the program. The data for its calculation are more subjective and usually less reliable than the data after the program is completed. Because of this factor, management may require a higher ROI for a diversity program in the proposal stage.

Annualized Values

All of the DROI formulas presented here use annualized values so that the first-year impact of the diversity initiative's investment is developed. Using annualized values is becoming a generally accepted best practice for developing DROI in organizations. This approach is a conservative way to develop DROI because many short-term diversity initiatives have added value in the second or third year. For long-term diversity initiatives, annualized values are inappropriate, and longer timeframes need to be used.

When selecting the approach to measure DROI, it is important to communicate to the target audience the formula used and the assumptions

made to arrive at the decision to use it. This action can avoid misunderstandings and confusion surrounding how the DROI value was actually
developed. Although several approaches are described in this chapter,
two stand out as the preferred methods—the benefit/cost ratio and the
basic DROI formula. These two approaches are described next, along
with brief coverage of the other approaches.

Benefit/Cost Ratio

One of the earliest methods for evaluating investments in diversity initiatives is the benefit/costs ratio (read as the benefits-to-costs ratio). This
method compares the benefits of the program to the costs in a ratio.
In formula form, the ratio is:

$$BCR = \frac{\text{Diversity Initiative Benefits}}{\text{Diversity Initiative Costs}}$$

In simple terms, the BCR compares the annual economic benefits of the
diversity initiative to the cost of the initiative. A BCR of 1 means that the
benefits equal the costs. A BCR of 2, usually written as 2:1, indicates that
for each dollar spent on the diversity initiative, two dollars were returned
as benefits.

The following example illustrates the use of the benefit/cost ratio.
A diversity leadership initiative, designed for managers and supervisors,
was implemented at an electric and gas utility. In a follow-up evaluation,
action planning and business performance monitoring were used to capture benefits. The first-year payoff for the initiative was $1,077,750. The
total fully loaded implementation cost was $215,500. Thus, the ratio was:

$$BCR = \frac{\$1,077,750}{\$215,500} = 5:1$$

For every one dollar invested in the diversity initiative, five dollars in
benefits were returned.

The principal advantage of using this approach is that it avoids traditional financial measures, so there is no confusion when comparing
diversity initiative investments with other investments in the organization. Investments in plants, equipment, or subsidiaries, for example, are
not usually evaluated with the benefits/cost method. Some executives
prefer not to use the same method to compare the returns in diversity

with the returns on other investments. Consequently, this method for calculating DROI stands out as a unique type of evaluation.

Unfortunately, there is no standard as to what constitutes an acceptable benefit/cost ratio for diversity. A standard should be established within an organization, perhaps even for a specific type of diversity initiative; however, a 1:1 ratio is unacceptable for most programs, and in some organizations, a 1.25:1 ratio is required, where 1.25 times the cost is the benefit.

The DROI Formula

Perhaps the most appropriate formula for evaluating an investment in a diversity initiative is the net initiative benefits divided by costs. The ratio is usually expressed as a percentage, where the fractional values are multiplied by 100. In formula form, the DROI formula is expressed as:

$$\text{DROI}(\%) = \frac{\text{Net Diversity Initiative Benefits}}{\text{Diversity Initiative Costs}} \times 100$$

Net benefits are diversity initiative benefits minus diversity initiative costs. The DROI value is related to the BCR by a factor of 1. For example, a BCR of 2.45 is the same as a DROI value of 145 percent. This formula is essentially the same as ROI in other types of investments. For example, when a firm builds a new plant, the ROI is found by dividing annual earnings by the investment. The annual earnings is comparable to net benefits (annual benefits minus the cost). The investment is comparable to the diversity initiative costs, which represent the investment in the initiative.

A DROI on a diversity investment of 50 percent means that the costs are recovered and an additional 50 percent of the costs are reported as earnings. A diversity investment of 150 percent indicates that the costs have been recovered and an additional 1.5 multiplied by the costs is captured as earnings. An example illustrates the DROI calculation. Magnavox Electronics Systems Company conducted an 18-week literacy program for entry-level electrical and mechanical assemblers (Ford, 1994). The results of the program were impressive. Productivity and quality alone yielded an annual value of $321,600. The total fully loaded costs for the program were $38,233. Thus, the DROI becomes:

$$\text{DROI}(\%) = \frac{\$321,600 - \$38,233}{\$38,233} \times 100 = 741\%$$

For each dollar invested, Magnavox received $7.41 in return after the cost of the program had been recovered.

Using the DROI formula essentially places diversity investments on a level playing field with other investments using the same formula and similar concepts. Key management and financial executives who regularly use ROI with other investments easily understand the DROI calculation.

Although there are no generally accepted standards, some organizations establish a minimum requirement or hurdle rate for an ROI in human resource–based programs such as training. An ROI minimum of 25 percent is set by some organizations. The same will eventually come true for diversity initiatives. This target value in training is usually above the percentage required for other types of investments. The rationale is that the ROI process for training is still relatively new and often involves some subjective input, including estimations. Because of that, a higher standard is required or suggested, with 25 percent being the desired figure for these organizations. It is critical that DROI calculations follow suit.

Cautions When Using DROI

Because of the complexity and sensitivity of the DROI process, caution is needed when developing, calculating, and communicating the ROI. Implementation of the DROI process is a very important issue and is a goal of many diversity organizations. Addressing the following issues can help make certain the process does not go off track (adapted from Phillips, Stone, Phillips, 2001).

☐ *The DROI process should be developed for an initiative where a serious needs assessment has been conducted.* Because of the evaluation problems that can develop when it is not clear that a need exists, it is recommended that the DROI study be conducted with initiatives that have had a comprehensive needs assessment; however, some practical considerations and management requests may prohibit this suggested requirement.

☐ *The DROI analysis should always include one or more strategies for isolating the effects of the diversity initiative.* Because of the importance of accounting for the influences of other factors, this step in the process must not be ignored. Too often, an excellent study—from what appears to be a very successful diversity effort— is perceived to be worthless because there was no attempt to account for other factors. Omission of this step seriously diminishes the credibility of the diversity initiative study.

□ *When making estimates, use the most reliable and credible sources.* Because estimates are critical to any type of analysis, they will usually be an important part of a DROI study. When they are used, they should be developed properly and obtained from the most reliable and credible sources—those individuals who best understand the overall situation and can provide accurate estimates.

□ *Take a conservative approach when developing both benefits and costs.* Conservatism in DROI analysis builds accuracy and credibility. What matters most is how the target audience perceives the value of the data. A conservative approach is always recommended for both the numerator of the DROI formula (diversity initiative benefits) and the denominator (diversity initiative costs).

□ *Use caution when comparing the ROI in diversity with other financial returns.* There are many ways to calculate the return on funds invested or assets employed. The ROI is just one of them. Although the calculation for DROI uses the same basic formula as in other investment evaluations, it may not be fully understood by the target group. Its calculation method and its meaning should be clearly communicated. More important, it should be accepted by management as an appropriate measure for measuring diversity results. This kind of credibility must be earned by taking the time to complete all of the assessment and measurement steps in the process.

□ *Involve management in developing the return.* Management ultimately makes the decision if a DROI value is acceptable. To the extent possible, management should be involved in setting parameters for calculations and establishing targets by which diversity initiatives are considered acceptable within the organization.

□ *Approach sensitive and controversial issues with caution.* Occasionally, sensitive and controversial issues will be generated when discussing a DROI value. It is best to avoid debates over what is measurable and what is not measurable unless there is clear evidence of the issue in question. The issue can be included in the overall measurement process as an intangible benefit. Also, some initiatives are so fundamental to the organization's survival that any attempt to measure them is unnecessary. For example, a diversity initiative designed to improve customer service in a customer-focused organization may escape the scrutiny of a DROI evaluation, on the assumption that if the initiative is well designed, it will improve customer service. As more organizations implement DROI studies and standards evolve, the diversity measurement discipline will have increasing evidence that DROI values can be trusted with accuracy and validity.

☐ *Develop case studies of your DROI calculations.* Creating case studies of your DROI studies can help educate your organization about the full value of your efforts and the benefits in measuring diversity results. These successes and learning opportunities can help other diversity initiatives and other diversity personnel throughout the organization. Hubbard & Hubbard, Inc.'s Diversity Measurement and Productivity Institute offers specific workshops designed to help you develop or turn your existing data into a diversity business case study.

☐ *Do not boast about a high return.* It is not unusual to generate what appears to be a very high DROI for a diversity initiative. This can open the diversity organization up to undue criticism and scrutiny even when the numbers are an accurate reflection of the facts. The value for DROI will be built as more members of the organization come to understand the processes through their own participation on diversity initiative teams and obvious improvements in organizational climate and performance.

☐ *Do not try to use DROI on every diversity initiative.* Some diversity initiatives are difficult to quantify, and a DROI calculation may not be feasible. Other methods of presenting the benefits may be more appropriate. It is helpful to set specific criteria for the selection of diversity initiatives that will be evaluated when using the DROI level of analyses.

IMPORTANCE OF RECOGNIZING INTANGIBLE MEASURES IN DIVERSITY

Most successful diversity initiatives result in some intangible benefits. Intangible benefits are those positive results that either cannot be converted to monetary values or would involve too much time or expense in the conversion to be worth the effort. The range of intangible outcomes is practically limitless.

Intangible benefits should be measured and reported. They can be used as additional evidence of a diversity initiative's success and can be presented as supportive qualitative data. Intangibles may not carry the weight of measures that are expressed in dollars and cents, but they are still a very important part of the overall evaluation, and many executives are interested in these measures.

Table 5-4. Typical Intangible Variables Linked with Diversity

Attitude Survey Data	Employee Transfers
Organizational Commitment	Customer Satisfaction Survey Data
Climate Survey Data	Customer Complaints
Employee Complaints	Customer Response Time
Grievances	Teamwork
Discrimination Complaints	Cooperation
Stress Reduction	Conflict
Employee Turnover	Decisiveness
Employee Absenteeism	Communication
Employee Tardiness	

It is important to note that, even though any of the intangible benefits may not be converted in one evaluation study, they may be converted in another study or in another organization. Not all measures can or should be converted to monetary values. By design, some should be captured and reported as intangible measures. Although they may not be perceived as valuable as the measures converted to monetary values, as stated earlier, intangible measures are critical to the overall evaluation process.

In some diversity initiatives such as diversity leadership training, managing multicultural conflict, intangible effects on teamwork, job satisfaction, communication, and customer satisfaction, the intangible or nonmonetary benefits can be more important than monetary or tangible measures. Consequently, these measures should be monitored and reported as part of the overall evaluation. In practice, every diversity initiative, regardless of its nature, scope, and content, will have intangible measures associated with it. The challenge is to efficiently identify and report them. Table 5-4 gives some of the more typical variables that are referred to as intangible.

The good news is that with the advent of processes such as causal pathway analysis and staple measurement processes such as correlation, linear and multiple regression, and even cross-tab correlation, we are pinpointing diversity contributions in many of the so-called intangible areas and converting diversity initiative contributions into monetary values. Nonetheless, if you need to report these variables as intangibles, the following procedures will help.

Identification of Measures

Intangible measures can be identified in several ways representing different timeframes. First, they can be uncovered early in the process, during the needs assessment. Once identified, the tangible data are planned for collection as part of the overall data collection strategy. For example, a multicultural marketing training for team leaders program has several hard data measures linked to the effort. An intangible measure, employee satisfaction, is identified and monitored, with no plans to convert it to a monetary value. Thus, from the beginning, this measure is destined to be a nonmonetary benefit reported along with the DROI results.

A second way in which an intangible benefit is identified is to discuss with the sponsors or management what the impact of the diversity initiative is as they see it. They can usually identify intangible measures that are expected to be influenced by the diversity initiative.

The third way in which an intangible measure is identified is during an attempt to convert the data to monetary values. If the process used to convert the data to monetary value loses credibility, the measure should be reported as an intangible benefit. For example, in a multicultural selling skills program, customer satisfaction is identified early in the initiative as one of the measures of the diversity initiative's success. A conversion to monetary values was attempted; however, the process of assigning a value to the data lost credibility, therefore, customer satisfaction was reported as an intangible. Currently, to remedy this problem, correlations can be made linking customer satisfaction to customer retention and then customer retention to dollars to calculate the benefits in hard dollar amounts.

The fourth way in which an intangible measure is identified is during a follow-up evaluation. Although the measure was neither expected nor anticipated in the initial diversity initiative design, the measure surfaces on a questionnaire, in an interview, or during a focus group. Questions are often asked about other improvements linked to the diversity initiative. Several intangible measures are usually provided, and there are no planned attempts to place a value on the actual measure. For example, in a diverse customer service initiative, participants were asked specifically what had improved about their work area and their relationship with customers as a result of the application of the skills they acquired in the diversity initiative. The participants provided more than a dozen intangible measures, which managers perceived to be linked directly with the diversity initiative.

Sources for Intangible Benefits

During needs assessments. While conducting a business needs assessments, there are numerous opportunities to address intangibles.

Many needs often start at Level 3, and as we begin to question how behavior influences outcomes, we can identify Level 4 intangible needs as well. As we identify needs, we should attempt to place a monetary value on the business problem/opportunity. For example, if we identify a Level 4 need to reduce excessive diverse workforce absenteeism, we have identified a Level 4 intangible. If we can place a value on absenteeism, we can calculate what it is costing the organization (cost of one absenteeism × number of excessive absences = cost to the organization). We now have a tangible value in management terms.

During early planning. As stated before, during the planning phase of the evaluation process, when linking objectives to business measures or addressing baseline measures, intangibles are often uncovered. The objectives of the training may also reveal intangibles.

Clients. Clients participating in the diversity initiative can often identify intangibles. A client who seeks diversity-related assistance often identifies a need in Level 3 language, such as: "My associates are not working together as a team, especially when people from different backgrounds are involved," or "Our lack of cross-cultural communication is hurting our ability to serve our diverse customers." Likewise, clients can identify when these intangible measures have improved.

Participants. Participants may be one of the best sources in identifying intangibles. Because we are trying to influence their performance, they can tell us how things change for them in the organization as they implement new skills.

Managers. Managers often have a broader view of the work setting and can see the overall behavioral changes and how they impact important intangible measures.

Customers. Customers often identify intangibles when they discuss the performance of an associate—comments like "She is so friendly and helpful," or "I feel like my account has been handled with care. It is great that she spoke to me in Spanish," or "Your office displays such a high degree of professionalism." Often, we can link such behavior to improved customer satisfaction.

During data collection. We often uncover intangible data during data collection from stakeholders. We may not always plan to collect intangible data, and we may not anticipate it in the initial planning; however, intangible data may surface on a questionnaire, during an interview, or during a focus group activity. When questions are asked about improvements influenced by the diversity training initiative, participants usually provide several intangible measures for which there are no plans to assign a value.

During conversion attempts. Intangibles are often identified when attempts at conversion are aborted. When Level 4 data cannot be converted to a monetary value (or we choose not to convert), we are inherently left with intangible outcomes. When this occurs, we should explain the reason we are unable to convert.

It is important to identify trends when capturing intangible benefits. It is tempting to use sparse comments or observations by clients, customers, participants, or supervisors of participants to draw conclusions about the intangible benefits resulting from a program. One positive comment about one associate from a customer or supervisor may be insufficient to claim an overall Level 3 intangible benefit from the initiative. An objective evaluator will look further and deeper for intangible benefits (Phillips, Stone, Phillips, 2001).

REPORT IT TO OTHERS

Once you have an understanding of the processes necessary to calculate the DROI impact, you are ready to develop a communications strategy to report it to others. This strategy includes tasks such as the following:

- ☐ Consider some general principles for reporting statistical data and results to others.
- ☐ Create a management summary.
- ☐ Communicate background information regarding the diversity research study.
- ☐ Describe the evaluation strategy.
- ☐ Discuss the data collection, analysis, and performance tracking plan.
- ☐ Detail the diversity initiative's costs and benefits.
- ☐ Profile an initiative's results and DROI impact.
- ☐ Identify your conclusions and recommendations.

Reporting the results is almost as important as producing results. It will do you and your department little good if you are making great progress and few people know about it. In effect, you must become a cheerleader and chief advocate for your diversity efforts. Regardless of the message, a few general principles are important when communicating your diversity initiative's results:

- ☐ The communication must be timely.
- ☐ The communication should be targeted to specific audiences.

- [ ] The media should be carefully selected.
- [ ] The communication should be unbiased and always modest.
- [ ] The communication must be consistent.
- [ ] Testimonials are more effective if they are from individuals with audience credibility.
- [ ] The audience's perception of the diversity department will influence communication strategy.

Key Questions to Answer When Selecting the Message

In order for your diversity initiative report to have the maximum impact, you must answer a few key questions:

- [ ] Is the audience interested in the subject?
- [ ] Do they really want to hear the information?
- [ ] Is the timing right for this audience?
- [ ] Is this audience familiar with the views of the diversity organization?
- [ ] How do they prefer to have results communicated?
- [ ] Are they likely to find the results threatening?
- [ ] What else is happening in the organization that may compete for their attention to focus on the diversity results?
- [ ] Which medium will be most convincing to this group?

To be an effective communicator, you must get to know the audience you will be working with, noting how others have been successful in reporting data to them in the past. Find out what information is needed and why. Try to understand each audience's point of view—some may want to see the results while others may not. Others may be neutral. Keep in mind that your reporting approach must reach all employees in a way that helps them understand the significance of the work you have completed.

Developing the Evaluation Report

The type of formal evaluation report used to communicate results depends on the amount of detailed information that is developed for various target audiences. In general, the objective is to keep the presentation to one or two pages. For senior leadership groups, it should be condensed in a management summary or briefing. For other audiences, the evaluation report can be layered into sections such that you present those portions that are most applicable to your target audience.

The following elements should be covered in a complete diversity evaluation report:

☐ Management summary
☐ Background information
☐ Evaluation strategy
☐ Data collection, analysis, and performance tracking
☐ Diversity initiative's costs and benefits
☐ Diversity initiative results and DROI calculations
☐ Conclusions and recommendations

Although this report format is an effective way to present DROI data, several cautions need to be followed. Because this document can report the success of a diversity initiative involving a group of employees, for example, complete credit for the success must go to the participants and their immediate leaders. Their performance generated the success. Another important caution is to avoid boasting about results. Although the DROI process may be accurate and credible, it still may have some subjective issues. Huge claims of success can quickly turn off an audience and interfere with the delivery of the desired message.

A final caution concerns the structure of the report. The methodology should be clearly explained, along with assumptions made in the analysis. The reader should readily see how the values were developed and how the specific steps were followed to make the process more conservative, credible, and accurate. Detailed statistical analysis should be placed in the appendix. While these components are key parts of a complete diversity evaluation report, the report can be scaled down, as necessary, to provide needed documentation to meet target audience needs.

When reporting a successful outcome, it is important to recognize those who participated in less visible ways, such as those who collect and analyze data or convert data to monetary values and the managers who support data collection and other aspects of the diversity training and the evaluation process.

In the end, the participants achieve the results. The participants must implement the learned diversity initiative behaviors or there will be no result. The process reaches closure when appropriate partnering occurs to ensure results in the organizational settings. It is appropriate for the diversity staff to take credit by claiming that the diversity initiative caused the results. The truth is, the diversity process causes the results. The process (not a program or the diversity department) should get the credit, and the focal point should be on the participants and their managers.

FINAL THOUGHTS

This chapter outlined the remaining stages of the Hubbard Diversity ROI Process: isolating diversity's contribution, converting the contribution to money, calculating cost and benefits, calculating diversity's return-on-investment, identifying intangible effects, and reporting the contribution to others. Each stage is a required element that forms an essential link in the chain to build compelling causal evidence that your diversity initiative helped produce tangible and intangible effects on the organization's performance. Without them, there is little to support the notion that your diversity initiative made measurable difference.

In the next chapter, we will discuss several options for tracking and assessing your progress to sustain the value of your diversity efforts.

REFERENCES

Ford, D. "Three Rs in the Workplace." In J. Phillips (Ed.), *In Action: Measuring Return on Investment,* Vol. 1. Alexandria, VA: American Society for Training and Development, 1994, pp. 85–104.

Hubbard, Edward E. *How to Calculate Diversity Return on Investment.* Petaluma, CA: Global Insights, 1999.

Phillips, Jack J., Ron D. Stone, and Patricia P. Phillips. *The Human Resources Scorecard.* Boston: Butterworth–Heinemann, 2001.

FURTHER READING

Brinkerhoff, Robert O., and Stephen J. Gill. *The Learning Alliance: Systems Thinking in Human Resource Development.* San Francisco: Jossey-Bass, 1994.

Casio, Wayne F. *Costing Human Resources: The Financial Impact of Behavior in Organizations.* Boston: PWS-Kent Publishing, 1987.

Casio, Wayne F. *Applied Psychology in Human Resource Management,* 5th ed. Englewood Cliffs, NJ: Prentice-Hall, 1997.

Fleming, Maureen J., and Jennifer B. Wilson (Eds.). "Effective HR Measurement Techniques." Alexandria, VA: Society for Human Resources Management, 2001.

Phillips, Jack J. *Accountability in Human Resources Management.* Boston: Butterworth–Heinemann, 1996.

Phillips, Jack J. *Return on Investment in Training and Performance Improvement Programs.* Boston: Butterworth–Heinemann, 1997.

Sloma, Richard S. *How to Measure Managerial Performance.* New York: Macmillan, 1980.

CHAPTER 6

Track and Assess Progress

IMPORTANCE OF TRACKING AND ASSESSING YOUR PROGRESS

Tracking and assessing the overall progress of your diversity ROI initiative is critical for institutionalizing any gains achieved in the process. A tracking system is usually fueled by the documents and procedures you used to collect and summarize the data for feedback purposes. Although it is an often-overlooked part of the process, an effective diversity scorecard tracking and monitoring plan can help keep your diversity initiatives on target and let others know what progress is being made for the organization. By using DROI techniques, you can establish your diversity efforts on a solid business foundation like any other organizational initiative.

CREATING TRACKING AND MONITORING SYSTEMS

An effective tracking system has the following attributes:

- ☐ *Relevant.* The organization receives information directly related to the diversity measures and metrics being used.
- ☐ *Frequent.* Generally, the more frequent the feedback on key items the better. The goal is to provide feedback often enough to prevent the organization from drifting off the diversity and business performance target.
- ☐ *Immediate.* Feedback should come as soon as possible after work is completed or on a regularly scheduled basis once processes are placed in an implementation mode.
- ☐ *Specific.* Feedback should state exactly how the organization did in accomplishing the diversity initiative's goals and objectives.

This includes meeting any BCR and DROI targets as well as stories of success (anecdotal) achieved along the way.

Remember: You cannot manage what you do not measure, and you cannot know if you are making progress if you are not tracking the diversity results to compare. Unless the organization knows how it is doing in meeting its diversity initiative targets, it cannot improve. Honest, two-way communication between the diversity implementation team and the organization begins with accurate data about how well the organization is performing relative to meeting its diversity goals and objectives. Without it, both the diversity implementation team and management can only exchange subjective opinions about how the diversity initiatives have performed.

MONITORING YOUR SCORECARD INDICES

The initial implementation schedule of the DROI study provides a variety of key events or milestones. Routine progress reports need to be developed to present the status and progress of these diversity initiative events and their key milestones. Reports are usually developed at six-month intervals; however, they can be more frequent depending on the informational needs of your audience. Two target audiences, the diversity organization staff and senior managers, are critical for progress reporting. The entire human resources and operations communities within the organization should be kept informed of the initiative's progress. In addition, senior managers need to know the extent to which the DROI study is being implemented and how it is working in the organization. To maintain this level of information and reporting capability, automated systems may be necessary.

MetricLINK: AN AUTOMATED DIVERSITY MEASUREMENT SYSTEM FOR TRACKING IMPROVED PERFORMANCE

Developing diversity measurement strategies, business objectives, and tactics, calculating formulas for diversity metrics, and keeping everyone informed on the diversity initiative's progress can be tedious work. Someone must take the responsibility to develop procedures and a method to systematically monitor and track each diversity measure and set of metrics used to implement the initiative, then summarize the results over time.

This task is best done by a computer or an automated measurement system (Hubbard, 1999).

As stated earlier: If you do not measure it, you cannot control it, and, if you cannot control it, you cannot manage it. MetricLINK, a comprehensive diversity strategy alignment and performance-tracking tool developed and distributed by Hubbard & Hubbard, Inc., has been found to be an easy-to-use, highly effective measurement planning, analysis, and reporting system that provides all the information you need to manage by facts (see Figure 6-1). MetricLINK allows you to manage your entire diversity strategic plan and its metrics in one system. It integrates and organizes diversity measures, strategies, tactics, action plans, diversity initiative history files, and strategic diversity reporting templates all in one place.

The system frees the diversity professional up from some of the time-consuming tasks of tracking, calculating, and reporting a

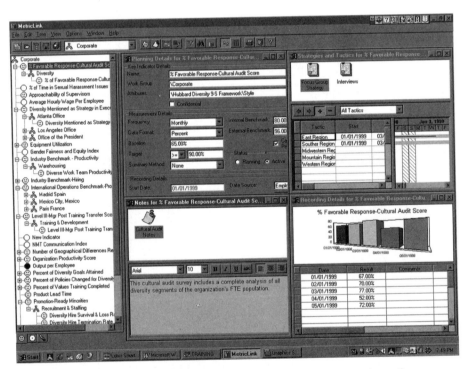

Figure 6-1. MetricLINK diversity strategy alignment and performance-tracking tool.

diversity initiative's results. Some of the benefits of MetricLINK are as follows:

☐ Aligns diversity measures with strategic business objectives and the organization's operations structure.

☐ Multiple views allow diversity measures to be reviewed in different contexts.

☐ Drill-down capabilities are available to view diversity measures by component, location, workgroup, or results area.

☐ Multiple comparisons of actual diversity initiative performance to organizational targets, stretch goals, historical performance, benchmarks, or other reference points is available.

☐ Target specifications can be varied over multiple periods to reflect changing objectives over time.

☐ Weights, performance scaling, and diversity initiative indexing capabilities can be used to combine several measures into meaningful summary values.

☐ Color-coded reporting allows you to easily monitor performance at a glance.

☐ Team or individual ownership can be assigned for each diversity measure, promoting accountability and communication.

☐ Customized reporting and printout capabilities are available.

☐ Notes, Task, and Project Planning features complete with Gantt charts are built in to capture ideas and actions for diversity and organizational performance improvement.

☐ Easy-to-use menus and icons are available throughout MetricLINK to intuitively locate features and functions with a point and click.

☐ Reporting capability allows a wide range of reporting, including reports that generate a comprehensive scorecard.

Using the MetricLINK approach, no programming is required, and typical administrator training takes only about 4 hours to get up and running on the system. MetricLINK software options allow the use of diversity measurement templates for key diversity benchmark measures you can use immediately. Setup and the ready-to-use timeframe is less than a day if standard measures are used and organization-specific measures are ready and well defined. MetricLINK offers options to run on a stand-alone personal computer (PC, lap, or desktop) or using the network option, MetricLINK can be networked with up to 100 users anywhere in the world.

SURVEY ANALYSIS SYSTEM (SAS): A TIMESAVING SURVEY DEVELOPMENT TOOL

Survey Analysis System (SAS) is a great companion measurement tool to MetricLINK. Also distributed by Hubbard & Hubbard, Inc., SAS is an all-in-one survey development software package with a variety of specific application modules that takes the guesswork out of assembling survey questionnaires of any kind using a fast, easy-to-use process. A brief list of SAS modules includes applications such as the following:

- ☐ Culture and Systems Audit Module
- ☐ Organizational Climate Module
- ☐ Customer Service Module
- ☐ Employee Opinion Module
- ☐ Focus Group Summary Module
- ☐ 360° Feedback Analysis Module
- ☐ Diversity Baseline Metrics Module

The SAS's flexible and powerful tools are designed to suit any application, making survey development quick and cost effective. For survey design, SAS quickly generates polished layouts for paper or Internet forms. SAS is an excellent tool for developing, tracking, and reporting all survey, focus group, interview, and other data that generates scores, which get reflected in the diversity scorecard.

SAS can help you accomplish the following tasks:

- ☐ Develop survey questionnaires.
- ☐ Gather answers from respondents.
- ☐ Organize responses for graphical reporting using a wide variety of layouts, such as summary tables, pie charts, bar charts, 3-D charts, stacked bar charts, comparison profile graphs, X-Y plots, written comment summaries, and much more.
- ☐ Present conclusions.
- ☐ Monitor and compare changes in the data.
- ☐ Generate survey-based scoring for scorecard reports.

SAS operates very quickly because of its library of common measurement scales, which requires simple entries of customized question text. Or the user can design his or her own scales. SAS can accommodate up to 500 scales and 2,000 questions in each survey file. This product makes developing and analyzing survey data as part of a DROI study a breeze!

OTHER MEASUREMENT SOFTWARE OPTIONS

Other measurement software options include using popular spreadsheet programs such as Microsoft Excel, Lotus 1-2-3, and so on, and project management software programs such as Microsoft Project, as well as using database management programs such as Microsoft Access or Lotus Approach. These software solutions will, however, require time to design and program formula calculations, recording, and data input elements to track and monitor progress. Additional automation options could include a formal software development process using the organization's Management Information Systems (MIS) or Information Technologies (IT) department. Regardless of the system selected, it must allow the diversity organization to respond quickly and effectively with up-to-the-minute information regarding the status of diversity initiatives. Tracking and assessing progress as the diversity initiative matures must become a routine, integral part of the organization's systems of measurement.

INSTITUTIONALIZING YOUR SCORECARD SYSTEM

Institutionalizing the diversity measurement tracking and monitoring process is a three-part challenge:

1. Create and refine the DROI process and other measurement systems that support it. Managers must be instrumental in helping to create the measurement model and align with it to create buy-in.
2. Create management alignment around the use of the DROI measurement model to run the organization.
3. Deploy the DROI measurement model so as to build business literacy and trust among everyone who participates in or is affected by these measurement methods.

First, it is important to build alignment around the DROI measurement process and its techniques: The DROI model and its measures (e.g., Survival and Loss Rates, Stability, Instability Factors, BCR,

DROI calculations, % of Favorable Responses) make up a single system that gets reflected in the diversity scorecard. This system must become a cornerstone for management decision making. Therefore, every manager, especially those at the top, must understand the system and buy into it.

Second, it is essential to deploy the diversity measurement system properly in order to create a sense of ownership among employees and staff. This is more than simple communication. It requires a well-developed plan that analyzes key business and individual needs and that creates accountability.

Third, it is a task of building trust and financial literacy among employees about numbers, processes, and diversity metrics that drive the business. Unless employees grasp the purpose of the system, understand the economics of the organization and industry, and have a clear picture of how their own work fits into the diversity value chain, the organization will never succeed in making the whole system work to leverage diversity for performance improvement.

Institutionalizing diversity is a key business strategy for reaping the benefits of a diverse workforce. It is one thing to have diversity in your workforce, but it is quite another to consciously utilize diversity as a competitive advantage. To become an employer of choice and to meet key competitive realities of the future, the use of diversity for performance improvement and DROI must become mandatory.

Final Thoughts

An effective diversity scorecard tracking and monitoring plan can help keep your diversity initiatives on target and let others know what progress is being made for the organization. As stated earlier, it is usually fueled by the documents and procedures you used to collect and summarize the data for feedback purposes. Without continual tracking, monitoring, and updating, the organization will not know if the diversity initiative results achieved were fleeting or a solid source for improved organizational performance. With automated, comprehensive measurement system tools such as Hubbard & Hubbard Inc.'s MetricLINK, SAS, and the like, this task can be completed with relative ease.

In the next chapter, we will learn what it takes to build an effective diversity scorecard by examining basic diversity scorecard components. It will provide fundamental insights into the diversity scorecard structure and a brief look at some of the measurement perspectives that apply.

REFERENCE

Hubbard, Edward E. *How to Calculate Diversity Return on Investment.* Petaluma, CA: Global Insights, 1999.

FURTHER READING

Hubbard, Edward E. "Assessing, Measuring, and Analyzing the Impact of Diversity Initiatives." In Deborah L. Plummer (ed.), *Handbook of Diversity Management.* Lanham, England: University Press of America, 2003.

Phillips, Jack J., and Ron D. Stone. *How to Measure Training Results.* New York: McGraw-Hill, 2002.

Phillips, Jack J., Ron D. Stone, and Patricia P. Phillips. *The Human Resources Scorecard.* Boston: Butterworth–Heinemann, 2001.

PART III

Building a Diversity Scorecard

CHAPTER 7

Basic Diversity Scorecard Components

While you may be anxious to get right to the work of developing your diversity scorecard, it is important that you spend some time on this chapter because it essentially serves as the foundation for the rest of the book. When you begin developing a balanced diversity scorecard, your organization will rely on you not only for advice on the technical dimensions of this new process, but also on the broader subject of diversity performance measurement and diversity management. You can enhance your expert credibility within the organization by learning as much as possible about this subject. This is especially important if your current function is one that typically has not gotten involved in the diversity process and you only recently acquired responsibility for managing the diversity effort and direction for your business unit. Think of this chapter as a primer for the exciting work that lies ahead.

The diversity scorecard assists organizations in maximizing two key issues: (1) achieving effective diversity performance, and (2) implementing a comprehensive diversity strategy and measurement process. We begin the chapter by discussing diversity and performance measurement, especially our reliance on financial measures of performance despite their inherent limitations. From there we will discuss the notion of a balanced scorecard. Our balanced scorecard overview begins with a look back at how and when the scorecard was originally conceived and the genesis of the diversity scorecard. Next, you will be introduced to the theory underlying the diversity scorecard and the six perspectives of performance analyzed using this process. The chapter concludes with two important topics: (1) the critical task of linking diversity scorecard measures through a series of cause-and-effect relationships, and finally, (2) a discussion of what is actually meant by the word *balance* in creating a balanced diversity scorecard.

FINANCIAL MEASUREMENT AND ITS LIMITATIONS

As long as business organizations have existed, the traditional method of measurement has been financial. Bookkeeping records used to facilitate financial transactions can literally be traced back thousands of years. At the turn of the twentieth century, financial measurement innovations were critical to the success of the early industrial giants like General Motors. That should not come as a surprise because the financial metrics of the time were the perfect complement to the machine-like nature of the corporate entities and management philosophy of the day. Competition was ruled by scope and economies of scale, with financial measures providing the yardsticks of success.

Financial measures of performance have evolved, and today the concept of economic value added (EVA) is prevalent. This concept suggests that unless a firm's profit exceeds its cost of capital, it really is not creating value for its shareholders. Using EVA as a lens, it is possible to determine that despite an increase in earnings, a firm may be destroying shareholder value if the cost of capital associated with new investments is sufficiently high. Effectively utilizing workforce diversity and diversity management strategies can help lower the cost of capital by lowering operating costs, improving productivity, and increasing profits.

The work of financial professionals is to be commended. As we move into the twenty-first century, however, many are questioning our almost exclusive reliance on financial measures of performance. Perhaps these measures would better serve as a means of reporting on the stewardship of funds entrusted to management's care rather than charting the future direction of the organization (Niven, 2002). Let's look at some of the criticisms levied against the overabundant use of financial measures:

☐ *Not consistent with today's business realities.* Value-creating activities are not captured in the tangible, fixed assets of the firm. Instead, value rests in the ideas of people (intellectual capital) scattered throughout the organization, in customer and supplier relationships, in databases of key information, and in cultures of inclusion, innovation, and quality. Traditional financial measures were designed to compare previous periods based on internal standards of performance. These metrics are generally not helpful in providing early indications of customer, quality, or diverse workforce problems or opportunities. They tend to give us information about what happened after the fact.

☐ *Driving by rearview mirror.* Financial measures provide an excellent review of past performance and events in the organization. They represent a coherent articulation and summary of activities of the organization in prior periods; however, this detailed financial view has no predictive power for the future. As we all know, and experience has shown, great financial results in one month, quarter, or even year in no way indicate future financial performance. In a diverse, competitive, global world, organizations cannot operate on financials alone. Having predictive power for the future is essential.

☐ *Tend to reinforce functional silos.* How are your financial statements prepared? Does your functional area prepare them in a team across lines of business or individually as a department? Financial statements are normally prepared by functional area: Individual department statements are prepared and rolled up into the business unit's numbers, which are ultimately compiled as part of the overall organizational picture. This approach is inconsistent with today's organization in which much of the work is cross-functional in nature. Today, we see diverse work teams comprising many functional areas and diverse people coming together to solve pressing problems and create value in previously unimagined ways. Our traditional financial measurement systems have no way to calculate the true value or cost of these relationships.

☐ *Sacrifice long-term thinking.* When organizations go through large and even small-scale change, long-term thinking is often sacrificed. Many change programs feature severe cost-cutting measures that may have a positive impact on the organization's short-term financial statements; however, these cost-reduction efforts often target the long-term value-creating activities of the firm such as diverse workforce development for critical downstream capability, research and development, and diverse customer relationship management. This focus on short-term gains at the expense of long-term value creation may lead to suboptimization of the organization's resources. This organizational behavior results in a negative effect that catches up with the organization at some point in the future.

☐ *Not relevant to many levels of the organization.* Financial reports by their very nature are abstractions. *Abstraction* in this context is defined as moving to another level, leaving certain characteristics out. When we roll up financial statements throughout the organization, that is exactly what we are doing—compiling information at a higher and higher level until it is almost unrecognizable and useless in the decision making of most managers and employees.

Employees at all levels of the organization need performance and environment data they can act on. This information must be imbued with relevance for their day-to-day activities that operate in a fast-paced, diverse, internal and external climate (Niven, 2002).

Given the limitations of financial measures, should we even consider saving a space for them in our balanced diversity scorecard? With their inherent focus on short-term results, often at the expense of long-term value-creating activities, are they relevant in today's environment? The answer is "yes" for several reasons. As discussed shortly, a balanced diversity scorecard is just that: balanced. An undue focus on any particular area of measurement will often lead to poor overall results. Precedents in the business world support this position. In the 1980s the focus was on productivity improvement, while in the 1990s quality became fashionable and seemingly critical to an organization's success. In keeping with the principle of what gets measured gets done, many businesses saw tremendous improvements in productivity and quality during these focus periods.

What they did not necessarily see was a corresponding increase in financial results, and in fact some companies with the best quality in their industry failed to remain in business. Some of the so-called "Excellent Companies" and "Baldridge Winners" are no longer at the top of the financial heap and/or have been taken out of the picture. Nonetheless, financial statements will remain an important tool for organizations because they ultimately determine whether improvements in diverse customer satisfaction, quality, on-time delivery, workplace culture, leadership competencies for a diverse workforce, and innovation are leading to improved financial performance and wealth creation for shareholders. What we need is a method of balancing the accuracy and integrity of our financial measures with the drivers of future financial and diversity performance of the organization.

ORIGINS OF THE BALANCED SCORECARD

Two colleagues, Robert Kaplan, a professor at Harvard University, and David Norton, a consultant also from the Boston area, developed the balanced scorecard. In 1990, Kaplan and Norton led a research study of a dozen companies exploring new methods of performance measurement. The impetus for the study was a growing belief that financial measures of performance were ineffective for the modern business enterprise. The study companies, along with Kaplan and Norton, were convinced that a reliance on financial measures of performance was affecting their ability to create value. The group discussed several possible alternatives but settled on the idea of a scorecard featuring performance measures capturing activities from throughout the organization—customer issues, internal business processes, employee activities, and of course shareholder concerns. Kaplan and Norton labeled this new tool the balanced scorecard and later summarized the concept in the first of three *Harvard Business Review* articles, "The Balanced Scorecard: Measures that Drive Performance" (Kaplan and Norton, 1992).

Over the next four years several organizations adopted the balanced scorecard and achieved immediate results. Kaplan and Norton discovered that these organizations were not only using the scorecard to complement financial measures with the drivers of future performance but were also communicating their strategies through the measures they selected for their balanced scorecard. As the scorecard gained prominence with organizations around the globe as a key tool in the implementation of strategy, Kaplan and Norton summarized the concept and learning generated from the study in their 1996 book *The Balanced Scorecard* (Kaplan and Norton, 1996).

Since that time the balanced scorecard has been adopted by nearly half of the *Fortune* 1000 organizations, and the momentum continues to grow. Once considered the exclusive domain of the for-profit world, the balanced scorecard has been translated and effectively implemented in both the not-for-profit and public sectors. These organizations have learned that by slightly modifying the scorecard framework they are able to demonstrate to their constituents the value they provide and the steps they are taking to fulfill their important missions. In future chapters, we will take a closer look at how the balanced diversity scorecard is being successfully implemented in both the public and not-for-profit sectors. So widely accepted and effective has the scorecard been that the *Harvard Business Review* recently hailed it as one of the 75 most influential ideas of the twentieth century.

What Is a Balanced Scorecard?

We can describe the balanced scorecard as a carefully selected set of measures derived from an organization's strategy. The measures selected for the scorecard represent a tool for leaders to use in communicating to employees and external stakeholders the outcomes and performance drivers by which the organization will achieve its mission and strategic objectives. A simple definition, however, cannot tell us everything about the balanced scorecard. In many organizations, and research into best practices of scorecard use, this tool serves at least three functions:

1. A measurement system
2. A strategic management system
3. A communication tool

THE BALANCED SCORECARD AS A MEASUREMENT SYSTEM

Earlier in the chapter we discussed the limiting features of financial performance measures. Although they provide an excellent review of what has happened in the past, they are inadequate in addressing the real value-creating mechanisms in today's organizations—the intangible assets such as knowledge and networks of relationships. We might call financial measures *lag indicators*. They are outcomes of actions previously taken. The balanced scorecard complements these lag indicators with the drivers of future economic performance, or *lead indicators*. Where do these performance measures (both lag and lead) come from? The answer is the organization's strategy. All of the measures on the balanced scorecard serve as translations of the organization's strategy. Look at Figure 7-1 (Kaplan and Norton, 1996).

What is striking about this diagram is that vision and strategy are at the center of the balanced scorecard system, not financial controls, as in many organizations.

Many organizations have inspiring visions and compelling strategies, but they are often unable to use those beautifully crafted words to align employee actions with the firm's strategic direction. The balanced scorecard allows an organization to translate its vision and strategies by providing a new framework, one that tells the story of the organization's strategy through the objectives and measures chosen. Rather than focusing on financial control devices that provide little in the way of guidance for long-term employee decision making, the scorecard uses measurement as a new language to describe the key elements in the achievement of the strategy. The use of measurement is critical to the achievement of strategy. In his book *Making Strategy Work,* Timothy Galpin (1997) notes "measurable goals and objectives" as one of the key success factors of making strategy work. While the scorecard retains financial measures, it complements them with three other, distinct perspectives: Customer, Internal Processes, and Learning and Growth (Kaplan and Norton, 1992; Niven, 2002).

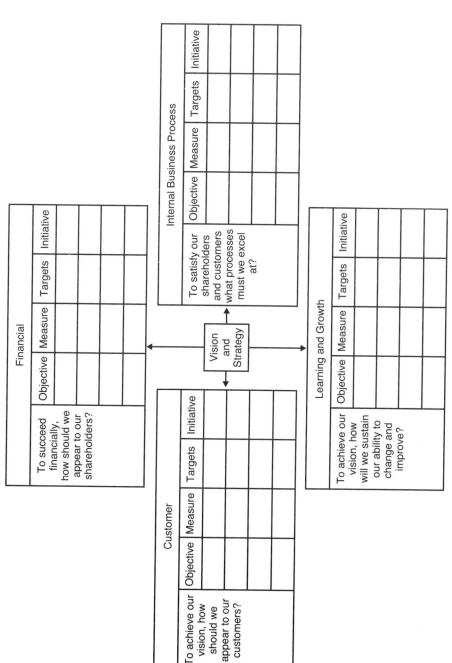

Figure 7-1. The balanced scorecard. (Source: Kaplan and Norton, January/February 1996.)

PERSPECTIVES

The use of the word *perspective* is intentional and represents the preferred method when discussing a balanced scorecard. You may hear others refer to the four quadrants instead of perspectives; however, this reference to quadrants is somewhat limiting compared to the flexible approach inherent in the notion of a scorecard. For your diversity scorecard, you might have six perspectives or only three. Sticking to the word *perspective* is preferred because it is more generic and merely reflects a viewpoint, not a fixed number. In this regard, your scorecard can adjust to meet the changing nature of the organization's business.

Customer Perspective

The customer perspective of the scorecard suggests that organizations answer at least two critical questions: (1) Who are our target customers? and (2) What is our value proposition in serving them? Sounds simple enough, but both of these questions offer many challenges to organizations. Most organizations will state that they do have a target customer audience, yet their actions reveal an "all things to all customers" strategy. This lack of focus will prevent an organization from differentiating itself from competitors. Choosing an appropriate value proposition poses no less of a challenge to most firms. Many will choose one of three disciplines articulated by Treacy and Wiersema in *The Discipline of Market Leaders* (1995):

1. *Operational Excellence.* Organizations pursuing an operational excellence discipline focus on low price, convenience, and often no frills. Wal-Mart provides a great representation of an operationally excellent company.
2. *Product Leadership.* Product leaders push the envelope of their firm's products. Constantly innovating, they strive to offer simply the best product in the market. Nike is an example of a product leader in the field of athletic footwear.
3. *Customer Intimacy.* Doing whatever it takes to provide solutions for unique customers' needs help define the customer-intimate company. They do not look for one-time transactions but instead focus on long-term relationship building through their deep knowledge of customer needs. In the retail industry, Nordstrom epitomizes the customer-intimate organization.

Regardless of the value discipline chosen, this perspective will normally include measures widely used today (e.g., customer satisfaction, customer loyalty, market share, and customer acquisition). Equally as important, the organization must develop the performance drivers that will lead to improvement in these lag indicators of customer success (Niven, 2002). We will take a closer look at the diverse customer perspective and identify what specific steps your organization should take to develop customer measures as we explore the diversity scorecard.

Internal Process Perspective

The internal process perspective of the scorecard helps us address the question: What processes generate the right forms of value for customers and lead to the fulfillment of shareholders' expectations? Each of the customer disciplines outlined previously will entail the efficient operation of specific internal processes in order to serve the organization's customers and fulfill the organization's value proposition. The organization's task in this perspective is to identify those processes and develop the best possible measures with which to track its progress. To satisfy customer and shareholder expectations, the organization may have to identify entirely new internal processes rather than focusing its efforts on the incremental improvement of existing activities. Product development, production, manufacturing, delivery, and post-sale service may be represented in this perspective.

Many organizations rely heavily on supplier relationships and other third-party arrangements to effectively serve customers. In those cases, it is important to consider developing measures in the internal process perspective to represent the critical elements of those relationships (Kaplan and Norton, 1992; Niven, 2002).

Learning and Growth Perspective

The learning and growth perspective enables the organization to ensure its capacity for long-term renewal, a prerequisite for survival in the long run. If the organization wants to achieve ambitious results for internal processes, customers, and ultimately shareholders, where will it find these gains? Measures in the learning and growth perspective of the balanced scorecard serve as enablers of the other three perspectives. In essence, they are the foundation on which this entire house of a balanced scorecard is built. In this perspective, the organization should consider not only what it must do to maintain and develop the know-how required for understanding and satisfying customer needs, but also how it can sustain the necessary efficiency and productivity of the processes that presently create value for the customer. Because know-how is largely a perishable commodity, it will become increasingly important to decide which core competencies the organization should cultivate as the basis for its future performance.

As a consequence of this strategic choice, the organization must also determine how to obtain this know-how, which is still needed in areas that are not core competencies. Once you identify measures and related initiatives in your customer and internal process perspectives, you can be certain of discovering some gaps between your current organizational infrastructure of employee skills and information systems and the level necessary to achieve your results. The measures you design in this perspective will help you close that gap and ensure sustainable performance for the future.

Like the other perspectives of the scorecard, there should be a mix of core outcome (lag) measures and performance drivers (lead measures) to represent the learning and growth perspective. Employee skills, employee satisfaction, availability of information, and alignment certainly apply to this perspective. Many organizations struggle with the development of learning and growth measures. It is normally the last perspective to be developed in a balanced scorecard process, and perhaps the teams are intellectually drained from their earlier efforts of developing new strategic measures or they simply consider this perspective soft stuff best left to the human resources group. No matter how valid the rationale seems, this perspective cannot be overlooked in the development process or left to someone else to develop. As mentioned earlier, the measures developed in the learning and growth perspective are really the enablers of all other measures on the scorecard. Think of them as the "roots of a tree that will ultimately lead through the trunk of internal processes to the branches of customer results, and finally to the leaves of financial returns" (Nivens, 2002).

Financial Perspective

Financial measures are an important component of the balanced scorecard, especially in the for-profit world. The measures in this perspective tell whether the organization's strategy execution, which is detailed through measures chosen in the other perspectives, is leading to improved bottom-line results. We could focus all of our energy and capabilities on improving customer satisfaction, quality, on-time delivery, or any number of things, but without an indication of their effect on the organization's financial returns, they are of limited value. Classic lagging indicators are normally encountered in the financial perspective. Typical examples include profitability, revenue growth, and economic value added.

THE BALANCED SCORECARD AS A STRATEGIC MANAGEMENT SYSTEM

For many organizations the balanced scorecard has evolved from a measurement tool to what Kaplan and Norton have described as a strategic management system. Although the original intent of the scorecard system was to balance historical financial numbers with the drivers of future value for the firm, as more and more organizations experimented with the concept, they found it to be a critical tool in aligning short-term actions with their strategy. Used in this way the scorecard alleviates many of the issues of effective strategy implementation.

THE BALANCED SCORECARD AS A COMMUNICATION TOOL

The preceding sections have discussed the use of the balanced scorecard as a pure measurement system and its evolution into a strategic management system; however, the most basic and most powerful attribute of the entire balanced scorecard system is its ability to communicate the translation of the organization's strategy and telling its story to all employees. A well-constructed scorecard eloquently describes the organization's strategy and makes the vague and imprecise world of visions and strategies come alive through the clear and objective performance measures chosen.

Much has been written in recent years about knowledge management strategies within organizations, and many schools of thought exist. One common trait of all such systems may be the desire to make the implicit knowledge held within the minds of the diverse workforce explicit and open for discussion and learning. We live in the era of knowledge workers—employees who, unlike their organizational descendants who relied on the physical assets of the company, own the means of production: knowledge. There may be no greater challenge facing the organization today than codifying and acting on that knowledge. Sharing scorecard results throughout the organization provides your diverse workforce with the opportunity to discuss the assumptions underlying the strategy, learn from any unexpected results, and dialogue on future modifications as necessary. Simply understanding the organization's strategies can unlock many hidden organizational capacities as diverse employees, perhaps for the first time, know where the organization is headed and how they can contribute during the journey.

Now that you understand the definition, structure, scope, and strategic importance of the balanced scorecard, let's begin our examination of the diversity scorecard process.

WHAT IS A DIVERSITY SCORECARD?

As we said earlier, we can describe the diversity scorecard as a balanced, carefully selected set of objectives and measures derived from an organization's strategy that link to the diversity strategy. The measures selected for the diversity scorecard represent a tool for diversity leaders to use in communicating to executives, managers, employees, and external stakeholders the diversity outcomes and performance drivers by which the organization will achieve its diversity mission and strategic diversity objectives. Because each organization's strategy will be different as a result of the specific industry and type of products and services it provides, its key diversity scorecard perspectives will also vary. Nonetheless, the basic objectives and measures of a diversity scorecard will generally view the organization's diversity performance from six perspectives:

1. Financial impact
2. Diverse customer/community partnership
3. Workforce profile
4. Workplace climate/culture
5. Diversity leadership commitment
6. Learning and growth

All of the measures on the diversity scorecard serve as translations of the organization's strategy and link them to the diversity strategy (see Figure 7-2).

The diversity scorecard is rooted in the organization's vision and strategy and is driven by its leadership.

Financial Impact Perspective

This perspective of the diversity scorecard should show the results of the strategic choices made in the other diversity scorecard perspectives, while

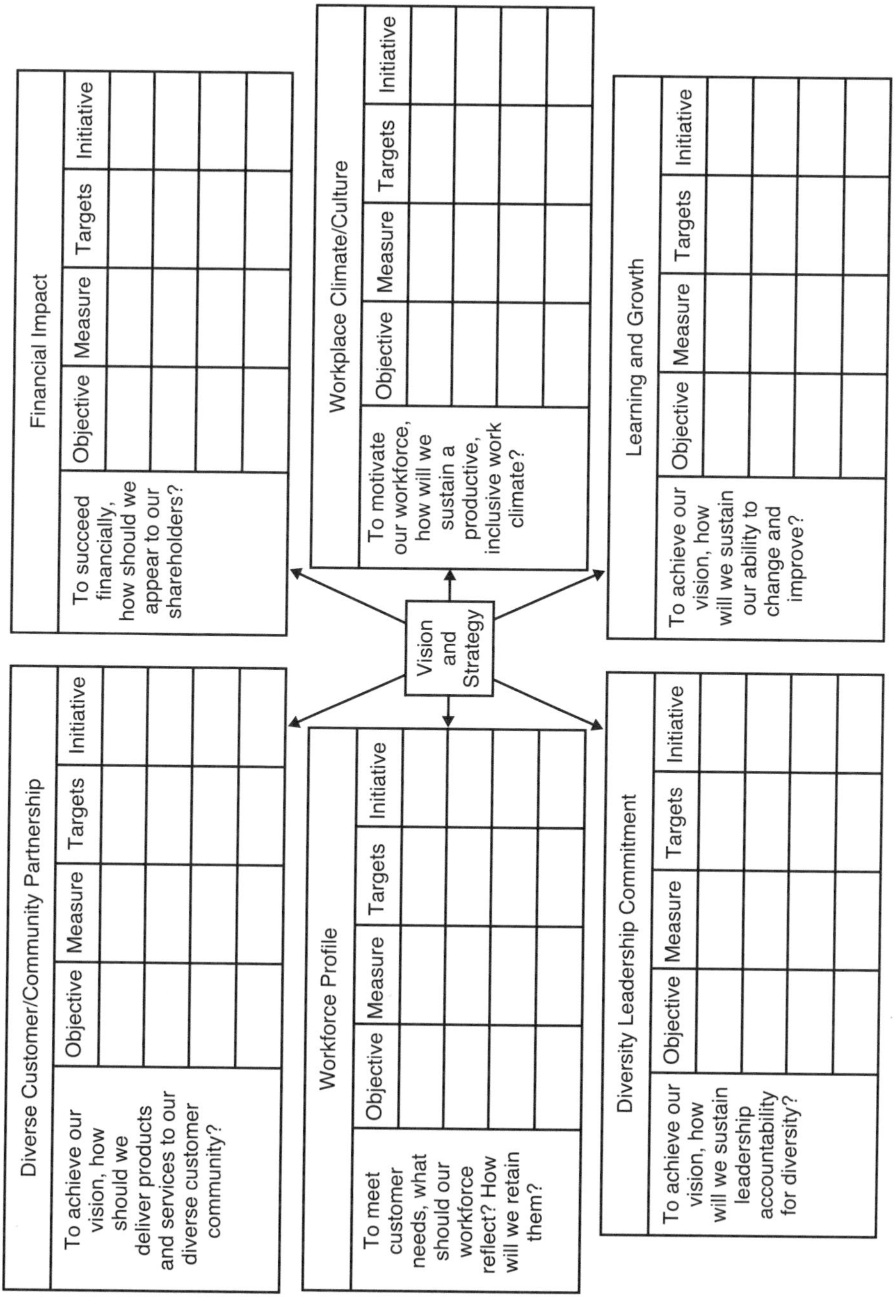

Figure 7-2. The diversity scorecard perspectives.

establishing several of the long-term goals and thus a large part of the general ground rules and premises for the other perspectives. Here we find a description of what the executive team and shareholders expect of the organization in terms of growth and profitability. In this perspective, it is also appropriate to describe which financial risks, such as a negative cash flow, are acceptable. Other issues that may be covered relate to cost and investment strategies, to the maximum permissible amount of accounts receivable, and so on. This perspective is similar to any other balanced scorecard an organization or business unit would create. In other words, this is where you will find many of the traditional instruments of management control in the form of financial measures and key ratios.

Diverse Customer/Community Partnership Perspective

This perspective of the diversity scorecard describes the ways in which value is to be created for diverse customers, how diverse customer demand for this value is to be satisfied, operational excellence required to achieve this value, and why these diverse customers will be willing to pay for it. It also describes the degree to which the community views the organization as a strategic partner and sees its presence as value added. We live in an increasingly global world that is diverse. Whether the organization's business includes marketing financial services, computers, telecommunications products, social services, health care equipment, manufacturing processes, or engineering expertise, know-how in addressing a diverse customer market and building relationships with the communities it serves will be essential to success.

For example, on the customer side, an automobile manufacturer in Japan cannot afford to ignore the fact that nearly half of all new-car buyers in the United States are women. This is true regardless of the gender makeup of car buyers in Japan. Likewise, no reasonable person in the consumer-goods industry can afford to ignore the fact that roughly one-quarter of the world's population is Chinese, and immigration to the United States from mostly Asian and Latin American countries is occurring at a rate of more than one million people per year.

In the United States, Asians, African Americans, and Hispanics combined now collectively represent more than $1 trillion annually in consumer spending. The Selig Center for Economic Growth's (from the University of Georgia Terry School of Management) estimates and projections of buying power for 1990–2007 show that minorities—African

Americans, Asians, Native Americans, and Hispanics—definitely share in this success, and together wield formidable economic clout. As these groups increase in number and purchasing power, their growing shares of the U.S. consumer market draw avid attention from producers, retailers, and service providers alike.

The buying power data presented here and differences in spending by race and/or ethnicity suggest that one general advertisement, product, or service geared for all consumers increasingly misses many potentially profitable market opportunities. As the U.S. consumer market becomes more diverse, advertising, products, and media must be tailored to each market segment. With this in mind, new entrepreneurs, established businesses, marketing specialists, economic development organizations, and chambers of commerce now seek estimates of the buying power of the nation's major racial and ethnic minority groups. The Selig Center projected that the nation's total buying power would rise from $4.3 trillion in 1990 to $7 trillion in 2000, to $7.6 trillion in 2002, and to $9.9 trillion in 2007. The percentage increase for the 17-year period, 1990–2007, is 130.8 percent, which far outstrips cumulative inflation. These diverse forces support this substantial growth.

Buying Power Statistics by Race

In 2007, the combined buying power of African Americans, Asians, and Native Americans will more than triple its 1990 level of $453 billion and will total almost $1.4 trillion, a gain of $912 billion or 201 percent. In 2007, African Americans will account for 62 percent of combined spending, or $853 billion. Over this 17-year period, the percentage gains in minority buying power vary considerably by race, from a gain of 287 percent for Asians to 197 percent for American Indians to 170 percent for African Americans. All of these target markets will grow much faster than the Caucasian market, where buying power will increase by only 112 percent.

The combined buying power of these three groups will account for 13.8 percent of the nation's total buying power in 2007, up from 10.6 percent in 1990. This 3.2 percent gain in combined market share amounts to an additional $316 billion in buying power in 2007. The market share claimed by a targeted group of consumers is important because the higher their market share, the lower the average cost of reaching a potential buyer in the group. To be effective, managers in organizations must possess effective multicultural marketing savvy to meet specific needs of a diverse marketplace to affect buying behavior (The Selig Center for Economic Growth, 2002).

In addition, organizations can gain a lot from the insights of its diverse workforce to understand the cultural effects of buying decisions and mapping strategies to respond to them. Depending on the product or service delivered by the organization, many employees may also represent part of the firm's customer base! A good reputation inside the organization can help product and service sales outside the organization. Another key marketing strategy includes tapping employee network or resource groups. They can be an excellent resource for focus groups, feedback, and ideas for honing the organization's reach into diverse marketplace opportunities.

If an organization plans to sell or deliver goods and services in a diverse marketplace, it must be fully capable of effectively utilizing its diverse workforce in key strategic ways. For instance, it is important from a public relations point of view to be viewed as a company that is known for managing and utilizing its diverse workforce assets well. Nonetheless, a word of caution: Employees from diverse backgrounds also want to be valued for who they are, to have their humanity and dignity respected along with their skills, competencies, and talents. This will not happen if they believe the organization regards them as just another revenue stream, benefiting the shareholders, but not them.

From a community perspective, the diversity scorecard must also reflect the organization's efforts as a good corporate citizen to all external constituent and stakeholder communities represented in its marketplace. This includes its philanthropic activities, volunteerism, vendor/supplier diversity efforts, board member participation, and the like. Activities such as these help mold the community's view of the organization. There are several well-publicized ratings for "The Best Company for Working Women and Working Mothers," "The Most Admired Company," and "The Top 50 Companies for Women and Minorities." This fuels a public relations climate in which workforce talent and consumers make choices about the organizations they would work for and buy from. This line of thinking is also supported by a study of stock price responses to publicity that changed either positively or negatively on an organization's ability to manage diversity. The study authors found that announcements of awards for exemplary efforts resulted in significant positive changes in stock prices while announcements of discrimination suits resulted in significant negative changes in stock prices (Wright et al., 1995).

Workforce Profile Perspective

This perspective of the diversity scorecard typically reflects the recruitment, selection, and retention efforts of the organization beyond the normal affirmative action reporting. Recruitment and selection is often the first place organizations will start when building a diverse work environment. The current changing landscape of American demographics, both native and foreign born, reflects a labor pool that comprises a large population of educated, capable people from diverse backgrounds, especially in the high-tech and service-based industries.

Any organization that desires to stay competitive for now and in the future is going to have to find, recruit, and retain the best employees, regardless of their diverse backgrounds. Too often, recruiters and their organizations evaluate new recruits solely on the basis of how they fit the organization's culture, which is somewhat antiquated in today's hiring practices and requirements (today, many organizations try to avoid hiring in their own image). Many of these interviews are unstructured and haphazard; the interviewers are often poorly trained in how to conduct a culture-fair, objective interview. In addition, very few metrics and incentives encourage the interviewers to make certain they obtain a diverse candidate pool.

This portion of the diversity scorecard is designed to provide feedback on progress in the recruitment, selection, and retention areas to ensure a stable, competitive workforce. Your diversity scorecard workforce profile should help you respond to questions like the following about the organization's commitment to diverse workforce representation:

- ☐ What is the ethnic, racial, and gender composition of the workplace?
- ☐ What is the age span of the workforce?
- ☐ What percentage of top management are women, minorities, or those who are differently abled?
- ☐ How do these percentages change when they are applied to middle management? First-line supervisors or staff?
- ☐ Is the ethnic and cultural distribution the same from top to bottom in the organization or are all white males in the executive suite and all Hispanic or African Americans in "environmental engineering"?
- ☐ What is the turnover rate by demographic group and age?

In addition to recruiting a diverse workforce, processes must be in place to retain and develop these employees. The ability to retain the diverse work group once recruited is a critical management competency. It helps avoid human capital depletion and revolving-door impact. Some organizations do a wonderful job of setting up systems to recruit diverse employees only to lose them 12 to 18 months later in voluntary turnover (human capital depletion). This often occurs because little thought is given to retaining employees once they are inside the organization. If this happens, they show up in the revolving-door statistics (poor survival rate). Workforce profile statistics help you effectively manage your recruitment and selection efforts and increase diverse workforce retention.

Workplace Climate/Culture Perspective

This perspective of the diversity scorecard is structured to provide feedback on the degree to which the organization has created a diverse, inclusive environment that fosters employee satisfaction and performance. It includes examining various aspects of the organization's operating culture in terms of how things are done and what's expected of its members, acculturation, cultural differences, intergroup conflict, people management practices, organizational adaptability, and change.

No change effort will get far without some form of organizational diagnosis of climate and/or culture. A formal measurement of the current state is necessary, both to guide action planning and to set a baseline for assessing progress. Although a thorough discussion of organizational climate and/or culture diagnosis methods is beyond the scope of this book, the following offers some principles for effectiveness based on work with several organizations. Detailed techniques for analyzing diversity climate and culture using manual and web-based cultural audit processes are taught in workshops at the Hubbard Diversity Measurement and Productivity Institute (HDMP), along with measurement software available from Hubbard & Hubbard, Inc.

Measurement is valuable only if it focuses on true indicators of success. To identify these it will be helpful to start with some kind of explicit, research-based conceptualization of the components of work climate that determine an organization's capacity to welcome and use workforce diversity as a resource for better performance. This model (shown in Table 7-1), with some elements adapted from Taylor Cox's model of the Components of Diversity Climate (Cox, 2001), is based on empirical organizational dynamics research that is known to be significantly relevant to workforce diversity and inclusion.

Table 7-1. Key Components of Diversity Climate

Individual-Level Measures	Definition
1. Amount of identity-group prejudice	Predisposition to dislike or have a negative attitude toward someone
2. Amount of stereotyping	Assuming that individuals have limited abilities or negative traits based on membership in a group
3. Amount of ethnocentrism	Preference for members of one's own "in-group"
4. Diversity-relevant personality traits	Examples: tolerance for ambiguity; authoritarian personality

Work Group-Level Measures	Definition
1. Level of intergroup conflict	Conflict that is explicitly related to sociocultural group differences
2. Group identity strength	The extent to which a person feels a strong bond with his or her group
3. Quality of intergroup communication	Frequency and effectiveness of communications across groups
4. Diverse work team productivity	Amount or rate of increased output produced versus traditional team output
5. Diverse work team innovation	Amount or rate of increased new product or process output produced versus traditional team product or process output
6. Cultural differences and similarities	Amount of cultural distance versus overlap between cultures of groups

Organization-Level Measures	Definition
1. Identity profile of workforce	Demographics of key differences in a defined work group or organization
2. Mode of acculturation	Method of handling cultural differences (assimilation vs. pluralism)
3. Content of organization culture	Key norms, values, beliefs
4. Power distribution among groups	Extent to which people of different identity groups have authority or power
5. People management practices and policies	Recruiting, promotions, compensation, physical work environment, member development, work schedules
6. Openness of informal networks	Extent to which people of all identity groups have access to social and communication networks
7. Adaptability to Change	Rate of absorption and integration of new environmental demands and content from internal and external sources

Source: Edward E. Hubbard, "Building a Diversity Measurement Scorecard," June 2002.

Even though all items are important, it is not necessary to include all of these items in order to have a usable diagnosis of the organization's climate or culture. In selecting items to include, one criterion is ease of measurement. Capturing some items, such as identity profile of workforce and power distribution among groups, is straightforward; however, others, such as content of organization culture and openness of informal networks, are much more complicated.

Unless you are thoughtful and insightful about the factors that define the climate for diversity, you are likely to miss key components. For example, consider the item labeled mode of acculturation. The term *acculturation* refers to the way cultural differences are handled when parties from different cultural traditions are merged into one group. It applies to multiple types of group identifications, including gender, national origin, race, and organizational identity. The possibilities for acculturation mode include separation, with each party retaining its own identity and making little movement toward the work norms, values, and beliefs of the other. A second form is *assimilation,* in which the norms, values, and beliefs of the stronger, more dominant party or group are imposed on the other, less powerful party. Still another form is *pluralism,* in which each party is open to movement toward the culture of the other, the best traditions of each culture are carefully considered for adoption by the total enterprise, and each party retains some of their identity with the premerger culture.

The mode of acculturation in organizations in which acquisitions and joint ventures are prominent in the business strategy will have a great effect on the ability to integrate the workforces of the combining units and get them working together with maximum effectiveness as members of a newly defined team. Yet without an insightful model of what to study in diversity climate or culture assessments, this aspect of the climate is easily omitted. This example makes the point that we must marry content expertise with data collection savvy in order to get the best results when diagnosing a work climate or culture with respect to a specific aspect of organizations, such as diversity. This is another area where many organizations will need help from external consultants (Cox, 2001).

Making a commitment to diversity means more than striving for immediate results such as improved demographics. Employees must feel welcomed and supported as part of the organization's climate. They need to know that the organization has systems, processes, and people in place to help give them the best possible chance for success and allow them to build an invigorating career.

Diversity Leadership Commitment Perspective

This perspective of the diversity scorecard gauges the degree to which the organization's leaders are utilizing behaviors that set the vision, direction, policy, and a personal model for the diversity effort through demonstrated actions.

Leadership is the first requirement for a diversity change initiative. To be fully effective, leadership *must* start at the top in creating a high-performing diverse organization that is steeped in skills for effective diversity management. In the context of organizational change, leadership is behavior that establishes a direction or goal for the diversity change initiative (a vision), provides a sense of urgency and importance for the vision, facilitates the motivation of others, and cultivates necessary conditions for achievement of the vision. Leadership is the most essential element for the diversity change effort. Without it, nothing happens to sustain the effort. Although commitment and strong leadership at the top is necessary, it is not sufficient for effective leadership in managing diversity throughout the organization. Success requires many leaders.

It is clear that the CEO of the organization and heads of the main operating units have primary responsibility for breakthrough progress on diversity. If they do not hold themselves accountable for executing the diversity initiative, this change effort is doomed to failure. Diversity officers and their staff have a crucial role to play as facilitators of the diversity change process, but they alone cannot be held responsible for making it happen. Examples of real, top-down commitment to diversity can be seen in the following synopsis of corporate diversity activities (Schreiber, 2001):

☐ American Express has created a Diversity Council, made up of members of senior management, that meets every six or eight weeks to discuss the corporate diversity initiative.

☐ Hewlett-Packard's Diversity Leadership Council, also comprising members of the top executive team, conducts an ongoing appraisal of diversity efforts in all company areas. Key to the effort is an ongoing policy of reminding all managers of the corporation's commitment to diversity in all areas of operations.

☐ DaimlerChrysler has undertaken similar initiatives and places emphasis on benchmarking against other companies in their diversity undertakings. Their commitment to being state of the art with regard to diversity issues might well reward the company with increased competitiveness in the coming decades.

☐ At Mobil, the diverse constituency of its consumer base mandated the move toward greater diversity, both domestically and abroad. Mobil's operations, after all, take place in more than 125 countries. Back in 1984, Lou Noto, Mobil's chair and CEO, began a new diversity initiative by establishing a Leadership Council to spearhead its Global Inclusion and Diversity initiative. The key working points for the program were culture and communication, leadership and accountability, recruitment and outreach, and retention. In an effort to make these priorities operative down through the ranks, Mobil included them among the list of "Score Card" traits used to evaluate each manager's performance.

☐ In the early 1990s, several important lawsuits were filed against the Denny's restaurant chain, alleging discrimination against African-American clients. But by 1994, when the suits were settled, Denny's had already begun to demonstrate a strong commitment to diversity. Among other steps, Denny's instituted a special toll-free number on which customers could report any instances of discrimination they had observed in Denny's establishments and set up an active program of diversity recruitment and training for all current managers.

Denny's not only talked about diversity, it put money behind its words. In 1992, at the time of the discrimination suits, Denny's had no minority-owned vendors. By 1996, the company paid $80 million in contracts to vendors who were minority owned. CEO Jim Adamson was a motivating force in bringing about the transformation, and his efforts did not go unnoticed. In fact, he was awarded the NAACP's Corporate CEO Achievement Award in 1996, and Denny's continues to top *Fortune* magazine's list of the Best Companies for Asians, African Americans, and Hispanics. In less than a decade, Denny's transformed its image in the marketplace through its diversity efforts. This type of leadership commitment and other diversity leadership–based metrics should be tracked in the diversity scorecard.

Learning and Growth Perspective

This perspective of the diversity scorecard assesses the degree to which key strategic capabilities are being developed among all segments of the diverse workforce. As mentioned earlier, the learning and growth perspective enables the organization to ensure its capacity for long-term renewal, a prerequisite for survival in the long run. A diverse workforce, given proper attention to development, mentoring, growth-enabling assignments, flexibility, and the like, can create a whole new level of competitive performance and innovation in a diverse, global marketplace. Developing, training, and implementing competency models for diversity is an important first step in the evolution of a high-performing, diversity-enriched organization. Managing these competencies includes cultivating the performance of diversity-competent employees at all levels, assessing their performance against the models, and rewarding that performance appropriately.

The learning and growth perspective is really an enabler of all other measures on the scorecard. It helps produce diversity-competent employees who are well positioned to facilitate the pace and extent of change necessary to meet the demands of an ever-increasing diverse, multicultural society. Strategically, it helps the organization monitor its alignment and intellectual capability to execute strategy. It challenges the organization's growth paradigm to determine if it is ready to meet the demands of competing in a global economy by addressing questions such as the following:

☐ What portion of the organization's existing infrastructure (e.g., people, capabilities, systems, technology) can be leveraged to pursue the new emerging multicultural market opportunities?
☐ What new skills and abilities must we have to compete?
☐ Do people in the organization have access to information in time to capitalize on new opportunities?

If you are going after an ethnic segment within the United States, there are certain elements of your existing infrastructure you can leverage and others you cannot use in their present form. You may want to use the same distribution channels and the same sales force, but you have to ask yourself if this will be effective. Is some new kind of thinking required?

The learning and growth implications of the following marketing problem can help highlight examples of new learning and competency requirements if organizations are to survive. Suppose you are a skin-care company and you have products of high-potential usage by African Americans—perhaps an effective remedy lotion for razor bumps. African-American men have a very high incidence of razor bumps and ingrown hairs on their skin after shaving. If your company already has a product that addresses this problem, how well are you reaching African-American consumers? Do they have to go to Macy's or another department store to purchase your product? If so, is that the optimal channel for selling your product? The answer is "no." The sales the company is getting are merely general market sales. To tap the real potential of the African-American consumer market, you have to have the cultural competencies to repackage the product to be more culturally relevant (without offending the consumer), you need to know how many African-American men have razor bumps, and you must also know the best way to distribute the product.

Building competencies relevant to distributing the product would reveal that the best way will be through barber shops and beauty shops that cater to African Americans because, in general, African Americans do not get their haircuts or shaves at typical mainstream salons and boutiques. Instead, they have their own hair-care channel, which is unique and different from going to a typical salon. African Americans are brand loyal, so you are also building strong customer franchise and loyalty. Once an African-American consumer knows you have a product that works and it is sold at a point of need and a place with easy access (i.e., the barber shop), you have the makings of high customer value, repeat business, and profits.

If you are able to develop and package a skin-care product for African-American men and sell it through appropriate distribution channels, you must logically ask, "Who should be our marketing and sales manager for this product line?" and then define the competencies for that position through a multicultural lens. The competency definition for this position might be someone who understands the skin problems that are unique to African Americans and who can go to the beauty salons and barber shops to build the required channel relationships. What emerges is a competency definition that consists of the required marketing and sales capabilities. But in addition, it defines an individual who understands African-American culture and can relate to African-American merchants. It's very likely that the individual to fill this position will be an African American.

The candidate profile stops being a race-based definition and becomes a competency definition. Nine out of ten times that competency definition defines an African-American individual, even though there is nothing about race in the profile. Your skin-care company might well end up with a Caucasian who can do the job, but whomever you select must understand and be able to relate to that marketplace. The learning and growth perspective helps monitor process and outcome measures that build organizational competencies, growth, and capacity to capitalize on opportunities such as the African-American skin-care scenario described above. It assesses the strategic capability of the organization to execute its strategy in a multicultural world and helps maintain competitive performance.

An effective diversity scorecard is more than an ad-hoc collection of financial and nonfinancial measures. A well-crafted diversity scorecard should tell the story of the organization's diversity strategy and alignment through a series of cause-and-effect linkages inherent in the scorecard measures. The relationships are revealed through a series of if-then statements: If we increase diverse customer loyalty, then we expect revenue to increase. By explicitly documenting the assumptions in your diversity strategy through a cause-and-effect network of measures, you greatly enhance the opportunities for strategic learning and lay the groundwork for quantum performance in a global economy.

FINAL THOUGHTS

Understanding the basic diversity scorecard components and their application is critical to the creation of value-added performance in any organization. The best diversity scorecards will reflect the strategy of the organization and link the diversity change initiative(s) to it. A good test is whether you can understand the organization's strategy and diversity's role by looking only at the scorecard. Many organizations, especially those that created constituent/stakeholder scorecards or key performance indicator (KPI) scorecards, fail this test.

Strategy-based scorecards provide a logical and comprehensive way to describe the diversity organization's strategy. They communicate clearly the organization's desired diversity outcomes and its hypotheses about how these outcomes can be achieved. They enable all organizational units and employees to understand the diversity strategy and how its implementation produces value-added results. Armed with a diversity scorecard that tells the story of the diversity strategy, we now have a reliable foundation for reviewing each diversity scorecard perspective in more detail.

REFERENCES

Cox, Taylor, Jr. *Creating the Multicultural Organization*. San Francisco: Jossey-Bass, 2001.

Galpin, Timothy J. *Making Strategy Work*. San Francisco: Jossey-Bass, 1997.

Hubbard, Edward E. "Building a Diversity Measurement Scorecard." *Hubbard Diversity Measurement & Productivity Newsletter*, June 2002.

Hubbard, Edward E. *How to Calculate Diversity Return on Investment.* Petaluma, CA: Global Insights, 1999.

Kaplan, Robert S., and David P. Norton. *The Balanced Scorecard.* Boston: Harvard Business School Press, 1996.

Kaplan, Robert S., and David P. Norton. "The Balanced Scorecard: Measures that Drive Performance," *Harvard Business Review,* January-February 1992, 71–79.

Kaplan, Robert S., and David P. Norton. "Using the Balanced Scorecard as a Strategic Management System." *Harvard Business Review,* January-February 1996, 76.

Niven, Paul R. *Balanced Scorecard Step-by-Step: Maximizing Performance and Maintaining Results.* New York: John Wiley & Sons, 2002.

Schreiber, Alfred L. *Multicultural Marketing.* Chicago: NTC Business Books, 2001.

The Selig Center for Economic Growth, University of Georgia, Terry School of Management, www.selig.com, 2002.

Treacy, Michael, and Fred Wiersema. *The Discipline of Market Leaders.* Reading, MA: Perseus Books, 1995.

Wright, Peter, Stephen P. Ferris, Janine S. Hiller, and Mark Kroll. "Competitiveness through Management of Diversity: Effects on Stock Price Valuation." *Academy of Management Journal,* 1995, 272–287.

CHAPTER 8

Diversity Leadership Commitment Perspective

DEFINITION

Diversity leadership commitment can be defined as demonstrated evidence and actions taken by leaders to support, challenge, and champion the diversity process within their organization. It reflects the degree to which the organization's leaders utilize behaviors that set the diversity vision, direction, and policy into actual practice. It also reflects the individual level and degrees of accountability leaders have in forging an implementation strategy, and it analyzes the level of specific behavior they exhibit as a model diversity champion.

From an organizational change point of view, diversity leadership commitment is the behavior that helps establish a direction or goal for change (a vision), provides a sense of urgency and importance for the vision, facilitates the motivation of others, and cultivates necessary conditions for achievement of the vision. Diversity leadership commitment is critical to the diversity change process. It cannot be delegated or given just tacit consideration. It is clear that the CEO of the organization and heads of the main operating units have primary responsibility for breakthrough progress on diversity. If they do not hold themselves accountable for the leadership requirements to execute diversity initiatives, the change effort is doomed to failure. Diversity officers and their staffs have a crucial role to play as facilitators of the diversity change process. Leaders alone cannot be held responsible for making it happen. As a unifying force, diversity leadership commitment throughout the organization serves as a key linchpin for success that is combined with the efforts of others to sustain forward progress.

Here are some signals that will tell you where your organization stands on meeting key diversity leadership commitment requirements:

1. Check the composition of your diversity steering groups or task forces. They should not have more than one or two representatives from the HR function. Senior members of the line organizations must be full participating strategic partners.
2. The chair of your main planning group should not be an HR person or a diversity officer; it should be someone in a senior leadership, decision-making position. This is especially applicable in organizations where the diversity function is not a full strategic partner at the top or where the head diversity person does not report directly to the CEO.
3. If you are using consulting help, the lead consultant for the work on diversity should have access to, and be in contact with, key senior and operational leaders in your organization. If this person is limited to talking through the HR organization or diversity officer, then you have not established the right concept of leadership.

Let's elaborate on this third point to give you a better feel for the general principle of nondelegation of responsibility for diversity leadership and change. Taylor Cox (2001) offers these examples of effective diversity leadership commitment:

1. A general manager personally conducts feedback meetings to present the results of an assessment of the organization's climate for diversity.
2. A high-level manager who has been assigned to serve on a business-unit diversity steering committee is scheduled to attend the first meeting of this group. The committee has invited a senior outside consultant to attend this meeting and help them kick off their work. After the meeting is scheduled, this manager is asked by his supervisor (the head of the operation) to attend another meeting out of town on the same day. The manager insists that he cannot attend the meeting with his supervisor because he must attend the diversity steering group meeting. The Operations General Manager accepts this and excuses him from attending the out-of-town meeting.
3. While attending a training session for leaders of diversity change work, the president of the business unit notices that some of his direct reports who are attending the meeting are not focused on the business at hand (they are whispering to one another about

a business problem unrelated to diversity). During a break, the president calls these people aside and gives them a firm reminder of the importance of refocusing their attention on learning about diversity.

4. The top management team at a manufacturing plant commits to kick off and close *every* session of diversity awareness training. This requires three people to share responsibility for a total of one hundred training sessions conducted over a ten-month period, including sessions occurring during the midnight shift.

5. The vice president of human resources of a business unit personally designs and delivers a series of short seminars teaching principles about managing diversity, based on the book written by the lead consultant for their change process. His plan is to provide ongoing education by teaching a different portion of the book at each of their leadership meetings over an extended period of time.

6. The president of the local Steel Workers Union works with the general manager of a manufacturing operation to create a video to express their joint commitment to the change process for creating a positive diversity climate.

7. The CEO of the company agrees to be interviewed by a middle manager to discuss his views on people issues, including diversity. The interview is videotaped and distributed to all business units for use in introductory education.

8. The CEO of the company mandates that all diversity initiatives will have performance metrics. These diversity metrics are included in appropriate management and operational reports. Diversity return on investment studies are required for any diversity initiative meeting key business impact and cost criteria.

These are just a few examples of leaders who "get it" and demonstrate commitment to diversity through their actions.

To begin the process of integrating diversity and inclusion considerations into mainstream thinking, you need sponsors, people with clout and influence. You can start with the obvious choices—leaders who put people first—but take a closer look. They may not be the ones who are the most creative and influential. Find the high-performing leaders who have a record of achieving results through others—leaders who have mobilized change efforts, forged new ground, championed causes, and have a vested interest in your organization's achievement. Leaders with these attributes can also use their influence to help you begin to integrate diversity and inclusion into the fabric of your organization. Your job is to find them, establish a relationship with them, and develop that compelling business reason, global reality, or moral imperative that is just right to engage their support of the diversity process.

A committed diversity leader must walk the talk. He or she sets the formal and informal tone for inclusion in the organization. This leader's messages and actions taken must be congruent in order for the organization to take the diversity effort seriously. For example, it is incongruent to espouse valuing differences while continuing to support job performance evaluations that judge people on style and not substance. This kind of incongruence is immediately visible to employees and increases skepticism that meaningful change is possible within the organization (George, Jackson, LaBella, 1995).

The following example illustrates this impact: In an organization where Martin, the CEO, had come forth as a strong advocate for diversity, he continued to work in an autocratic, hierarchical manner with the vice presidents one layer beneath him. Martin received feedback from some of these vice presidents that he was advocating diversity yet was not fully including diversity in his own executive team. The vice presidents challenged him on continuing to work in the old way while advocating a more inclusive environment that valued and appreciated differences. They suggested that he model this new behavior by working more inclusively with his own layers of upper management, and they suggested that whenever feasible he "not conclude until he included." Martin took this advice and altered the way he worked with his vice presidents. Ultimately, this led Martin to working differently and more inclusively with general managers and others throughout the organization (George, Jackson, LaBella, 1995).

To the degree the leader shows and offers support, other key people will line up behind the effort. Some of the people who are major resisters may fall in line at least temporarily and allow the effort to get off to a strong start. Their behavior must be addressed with the appropriate support, training, incentives, performance metrics, and performance management feedback and actions if it is not consistent with the diversity vision.

The support and commitment of other leaders in the organization, such as the vice presidents, general managers, and other members of the executive team, are important because they have the authority to commit resources. Furthermore, managers and supervisors at all levels will look to the leadership team for support and guidance during the implementation of diversity initiatives. Their behavior and demonstrated actions reflecting commitment (or the lack of it) will speak volumes concerning the strategic importance of this effort.

The actual ongoing, day-to-day attitudes and behaviors of employees and supervisors will be most greatly influenced by these leaders. Although leaders can create the diversity vision and be role models, the managers and supervisors create the support and maintain the actual changes in everyday organizational life. The strength and clarity of the commitment of the leadership team will filter down to these people in a variety of ways and will be critical in creating buy-in. There will be multiple opportunities for supervisors and managers to practice the behavioral changes that a true diversity effort requires. Behavioral modeling may involve being more inclusive in decision making, holding oneself accountable for diversity results, becoming aware of and facilitating differences on a diverse team, helping people build on their individual strengths, pointing out and eliminating bias and stereotyping that may be present in the work group, and measuring diversity efforts to take corrective actions.

Organizational leaders who are well educated in the benefits of diversity are the strongest advocates. Leaders must take the time to educate themselves, personally orchestrate, and participate in actions that build an effective, high-performing inclusive climate. With diversity, often comes an element of tension in the workplace that must be managed effectively for diversity to be successful. Leaders must demonstrate effective diversity management behaviors and competencies that illustrate how diversity tension is managed to achieve organizational goals and objectives. Everyone else in the organization will look to the leaders to see where they are on the issue and how they respond when diversity challenges arise.

Leaders must clearly identify the benefits of building a diverse organization and tie them to the overall business strategy so people can see how a diverse organization will pay off. These payoffs must be measured in concrete ways that show their impact on the strategic and financial objectives of the organization. To be truly effective, leaders must drive diversity processes such that they become integrated into the fabric of the way business is done.

Leadership commitment is not limited to executives and managers inside the organization. Members of the board of directors can also do a great deal to promote the diversity initiative by carrying the message to the external community. What if the driving force to work with diversity is not initiated by the leadership? Then their lack of commitment and competency must be measured and fed back such that they can make an informed choice about their diversity leadership behavior. If leadership is still lacking regarding a commitment to diversity, then efforts should focus on champions anywhere in the organization; however, the diversity effort will be severely hampered without senior leaders' support.

Awareness, skill building, role modeling, and competent diversity leadership from senior management are needed to create ownership of working with diversity and to build strong commitment to support it over the long term. In sum, these aspects of diversity leadership reflect true commitment and are measured by the index in this strategic perspective.

COLLECTING DATA

The data collection process for the diversity leadership commitment index will depend on your organization's definition of leadership commitment in the area of diversity. As mentioned previously, it will be based partly on the business goals and objectives of the organization and the diversity strategic business plan. In general, it may include collecting data such as the following:

☐ *Level of participation in the organization's diversity vision formulation.* Executive and management participation in the formation of the diversity vision and mission is critical. By their very participation and leadership, it signals to the organization that this function is important to the organization's business.

☐ *Multirater, 360-degree feedback on a diversity leadership and/or climate assessment that asks specific questions regarding leadership accountability and commitment to the organization to the diversity process.* Organizational climate and cultural audits will often have questions that relate to the level of perceived support and leadership that is exhibited by top management. Often these questions probe for employee reaction to visible participation, behavior modeling, and the condition of the organization's or the department's diversity climate, among other things. The data found here, sorted by demographic group, can be a gold mine of information about leadership perceptions across the organization.

☐ *The impact of organizational leaders on their success in facilitating the achievement of employee Individual Development Plans (IDPs) within the year the IDPs were slated to be achieved (not 2 to 3 years later).* IDP implementation is the life-blood of developing an organization's intellectual asset value. The level of follow-through that is accomplished in making certain all groups of employees have the time can be a gauge of diversity leadership commitment. It can also be a reflection of the discriminatory support given to some groups to complete key strategic development activities within the timeframe specified during their performance reviews. It is not uncommon to note that employees from minority groups do not get the same level of IDP development and implementation support as other employees.

☐ *The number of diverse employees in formal mentoring programs with the leader (or manager) who get promoted.* Mentoring diverse workforce members and engaging in reverse mentoring—the practice of pairing mentors and protégés who reflect key differences such as race, gender, ethnicity, and so on.

☐ *The number of women and people of color personally selected by the leader for special assignments.* Getting a special assignment can often be tantamount to successfully making it in the promotion pool to a higher level. Diversity leadership commitment can be reflected in the leader's personal support and intervention in making certain that access to special developmental assignments is not impeding the progress of any employee group. In certain areas of the government, for example, if employees desire to move to higher levels of management, they must have a "visible Washington, DC assignment" as part of their career history. If not, he or she will find it difficult to advance beyond a certain level.

☐ *The percentage of diversity objectives that are aligned with key strategic business objectives, which are tied to the bonus and compensation system.* Leaders must make sure that the diversity organization is properly aligned with the business. This responsibility is no different from what would be done if the sales, marketing, operations, or manufacturing functions were out of alignment with the corporate strategy. Rarely, if ever, would you hear an executive who is responsible and accountable for the strategic results of the organization say, "It's too bad that the sales or marketing organization doesn't seem to align with the organization's strategy and results our shareholders expect. I hope they get their act together and are able to show how they add value. In the meantime, let's go on to something else." Instead, organizational leaders would help develop elaborate plans and strategies to get the department in alignment and probably take those in charge to task for letting the function slip away from its intended objectives.

☐ *The representation mix on the organization's board of directors.* Diversity leadership commitment can be reflected in the composition of an organization's board of directors. Most organizational leaders today know there are a wide range of people who can add tremendous value to the stewardship and other responsibilities that a corporate board requires. This is especially important when the demographic mix of employees and customers has changed over time and Board membership has not.

☐ *Leadership representation by level on the diversity steering committee and advisory boards.* Senior and other leaders in the diversity steering committee and advisory boards visually etch diversity leadership commitment—or the lack of it—in the minds of employees when they review the amount and level of participation that exist. In addition, diversity steering committees and advisory boards need members who have the resources and the authority to make decisions to change processes and address issues throughout the organization.

☐ *The degree of personal involvement and participation in diversity actions that drive organizational performance objectives and/or create a high-performing, inclusive climate.* Data collected here will feed back the level of personal leadership and impact leaders are having on changing the workplace environment. This data will help determine if leadership influence and management skill is driving real change in the organization.

☐ *Management competency in effectively dealing with diversity tension when it arises.* As mentioned earlier, a diverse workforce will naturally generate diversity tension. This is to be expected, if for no other reason than the fact that people have different ways of viewing and accomplishing things. Data regarding diversity leadership commitment can be assessed by examining the degree to which leaders and managers successfully utilize differences for performance and effectively manage the diversity tension that often accompanies it.

☐ *Multirater, 360-degree feedback on diversity leadership competencies that drive diversity process performance metrics.* This data reflects perceptions collected using a multirater survey instrument that helps determine if leaders are taking the time to build competencies using diversity to drive business performance.

☐ *Diversity budget dollars and resources allocated versus other major functions within the organization.* Diversity leadership commitment can also be reflected in the level of support the function receives in the form of its budget. Often, high-performing diversity leaders will go to bat during budget time to make certain the diversity function is properly funded and has the resources it needs to accomplish its mission.

☐ *The degree of diversity goal achievement.* Leaders have a significant amount of influence over the degree to which goals are attained and supported throughout the organization. The level of priority given to goals, their visibility on key performance and other reports, and resources allocated help demonstrate leadership commitment. Data reflecting what happens when diversity goals are not achieved is also a marker of commitment.

☐ *Specific evidence of the diversity vision elements in place and operating as a naturally occurring, integrated process.* Diversity leadership commitment can be seen in how well key themes, concepts, and implied actions from the diversity vision are translated into real policies, processes, and procedures in the organization.

☐ *The level of diversity-competent executives and managers as evidenced by training and diversity results achieved.* Diversity leadership commitment is often reflected in the support for diversity training, diversity skill development activities, and participation in diversity awareness-building events.

☐ *Decision impact on diversity-related issues in the organization.* Leadership behavior around issues such as family leave policies, flextime issues, glass-ceiling issues, willingness to address diverse customer needs, handling issues of customers not working with female leaders in a country that views women as nonplayers in the corporate landscape, and so on can be a refection of diversity leadership commitment.

☐ *Overall organizational climate and culture ratings and their effects on all represented groups.* Leaders are certainly responsible for the diversity climate of the organization. Their efforts to make deliberate changes that improve quality of work life and performance are important leadership commitment elements.

☐ *Succession management progress for underrepresented groups.* Leaders are accountable for management and development of talent for all employee groups in the organization. Diversity leadership commitment data can be reflected in the degree to which leaders build an inclusive succession management process to take full value of the organization's current and potential capability.

Typical Critical Success Factor Areas

Leadership and sponsorship are essential in any change initiative. Whether you want to assess a leader's readiness and awareness to begin a focus on diversity and inclusion or you want to evaluate your leader's readiness for new levels of action and involvement, the first step is defining the critical success factors that will help champion the diversity effort.

You can begin to create a clear picture of your leader's current awareness, readiness, and commitment to lead a diverse, inclusive environment by first defining what you need. Imagine what a leader would be like if he or she had a heightened awareness, a keen appreciation for diversity and inclusion and its important role in the success of your organization. What characteristics, behaviors, and actions best describe this kind of leadership style, values, receptiveness to new possibilities and differences, level of awareness, and ability to interact and relate well with others? Reflect on your own experiences and those of your team for ideas. Make a list of these leadership traits and behaviors. Refine the list to capture five to ten traits and behaviors you believe are essential. Think about each one of your current leaders. Make an informal evaluation of each one of them against your list of leadership essentials. Assign a numerical value (e.g., 1 to 10) or make a comparative word list describing their present characteristics, behaviors, and actions. Use this work to help you determine their common needs and to who is or might be a potential champion of diversity and inclusion.

Defining diversity performance metrics for a diversity scorecard index usually requires at least three distinct steps. In three steps, you can translate a general performance topic or strategic perspective into specific performance indicators. First, it requires that you have identified specific diversity objectives that are linked to the organization's strategy. Second, you have determined where and how the organization must succeed to accomplish each objective, spelling out the wheres and hows as a set of *critical success factor areas.*

A *critical success factor (CSF) area* is an important "must-achieve," "make-or-break" performance category for the organization. They typically focus on the organization's outputs and/or intended outcomes for success in that area. In general, a sample set of critical success factor areas might include outcomes such as the following:

- ☐ Quick access to demographic data by general and racial group
- ☐ Accurate information regarding turnover percentage within the first 18 months of service
- ☐ Improved satisfaction of women in the workplace
- ☐ Increased utilization of minorities in at least 25% of all job classes

Third, you would consider each critical success factor area and define diversity performance measures or indicators that will track success on it.

Let's look at an example that helps clarify this relationship. First, among the organization's strategic objectives, you find a series of crucial performance areas. One of these areas focuses on an objective of improved customer service. Based on the importance of this area to the business, the diversity organization has created a corresponding strategic objective to analyze and improve service across all demographic market segments. In the second step, you determine that for service to be improved in these targeted markets, the critical success factor areas must include improved communication, culturally appropriate interactions, quick access, increased satisfaction, and accurate information. Finally, these critical success factor areas lead you to select diversity performance measures and indicators that support each critical success factor area, such as the percentage of multilingual service transactions delivered, number of rings to answer, percentage of favorable responses on diverse customer satisfaction surveys, and so on.

In the area of diversity leadership commitment, you can choose from a wide variety of critical success factor areas. As stated earlier, this list will be driven by a combination of things, such as the organization's strategy, the diversity strategy, key stakeholders, the organization's mission, its values, and so on. A brief list of critical success factors for the diversity leadership commitment index might include the following:

- ☐ Vision formulation
- ☐ Improved diversity climate
- ☐ Personal leadership accountability (walking the talk)
- ☐ Vision communications impact
- ☐ IDP achievement
- ☐ Mentoring
- ☐ Succession management
- ☐ Compensation equity
- ☐ Board representation utilization
- ☐ Diversity process integration
- ☐ Organizational diversity management capability
- ☐ Litigation risk management
- ☐ Diversity-focused brand management
- ☐ Resource allocation

Your work in the leadership commitment area will undoubtedly result in dozens of possible critical success factor areas. How many critical success factor areas do you need, and how do you determine which to keep? As mentioned earlier, each critical success factor area should be reviewed to ensure consistency with your organization's mission, values, and vision. The critical success factor areas must also be examined to ensure that they represent a link to and translation of your diversity strategy. Ask yourself: Will achievement in this critical success factor area lead to the successful execution of our diversity strategy and thus help drive our organizational strategy?

Sample Measures to Drive the Index

Earlier in the chapter the process of defining diversity performance measures was broken down into three steps: (1) identifying specific diversity objectives; (2) determining where and how the organization must succeed to accomplish each diversity performance objective, spelling out the wheres and hows as a set of critical success factor areas; and (3) selecting diversity performance measures for each critical success factor area. These measures help determine if the organization is in fact performing well on its objectives. Diversity performance measures are the tools we use to determine whether we are meeting our objectives and moving toward the successful implementation of our strategy.

Specifically, we may describe diversity performance measures as quantifiable (normally, but not always) standards used to evaluate and communicate performance against expected results; however, no simple definition can truly capture the power that well-crafted and well-communicated performance measures can have on an organization. Measures communicate value creation in ways that even the most charismatic CEO's speeches never can. They function as a tool to drive desired action, provide all employees with direction in how they can help contribute to the organization's overall diversity goals, and supply management with a tool in determining overall progress toward the diversity vision. So diversity performance measures are critically important to your diversity scorecard, but generating diversity performance measures may not be as simple as you think. In a recent study by the American Institute of Certified Public Accountants, 27 percent of respondents stated "the ability to define and agree upon measures" as the most frequent barrier to implementing or revising a performance measurement system.

In addition, organizations have to be aware of the distinction between lagging and leading diversity performance measures. Lag indicators represent the consequences of actions previously taken, while lead indicators are the measures that lead to—or drive—the results achieved in the lagging indicators. For example, sales, market share, and lost time accidents may all be considered lagging indicators. What drives each of these lagging indicators? Sales may be driven by hours spent with diverse customers, market share may be driven by brand awareness, and the safety behaviors used drive lost time accidents. Leading indicators should predict performance of lagging measures.

Your diversity scorecard should contain a mix of leading and lagging indicators. Lagging indicators without performance drivers will fail to inform the organization about how to achieve its results. Conversely, leading indicators may signal key improvements throughout the organization, but on their own they do not reveal whether these improvements are leading to improved diverse customer and financial results. Developing lagging measures probably will not pose much of a challenge because our current measurement language is filled with these types of indicators: sales, profits, satisfaction, and many others. It is definitely appropriate to feature a number of these lagging indicators on your scorecard. Although you may share these lagging measures in common with many other organizations, your leading indicators set you apart by identifying the specific activities and processes you believe are critical to driving those lagging indicators of success.

The discussion of leading and lagging measures receives a lot of attention in the balanced scorecard and other literature because of their importance. Unfortunately, when it comes to actually developing a good balanced or diversity scorecard, many organizations fail to closely monitor their mixture of these important variables. Most people grasp the concept intellectually, but they are hard pressed to actually develop leading indicators, and instead place a great reliance on lagging measures of performance. To overcome this issue, build the discussion of leading measures into all of your measurement dialogues. A definitional look at lag and lead measures is shown in Table 8-1.

Your diversity scorecard should contain a mixture of lag and lead diversity measures of performance. To help you get started, a list of potential diversity leadership commitment measures are provided in Table 8-2.

Perfecting your diversity performance metrics will present you with numerous questions and issues, such as the following:

☐ How many measures should you have?
☐ How often should you measure?
☐ What about shared accountabilities?
☐ Could your measures be contaminated?
☐ Are your measures reliable?
☐ Which performance comparatives are best?
☐ Should you combine measures into an index?

Table 8-1. Lead and Lag Performance Measures

	Lag	Lead
Definition	Measures focusing on results at the end of a time period, normally characterizing historical performance	Measures that drive or lead to the performance of lag measures, normally measuring intermediate processes and activities
Examples	☐ Sales ☐ Market share ☐ Employee satisfaction	☐ Proposals written ☐ Hours spent with diverse customers ☐ Absenteeism
Advantages	Normally easy to identify and capture	Predictive in nature and allow the organization to make adjustments based on results
Issues	Historical in nature and do not reflect current activities; lack predictive power	May prove difficult to identify and capture; often new measures with no history at the organization

Source: Niven, 2002

Table 8-2. Potential Diversity Leadership Commitment Measures

☐ Diversity vision/mission written
☐ Percentage favorable response on diversity climate
☐ IDPs achieved
☐ Leadership benchstrength
☐ Percentage of diversity goals achieved
☐ Percentage gender pay differential
☐ Leadership participation rate
☐ Percentage High potential/business unit
☐ Extent to which employees are clear about the organization's diversity goals and objectives
☐ Extent to which the average employee can describe the organization's strategic diversity intent
☐ Percentage diverse employees mentored who are promoted

☐ Number of times diversity mentioned as strategy in executive presentations
☐ Critical skill attainment
☐ Internal promotion rate
☐ Percentage of diversity strategic plans implemented
☐ Percentage Board representation by group
☐ Percentage promotion-ready minorities
☐ Extent to which the organization has turned its diversity strategy into specific goals and objectives that employees can act on in the short and long run
☐ Diversity department's budget as a percentage of sales
☐ Competence development

Source: Hubbard MDR Stat Pak Diversity Measurement "Calculate and Go" Software.

☐ Is denominator management a risk?
☐ How can good measures be made better?

Whether this is the first time you have thought about diversity performance measures or you are well experienced in tracking organizational performance, you will be challenged by these issues. Here are a couple of examples:

How Many Measures?

Everyone wants the right number of metrics. Some authorities even recommend fixed limits (e.g., 10 to 15 measures, never more than 8, etc.). The reason, of course, is that it is important not to overwhelm the organization with too many measures. Action-oriented functions want to measure and manage the critical few things that will really make a difference. But there are three deadly arguments against arbitrarily limiting the number of metrics (Frost, 2000):

1. *Snoozing alligators.* These are things you must monitor, even if they may not change.
2. *Complexity.* Modern organizations are large and complex. Leaders need comprehensive pictures of performance to guide understandings and decisions. Managing with a keyhole view can lead to disaster. Ever look into the cockpit as you are boarding a flight? You probably saw that the pilot and copilot face a hundred or more dials and gauges. Would you want to limit them to 8 to 15? Actually, only a few gauges are important to a pilot at any one time. The airspeed indicator is not important while the plane is at the gate, for example, only a few gauges are critical during take-off or landing, and only a few are needed at cruising altitude. But they're not the same few! The critical few change with conditions, so the pilot needs, in total, a full complement of gauges. It is the same with diversity performance metrics. Not all of your metrics will demand focused attention all of the time, but if a few key ones are missing, your organization could be heading for a nosedive without realizing it.
3. *The rob-Peter-to-pay-Paul problem.* Stated simply: Anything not measured is subject to being sacrificed for the things that are measured. From a management perspective, this is a powerful argument for comprehensive metrics. One side of the coin says, "What gets

measured, gets done." The other side says, "What does not get measured, might not get done." And some of what might not get done can be very important.

Your challenge in establishing performance metrics is to ensure that everything important to successfully achieving the diversity vision is represented and monitored, *and* that the critical few occupy center stage. Is there any help? Yes. You might consider the designs of others who have solved, or partly solved, this problem. Some of the more common solutions involve foreground and background metrics, tiers of metrics available by drill-down links, and designs that distinguish between strategic metrics and monitored metrics. Special software packages like Hubbard & Hubbard Inc.'s MetricLINK are designed to manage a large number of metrics while keeping the focus on a critical few.

How Often Should You Measure?

How often should you take readings on your diversity performance indicators? In practice, this question is more complex than you might think. The right answer is unique to each measure. Some general guidelines recommended by Frost (2000) provide a good starting point:

- ☐ Other things being equal, you measure according to the rate of change you expect in the results. No point in measuring productivity every half hour, is there? But every month? Maybe. It depends on the nature of your work.
- ☐ The more you have at stake, the more often you measure. Even when you expect little change, additional tracking may be worth the price as a precaution.
- ☐ The longer it takes to respond, the more often you need to measure and the more finely tuned your metrics must be. You need the additional lead-time. When it takes a long time to alter course, your corrective action must begin at the earliest possible moment.
- ☐ The more short-term variability in your results, the more you want to average over time to separate what's really happening from the short-term changes. One or two satisfied, or dissatisfied, customers among thousands do not make a trend.
- ☐ Then there are administrative and political factors. You may be required to report results more frequently than you would otherwise feel the need to measure.

There is no formula for how often to measure because each situation is different. But the principles are clear, and those closest to the action must apply them to establish the right measurement frequency.

Analyzing Data

You might think that defining your diversity index and getting the data would be all there is to measurement. But it's not so. You still have to figure out how you are doing and what to conclude from the measures you track. Data, by itself, does not tell you much. Analyzing your diversity leadership data requires a planned approach. Begin by checking the data received for its completeness. In addition, review the formulas for calculation, making certain all of the elements are present for calculation and creating a summary. It is important to identify all of the variables that may be significant to respond to questions generated from the data and any key diversity leadership commitment issues that may be identified (Ainslie, 2001).

Determine the Relationships and Trends

The diversity leadership commitment measurements you will calculate allow a variety of paths for analysis. The following investigative questions will help you determine the relationships and trends in the data. Ask these and other questions to help unveil patterns in the data (Hubbard, 2001).

Examine the Facts

- ☐ What does the diversity leadership commitment index performance really look like taken as a group? What are the overall scores by business unit?
- ☐ What was the level of IDP achievement?
- ☐ What percentage of the diversity goals was achieved under the current leadership?
- ☐ What is the internal promotion rate by demographic group?
- ☐ What is the percentage of diversity-competent leaders?
- ☐ How many external diversity awards have we received based on demonstrated leader performance?

Examine the Relationships

- ☐ Which leaders are most likely to mention diversity as part of the organization's strategy? Why?

- [ ] Which business units are more likely to have diversity integrated into their strategy? Why? How?
- [ ] How many business unit leaders with the most favorable climates have the highest percentage of their diversity goal achieved?
- [ ] How many leaders with high participation rates in personal leadership activities also have high organizational climate ratings?

Examine the Trends

- [ ] Which department has the most improved diversity leadership commitment scores?
- [ ] Which strategic business unit leadership teams show the most improvement in diversity goal attainment over the last three years?
- [ ] What areas of the diversity strategic plan have not received attention by business units over the last 2 years?
- [ ] Over the last 3 years, has the gap in gender pay differentials decreased or increased?

Some general questions to use when exploring leadership commitment data include the following (Hubbard, 2001):

- [ ] How does this data compare with this same period last year, last month, over the last three years? In what way?
- [ ] Is the trend going down, up, staying the same? Why?
- [ ] How does this trend or figure compare with others in our industry? Our competition?
- [ ] What are the business implications and consequences of this number based on the organization's strategic objectives?
- [ ] What are the business implications and consequences of this number based on the organization's strategic diversity objectives?
- [ ] How does this number compare with best practices standards for this type of data?
- [ ] What should our next steps be in light of this information? Why? When? Who? How? What barriers exist?

REPORTING DATA

There are three key words in reporting performance: *graphs, consistency,* and *comparatives.*

In almost every case, *graphs* are the best way to present performance results. A picture is said to be worth a thousand words because we grasp meanings so much more quickly and easily in visual form. Graphs show you not only where you are but also where you have been and where you are likely to go. Use graphs and charts wherever you can.

The second essential in performance reporting is *consistency*. Your understanding of performance is more likely to be valid when:

☐ Your measurement definitions remain constant from period to period.
☐ Your charts show "up" as good, whenever possible.
☐ Your methods of data collection and analysis remain stable from period to period.

Every improvement in your metrics must be weighed against the loss of period-to-period consistency that will result from adopting the improvement.

Comparatives are important because we judge things so poorly in the abstract; our minds are better geared to making comparison judgments. Your diversity metrics need anchor points for these comparisons, benchmarks by which the results may be gauged. Examples might be a leadership team's past performance, its goals, diverse customer expectations, and so on. In particular, the organization should know how it compares to others in the industry and leaders in a particular business area. Think carefully about what comparatives will lead the organization to valid conclusions and sensible action.

The trend line offers a type of comparative that is generally very useful because it shows in what direction you are moving. When you show a trend line, you are implying that one comparative for the organization's current performance is its past performance. Generally, that's a very good thing; however, let's also recognize that a single comparative is seldom enough. We usually need to know where we stand in other terms. In today's global business economy, an organization may be doing consistently better in the areas of diversity than it did in the past, yet failing against its competitors who have taken diversity to a much higher level.

Like any other presentation you make, sharing your observations regarding the diversity calculation you have completed must be designed to suit the appropriate audience. A few key things should be kept in mind as you prepare to give your presentation:

☐ Make certain you chose the right forum for discussion. Executives often prefer a short summary before the meeting and a short one-hour briefing to ask questions. It is also important to share the observations in a variety forums, such as staff meetings, newsletters, "Lunch-n-Learn," and so on.

☐ During the presentation, present just the facts uncovered. There is no need to justify why the data appears as it does. Explore this in discussion.

☐ Highlight potentially significant patterns you found, such as significantly improved organizational climate scores, increased IDP achievement, reduced gaps in gender pay differentials, and so on. It is often helpful to point out what was not known before the analysis and what is known now (or what you think you know).

☐ Be certain to suggest alternatives, but do not solve the problem during the presentation. This involves further steps.

During the problem-solving step of the reporting process, it is important to identify the links between perception and reality. If a business unit's staff (based on the percentage of favorable response data) perceives an issue as real, they act on it as if it is real. It does not matter whether someone else agrees with that perception.

In addition, issues of cause and effect must be sorted out. If the data suggests that high turnover exists among women and minorities, the organization does not have a turnover problem. Turnover is a result or effect that was created. The cause of this turnover is what needs to be investigated as the problem.

In order for progress to be made, action and follow-through are required. Key questions to deal with at this stage include the following:

1. What actionable recommendations were proposed based on the data presented? To make effective decisions about the data, consider the following guidelines:

   ☐ Attack the root cause, not the symptom.
   ☐ Understand the cost-benefits (look deeper than just the obvious costs).
   ☐ Determine the likelihood that the results will be reasonable and measurable.
   ☐ Obtain commitment at all levels, especially senior management.
   ☐ Coordinate efforts across multiple solutions to build synergy.
   ☐ Track results.
   ☐ Change course of action when the data and/or objectives warrant it.

2. Is the organization following the proposed plan?
3. Did the actions taken make a difference toward building a more inclusive organization? What results have you obtained from surveys, interviews, and the like?
4. What has changed in the measured data?
5. What worked and what did not work?
6. What successes or failures did similar business units have?

Figures 8-1 and 8-2 present a few graphic examples to report your findings regarding the impact of diversity leadership commitment in the organization.

By using the analyses and reporting steps as a diversity evaluation strategy, you will be able to effectively assess the impact of your diversity leadership commitment measurement efforts.

FINAL THOUGHTS

Diversity leadership commitment is a mandatory prerequisite for diversity scorecard performance and success. Leadership behaviors set the stage

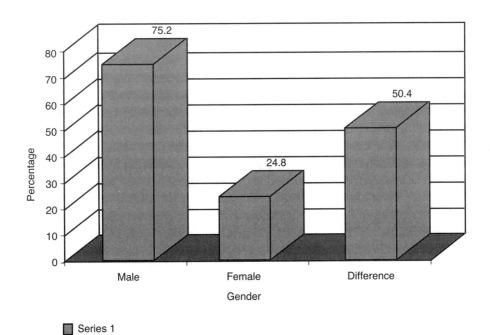

Figure 8-1. Gender-based pay differential.

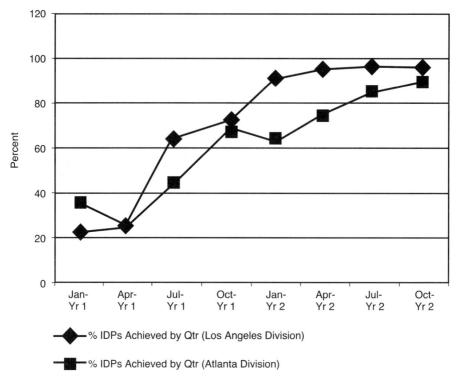

Figure 8-2. Percentage of IDPs achieved by quarter by division.

and model requirements that drive, direct, and select what is important and valued in the organization's culture. Measuring this perspective helps determine if the diversity change effort has a core support structure for success. A highly committed diversity leader or leadership team that walks the talk sends a message that diversity is a strategic partner in meeting the goals and objectives of the organization. Committed lead executives create a climate for change, the vision for what the diversity change can accomplish, and the governance process that promotes communication, interactive discussion, and learning about the diversity strategy.

The diversity scorecard strategic management system works best when it is used to communicate the diversity vision and strategy, not to control the actions of employees. This use is paradoxical to those who think that measurement is a control tool, not a communication tool. Organizational leaders who "get it" recognize that the biggest challenge they face in implementing strategic diversity change initiatives and new strategies is getting alignment on the diversity-focused behaviors that drive improved performance. Once the pillar of committed leadership is in place, organizations often turn their attention to addressing the workforce profile, which we will examine in the next chapter.

REFERENCES

Ainslie, Kenneth. "Turning Numbers into Strategy: Getting Management to Listen . . . And Take Action." IQPC HR Measurements Conference Presentation, January 2002.

American Institute of Certified Public Accountants and Lawrence S. Maisel. *Performance Measurement Survey*, 2001.

Cox, Taylor, Jr. *Creating the Multicultural Organization*. San Francisco: Jossey-Bass, 2001.

Frost, Bob. *Measuring Performance*. Dallas: Measurement International, 2000.

Bette, George, Tina Jackson, and Arleen LaBella. *A Practical Guide to Working with Diversity*. New York: AMACOM, 1995.

Hubbard, Edward E. *Metrics for Success: Pathways II*. Washington, DC: Minority Corporate Counsel Association (MCCA), 2001.

Niven, Paul R. *Balanced Scorecard*. New York: John Wiley & Sons, 2002.

FURTHER READING

Baytos, Lawrence M. *Designing & Implementing Successful Diversity Programs*. Englewood Cliffs, NJ: Prentice Hall, 1995.

Capowski, Genevieve. "Managing Diversity." *Management Review*, 85: 13–19.

Cox, Taylor, Jr., and Ruby L. Beale. *Developing Competency to Manage Diversity*. San Francisco: Berrett-Koehler, 1997.

Loden, Marilyn. *Implementing Diversity*. Chicago: Irwin, 1996.

Poole, Phebe-Jane. *Diversity: A Business Advantage*. Ajax, Ontario: Poole Publishing, 1997.

CHAPTER 9

Workforce Profile Perspective

DEFINITION

The diverse workforce profile perspective reflects a statistical summary of the organization's personnel makeup sorted by key demographic groups. This perspective often includes an analysis of personnel by race, gender, ethnicity, length of service, voluntary/involuntary turnover, organizational level, and sometimes by age and physical ability. This information is typically tracked to determine if the organization's employee population mirrors the demographic dimensions of its community and/or customer base.

Why would an organization concern itself with the level of diversity mix in its workforce and building skills for effective management of its diverse workforce? In the past, many organizations answered this question out of a sense of the right thing to do or because they were seeing more and more people who did not look like them in the workforce, or merely because they felt they had to meet the organization's requirement for working with diverse groups simply for Equal Employment Opportunity (EEO) and Affirmative Action (AA) reasons; however, today's organizations know that without a diverse workforce and an effective diversity management capability, organizational effectiveness is in jeopardy. Being effective at recruiting, retaining, managing, and leveraging a diverse workforce helps lift morale, improves business processes, brings access to new segments of the marketplace, and enhances organizational productivity. In essence, it is good for business (Hubbard, 2003).

Several studies have followed the changing mosaic of America. One of the most widely publicized studies was commissioned by the U.S. Department of Labor and conducted by the Hudson Institute.

Table 9-1. Changing Trend from a Homogeneous Workforce to a More Heterogeneous Workforce

Homogeneous	Heterogeneous
☐ White males	☐ Women and minorities
☐ 29 years old	☐ 40+ years old
☐ Married with children	☐ Variety of lifestyles
☐ Less than 12 years of education	☐ 12+ years of education

They have completed two studies: *Workforce 2000* in 1987, and 10 years later, *Workforce 2020* in 1997. The most significant trends in the U.S. population are as follows:

☐ Decreasing percentage of Caucasians
☐ Increasing percentage of people of color
☐ Decreasing birth rates
☐ Increasing percentages of people in their middle and older years

Table 9-1 shows that these trends translate into significant changes in the workforce composition, from more homogeneous to heterogeneous (Judy, D'Amico, 1987, 1997).

Because of these changes in the workforce, organizations must be prepared to deal with the following results:

☐ An equal balance of men and women
☐ Shrinking numbers of whites and increasing numbers of people of color
☐ The fact that most new entrants to the workforce will be women or people of color (over 85 percent)
☐ A shortage of new entrants in the workforce under age 24
☐ An increasing percentage of people aged 35 to 55 and older

The bottom line is that the workplace of the past no longer exists and has not for quite some time. It is not like past years when the typical workplace was made up of a homogeneous group of white men, who were 29 years old, married, with less than 12 years of education. During that time, most of them had wives who were stay-at-home mothers to care for the children. Compare that situation to today's reality of a workplace rich with diverse people from all walks of life, backgrounds, values, and ways of perceiving the world. Nonetheless, many organizations are structured for operation around the traditional homogeneous model that diminishes their ability to grow and ultimately compete in a global marketplace.

People in the homogeneous workplace naturally created an American work environment that worked for people present in the workforce at that time with similar backgrounds. When the organizational structure reflected their needs, backgrounds, and values, the system worked well for getting things accomplished for those who were in it. It makes little if any sense to blame those who created a system that supported and worked for the workplace needs of the time period; however, as the landscape of America changed, along with its workforce pools and composition, organizations fell woefully behind. Few organizations reflect the needs, backgrounds, and values of a diverse America and do not accommodate today's workforce in a way that effectively addresses its requirements for performance.

As far back as 1992, 52 percent of working adults were women, and 11 percent of the men were minorities, which means only 37 percent of working adults were white males—and the percentages are decreasing. It just makes good business sense to reexamine a situation in which 63 percent of the workforce may be less productive than they could be because they work in an outdated system!

With ever-increasing amounts of change in the workforce, workplace diversity cannot be ignored. It is a critical challenge that must be faced. The first part of addressing the current trend of a multicultural, diverse workforce lies in knowing how diversity can impact your organization (Hubbard, 2003). Therefore, it is critical to understand the workforce profile of your organization and their changes by demographic group.

Recruitment and selection is often the first place organizations will start when building their diverse workforce profile index; however, many organizations often demonstrate only a superficial commitment to building a diverse workforce despite the demographic and other evidence to the contrary. A common refrain heard by many goes something like this: "If only we could find some truly qualified women and minorities, we would be happy to hire them. Those folks don't seem to be interested in the type of work we do in our industry. If you find some, we'll hire them."

In reality, this type of statement is, at best, an unfounded assertion and, at its worst, reflects another form of racism, sexism, and bias, that stems from cultural programming that has effectively gone unchallenged. Qualified women and minorities are certainly out there if the work environment and the job offers are right. There's no secret in finding them; however, organizations need to rely on a variety of people and diverse recruitment approaches to attract and retain a diverse workforce. It is simply a matter of committing the organization to developing systematic, objective, rational, and fair recruiting strategies, implementing those strategies aggressively, and fostering a team environment that treats people fairly, regardless of their differences. In addition, the organization must build systems and a climate that retain these workers from diverse backgrounds once they come to work. Diverse workforce retention is absolutely essential for effective utilization and improved performance.

The current changing landscape of American demographics reflects a labor pool, both native and foreign born, that comprises a large population of educated, capable people from diverse backgrounds, especially in the high-tech and service-based industries. Any U.S. organization that desires to stay competitive for now and in the future is going to have to find, recruit, and retain the best employees, regardless of their diverse backgrounds. Too often, recruiters and their organizations evaluate new recruits solely on the basis of how they fit into the organization's existing culture, which is somewhat antiquated in today's hiring practices and requirements (today, many organizations try to avoid hiring in their own image). Many of these interviews are unstructured and haphazard; the interviewers are often poorly trained in how to conduct a culture-fair, objective interview, and very few metrics and incentives encourage interviewers to make certain they obtain a diverse candidate pool (Hubbard, 2003).

To be effective, recruiters and their organizations should look at potential employees' intellectual, technical, and professional skills and at their desire, their understanding of their personal culture, their strengths and weaknesses, their emotional intelligence, their ability to be empathetic, and their willingness to accept and value different race, ethnic, and gender groups. Recruiters, interviewers, and hiring managers need effective tools and skills to help them make good decisions regarding the best person for the job given all of the human resources available without the hindrance of bias. Table 9-2 presents the steps that can be helpful in avoiding race and gender bias in the recruitment and hiring process.

In addition, organizations must have clear, structured strategies to build inclusive pools of candidates. Table 9-3 presents a checklist that should be helpful.

It is also critical to have strategies to recruit seasoned employees to fill positions at all levels. Organizations cannot afford to overlook the

Table 9-2. Steps to Avoid Race and Gender Bias

Step	Activity
1	**Develop specific selection criteria.** It is essential to develop specific hiring criteria and to make sure that all of the interviewers and hiring managers use them.
2	**Develop specific instruments to measure the criteria.** Everyone in the interviewing and hiring process should be using them. A matrix usually works well as a summary tool. List the candidates down the left side and the criteria across the top row. For each cell created, enter the candidate's response on each criterion listed. In this way you can compare their responses against the same criteria.
3	**Train Interviewers.** Interviewers need to go through their own self-analysis to examine their own culture, norms, values, emotional intelligence, racial and gender attitudes, and the like. They should go through an assessment process to analyze their multicultural interviewing lenses to determine if they are "screening out versus screening in" and/or hiring only in their image. They should also receive feedback from recruits about their interviewing skills.
4	**Have Diverse Interviewers.** Because of our natural tendency to hire people like ourselves, it is crucial that women and minorities are recruiters and interviewers or part of a panel of interviewers.
5	**Use a Team Approach.** All parties to the process should meet as a team, to review candidates and to arrive at a team decision.
6	**Evaluate the Recruiters.** Recruiters should be evaluated in terms of their number of hires as well as of the race and gender, type of positions, and the success or failure of their recruits. This can be built in as part of the diverse workforce profile index.

recruitment of experienced employees to fulfill key strategic positions within the organization. Here are just a few ideas to get you started:

☐ Develop contacts with stakeholders from diverse backgrounds.
☐ Develop relationships with local and national religious, professional, political, and social organizations whose focus is people from diverse groups.
☐ Locate and develop relationships with recruitment firms dedicated to diverse groups.
☐ Develop a recruitment directory that contains listings for people from women and minority search firms, colleges and universities, sororities, fraternities, professional and political associations,

Table 9-3. On-Campus Strategies Checklist

✓	Activity
	Have formal and informal lunches and dinners with key students, faculty members, and administrators.
	Seek out and develop relationships with various student clubs and professional associations such as Historically Black Colleges and Universities (HBCU), Hispanic Association of Colleges and Universities (HACU), Catalyst (Women's Organization), INROADS (Inner City and Youth Development Organization), and others; and don't forget the organizations on campus that are devoted to meeting the needs of part-time, returning, and evening students.
	Volunteer to personally give lectures and conduct classes and/or recruit some suitable employees who are not on the team to help you out in this regard.
	Support student activities and provide financial or in-kind help as part of your organization's community development effort. This will help bolster the organization's image on campus.
	Provide year-round, ongoing internships for students, and get the jump on other organizations by letting them begin in their senior year of high school.
	Provide a Step Ahead Program for students where students work in the organization during their summer vacation and short periods of time (when school is out during other periods). Be sure that they get real experience on projects of substance, not just used as an extra pair of hands in the mailroom. Have their projects end with a written or oral report. This allows them to summarize what they learned and demonstrate their on-the-job training.

community organizations, publications to advertise in, and vocational and technical schools.

☐ Remember, this is not about quotas. It is about finding the person who is best qualified for the job given all of the talent pools available.

When you talk with diverse groups during the recruiting process, do not be surprised if they are skeptical. Based on different experiences, they may want to check out the organization to see if it is diversity-friendly. They may ask questions such as those in Table 9-4, which you must be prepared to answer or demonstrate in your behavior during the recruitment process.

Table 9-4. Diversity-Friendly Environment Question
Check/Preparation List

✓	Activity
	What is the level of women and minorities in senior positions?
	What is the company's philosophy of and commitment to developing women and minorities?
	What is the level of commitment of the organization to diversity and Affirmative Action?
	How has the organization handled charges of discrimination in the past?
	How sensitive, aware, and comfortable are interviewers with candidates of diverse backgrounds?
	How honest, straightforward, and candid are interviewers during the recruitment process?
	Does the company keep to the commitments it makes throughout the recruitment process? If so, to what extent?
	How do other women and minorities view the organization?
	How does the community perceive the organization's reputation and involvement?
	What is the organization's attitude regarding balancing work and personal life?

COLLECTING DATA

Collecting data for the diverse workforce profile index requires examining a variety of sources inside and outside of the organization. These sources can include some of the following:

- ☐ Internal recruitment processes
- ☐ External recruitment processes
- ☐ EEO and AAP statistics
- ☐ Turnover statistics
- ☐ Promotion processes
- ☐ Job transfer statistics
- ☐ External databases for comparative statistics

Let's examine some of these sources in more detail. Recruiting for a highly successful diverse workforce involves developing a vision for building and supporting a diverse workforce in your organization. This includes considering how you recruit both internally and externally.

Internal Recruiting

Left on its own, internal recruiting usually occurs without much thought given to issues of utilizing the diversity that exists within the organization unless a clear commitment to building and supporting a diverse work environment is made. There often seems to be a disproportionate number of people of color, women, people with disabilities, and so on in front-line worker positions versus management positions. There are both pros and cons to internal recruiting.

On the one hand, promoting from within is cost effective and can boost morale by letting employees know that hard work does pay off in opportunities for growth and development. On the other hand, your organization can miss the opportunity to bring in fresh new talent with new perspectives and approaches. Another downside of internal recruiting is that the organization can become so wrapped up in its own organizational programming that it stagnates as a result of excessive inbreeding of ideas and process. An inbred organization may approach problem solving and operational processes with tunnel vision. In addition, any new ideas that suggest changes and innovation may be met with resistance.

An effective internal recruiting process will take into account internal resources such as the following:

☐ *Promotions.* Examine your leadership development, specialized technical, and general managerial programs to locate candidates. This is a good place to assess whether your diversity efforts are working. Conduct a demographic analysis of the makeup of these groups. Do they include women and minorities or people who are part of an underrepresented group? How often have these programs graduated someone who is a part of a diverse group? What support programs have been put in place to help ensure a successful start?

☐ *Transfers.* Job shadowing opportunities can enhance learning and affect career choices. When this is done, however, it is critical to make certain the climate the transferee will experience is positive. The transfer group may need some diversity training before they are left to operate on their own.

☐ *Work Teams.* Work teams need diversity training as well. Simply because a team contains members with diverse backgrounds does not make it effective. Remember, diversity is about utilization, not representation. These teams can be another source of talent.

☐ *Committees.* Reviewing members who are a part of special committees can also be a source of possible talent for growth. This assumes that the process for accessing these committees is open to a variety of members from diverse backgrounds. In many cases, selection to participate on these committees can be tantamount to promotion and even succession. In some organizations, women and minorities rarely get nominated as part of the committee selection process.

External Recruiting

External recruiting is often well organized, having a systematic and consistent approach. Many organizations use the same resources to draw new employees year after year. The unspoken belief may be that if it's not broken, why fix it? The flaw in this type of thinking is that if you do not seek out new resources, you will not diversify your applicant pool. The challenge here is to expand your horizons and seek out additional and perhaps nontraditional sources of applicants.

As with internal recruiting, there are both pros and cons to external recruiting. If your organization is actively seeking a skill set that is not available internally, it is to your benefit to look outside. Also, if you are trying to improve your organization's diversity mixture, there is a larger pool of candidates outside; however, keep in mind that there are consequences involved. Employees who do not get promotional opportunities are left wondering: "Why not me?" They may not see the skill and qualification differences being brought in from the outside. This is made worse when this same employee is asked to show the new person how things should operate. Loss of morale, loyalty, and satisfaction can be the result of this action.

Be sure to use some of the following recruiting channels that involve traditional and nontraditional sources, as well as create specialized lists of your own:

- ☐ Chamber of commerce
- ☐ Church activities
- ☐ Sporting events
- ☐ Community organizations
- ☐ Family and friends of diverse groups (employee referrals)
- ☐ Career days
- ☐ Disabled student services
- ☐ Corporate-sponsored events that are diversity focused
- ☐ Service providers that have access to diverse groups
- ☐ Using multicultured media advertisements

Potential employees will usually get their first look at the organization based on your recruitment efforts and media exposure. It is one of the best places to start to analyze the impact of your efforts to attract and build a diverse workforce profile.

Looking at the Big Picture

As mentioned earlier, it is important to conduct a review of hires, job assignment changes, promotions, demotions, layoffs, transfers, and terminations. Sample 6 to 24 months' activity. Even if you see every change as it happened or you have reports that identify such activity, you will find a great benefit in reviewing all interrelated activity over a period of time. Your focused attention will help you see patterns and trends that will be helpful in knowing what is and isn't happening, as well as providing valuable input for your staffing and development planning needs.

Look at the people you are attracting and how you are going about it. If you are having difficulty attracting women, people of color, or other diverse talents, you may need to make changes in your approach. Here are a few possibilities to review that will help you determine where you have a weakness in recruiting:

1. *Identify who is involved in the recruiting process.* Review candidate sources, interviewing, and decision-making processes. Look for opportunities that were overlooked and processes that may be excluding quality applicants. Identify potential skill-building needs.

2. *Meet with recruiting sources, campus and professional organization contacts.* Talk with them about their experience working with you and the impressions they might share with you. Explore ways you can work together more closely to strengthen relationships and develop a more richly diverse candidate pool for future opportunities.

3. *Explore what others are doing that you might adapt for your environment.* Participate in a recruiting event so you can see first-hand *how* and *what* others are doing to reach the quality candidates they need.

4. *Investigate how other companies are recruiting and presenting themselves on the Internet.* Look not only for job listings, but also diversity, inclusion, and organizational values that are integrated into their website for prospective candidates and customers (Kennedy, 2000).

Many subtle actions often have far-reaching implications for attracting, hiring, developing, promoting, and retaining quality people. These subtleties do not show up in reports. Sometimes they are so ingrained into the organization's culture or within certain powerful individuals that they are not easily detected in a cursory review—they show up in *results,* or the lack of them. The best way to make an assessment is to step back and look at the big picture.

Here are six indicators to watch for:

1. Your board and senior leadership team remains primarily homogeneous after numerous opportunities for change.
2. Meetings and events have only a homogeneous group of presenters.
3. Key positions are filled with clones after repeated opportunities to bring in more diverse perspectives.
4. Women, people of color, and anyone representing a *difference,* although highly competitive, frequently come in second.
5. Women, people of color, or other different sorts and types are unintentionally, but repeatedly, overlooked when spontaneous inner circle meetings and gatherings are held.
6. Those in power often, but subtly, use intimidating, thoughtless language and behavior to keep new ideas and perspectives from influencing the status quo.
7. Women, people of color, and anyone who represents a difference are put in positions without supportive, involved sponsors.

What other subtle behaviors and actions are standing in the way of your organization learning and experiencing the value of a diverse, inclusive organization or community? Use examples to raise awareness in a nonaccusatory way. This can be a bold step in the right direction. Most people do not mean to be thoughtless, rude, or unsupportive. Sometimes an objective look and a little honest feedback can remedy these kinds of behaviors. At a minimum, it will help you identify who needs coaching and behavioral change counseling (Kennedy, 2000).

Who's up next? Bringing quality people with diverse perspectives into your organization is one important step. But keeping a perpetual stream of highly developed, diverse leadership talent, who are ready to assume senior levels of responsibility, is quite another. If you have set the stage to become a learning organization that ensures all of its people develop to their full potential, succession planning is a natural extension focused on senior leadership roles. Do you have a succession plan?

Are you identifying high-potential candidates early and working actively with them to develop their leadership and management skills? Have you assessed your future placement needs?

People represent the power in any organization or community. Measuring the organization's effectiveness in attracting, developing, promoting, and retaining the highest quality talent is the hallmark of a successful organization that truly will be competitive in the twenty-first century. Figuring out the strength of your infrastructure to support such talent is a critical assessment, and one you should review regularly in your diversity scorecard as the bar continues to rise.

Affirmative Action Data

The Affirmative Action (AA)/Assimilation model has been in place in most large companies for more than 20 years. Although AA programs have opened the door for countless individuals, many companies are distressed with the way in which individuals are concentrated at the bottom of the corporate pyramid. In organization after organization—even those that have had strong AA programs—women, people of color, and others who are different tend to be stuck below the glass ceiling. The acknowledged existence of barriers to advancement and a de facto limit to progress have yielded to a frustrating cycle entailing a variety of hidden costs, such as the following:

☐ The costs of underutilizing human resources
☐ The costs of underutilizing intellectual capital
☐ The cost of excessive turnover
☐ The cost of complaints and people to handle the complaints
☐ The cost of people checking out without quitting

Even the others who have broken through the glass ceiling often pay a price for it. In many companies, 90 percent of male executives are married and have children. On the other hand, it would not be unusual to find that only one-third to two-thirds of female executives are married with children. Minorities who reach key management levels talk about their continuing frustration and sense of isolation—not being accepted by their white peers and being distanced from the employee members of their own ethnic group.

The career pattern exemplified by the illustration often leads to a never-ending spiral of affirmative action efforts. This frustrating spiral highlights five sets of affirmative actions that have been repeated in many organizations with distinguishable phases that include the following (Kennedy, 2000):

1. *Problem discovery.* Management suddenly realizes that the numbers and distribution of females and minorities is not adequate. The problem has been created through excessive turnover, lack of upward mobility, an unsupportive environment, and so on.
2. *Target recruiting intervention.* When the diversity dearth is recognized, the initial response is typically affirmative action recruitment efforts directed at bringing in more members of protected class groups.
3. *Full inventory.* The organization's talent inventory has now been filled with the "best" qualified females and minorities that could be attracted. Corporate management relaxes because they assume that the newly hired individuals will trickle up through the organization, readily permeating the glass-ceiling barrier.
4. *Disappointment.* Because there have been no changes in the culture and systems of the organization, the others in the pipeline find that the environment is not as supportive and accepting of their diversity as they had hoped. Management disappointment centers around the inability of the others to fit in, become accepted team players, and so on.
5. *Departure.* Issues fester and people get tired of waiting for things to get better. If the job market is strong enough, they vote with their feet. The high turnover leads to recognition of another crisis, and the cycle begins all over again. If the job market is not strong, the individual's energy and commitment may dissipate, even though the individual remains on the payroll.

Companies have come to recognize that they must focus attention beyond the point of bringing diversity in the doors of the organization. Sustainable progress requires a change in the basic assumptions about those who are different from the mainstream. Our organizational successes, each with their unique mission, will depend on the diversity of talent we are able to attract, develop, and keep. Thus, paying attention to recruitment and retention is critical. For the best organizations, this will mean continually reevaluating the effectiveness of staffing and development methods, processes, programs, and supporting relationships that build an inclusive workplace that encourage a diverse workforce profile.

Workforce Turnover Data

Turnover is costly to organizations. Additional recruitment, training and retraining, and performance losses attributable to unwanted turnover cost the organization in time and money and affect employee morale. Analyzing turnover as part of your diverse workforce profile index can help reduce or prevent losses through targeted organizational improvements.

The calculation of turnover is a simple mathematical problem. The analysis of turnover is a powerful tool the diversity professional can use to interpret movement of the organization's diverse workforce into, within, and out of organizations. Turnover is often the first measurement that organizational leadership requests when it is contemplating proposals for scarce resources, implementing new programs, or looking at whether change efforts have been successful. Knowing turnover rates is a necessity in any organization, but rates alone may lack significance. Analysis and interpretation of turnover are a valued contribution the diversity department can make to the organization (Fleming and Wilson, 2001).

Although turnover analysis contributes to understanding the organization, it is rare that diversity practitioners can show a direct cause-and-effect relationship between turnover and specific organizational variables; however, diversity professionals, using the techniques taught in this book and those trained in the Hubbard Diversity Measurement and Productivity Institute, can usually illustrate a relationship between organizational changes and employee reactions such as turnover. Results of turnover analysis can help focus diversity as a strategic partner on areas of concern, targets for change efforts, or areas of success in the organization. Turnover is one widely accepted indicator of how the business is doing from an employment perspective.

Relevance of Turnover

Turnover is the permanent separation of employees from a position, a department, or an organization. Because there are numerous origins of turnover, it may be related to several aspects of the organization and its environment. Turnover originates from promotion or demotion, transfer, resignation, termination, or retirement of employees. Selection systems, compensation, benefits, performance management, managerial talent, training effectiveness, organizational policies, and the organization's external environment influence and are influenced by employee turnover. Increasing trends in turnover may be symptomatic of isolated or systemic issues that require change or intervention within the organization. Conversely, decreasing trends in organizational turnover may indicate changes in the labor market or other societal factors, or they may indicate the success of a specific new diversity initiative. Within an organization, diversity practitioners may use decreasing trends in turnover to indicate a relationship between diversity programs and organizational success. By using the Hubbard Diversity ROI Process, these relationships can be established with measurable compelling evidence of success (Hubbard, 1999). Turnover analysis helps illustrate this relationship between internal or external factors and organizational success.

For example, if new technologies were recently added to a job and turnover began to increase among employees in that job, several factors may be contributing to the increase in turnover. Turnover analysis prompts the questions, "Who is leaving?" "Is the turnover voluntary or involuntary?" And "What is this new skill worth in the labor market?"

First, if the employees who are leaving are predominantly employees who are new to the job, the turnover could indicate an out-of-date selection system that fails to address the new job skill requirements. Increasing turnover in the job among long-term employees may indicate ineffectiveness or lack of training in the new technology. Second, if the turnover is voluntary (such as in a transfer or resignation), employees may self-select out of the job or the organization because they do not have the skills needed to perform the work. If the turnover is concentrated mainly in a particular demographic group, it may suggest some of the reasons for leaving mentioned earlier are present, or it could mean that diverse work climate conditions for this particular group are not favorable to succeed using this new technology (e.g., poor interpersonal climate, discrimination, poor training access or lack of coaching support for this group in particular). If the turnover is involuntary, the manager of the work group may be releasing employees from the organization because they are unable to adequately perform the work. If the involuntary turnover is concentrated in a specific demographic group, it will require further study with "diversity lenses" to determine if issues of diversity management exist. Third, the market for employees who are familiar with the new technology may dictate a higher wage for their work than what the organization pays, and therefore they leave.

Looking for Causes Behind the Trends

In analyzing turnover, diversity practitioners need to contemplate what influences could be contributing to trends in turnover. There may be a new manager in a department that is experiencing increased turnover who lacks management skill and/or diversity management capability. The manager may not have a managerial style that meets organizational culture expectations. The manager may enforce policies more strictly, resulting in an increase in terminations, or may be less attentive to multicultural differences in development needs, resulting in an increase in resignations. The organization may have made changes that affect employees' personal lives, such as a change in hours of operation. The change may contribute to an increase in turnover because these employees seek positions with more desirable hours. Implementation of a stricter attendance policy may influence both voluntary and involuntary employee turnover.

The organization may also have implemented changes that contribute to a decrease in turnover. A recent increase in wages means the organization is more competitive in the labor market. Implementation of family-friendly programs may contribute to a better work and family balance, thus reducing turnover. It is important for diversity practitioners to understand the concept of turnover, measure it, analyze it, and discuss its relationship to organizational outcomes in a way that helps management understand how it directly affects organizational success.

Good Turnover Versus Bad Turnover

Organizations do not want zero turnover because not all turnover is bad for organizational outcomes. Turnover initiated by the organization is generally thought of as good or acceptable turnover; in other words, it is the result of upholding policy and performance expectations. For example, the turnover that results from terminating an employee for violation of harassment policies is good for the organization. Allowing harassment or similar situations to continue could have disastrous legal implications for the organization, be detrimental to the morale of other employees, damage the organization's brand in the marketplace, and actually contribute to other unwanted organizational outcomes (Fleming and Wilson, 2001).

Bad or unacceptable turnover generally exists when good employees leave voluntarily regardless of the diversity of their background. It is even more devastating when minorities and females leave because of poor diversity management, especially when the organization's track record on diversity has not been great to begin with. The organization is not meeting the desired employment outcomes and/or climate for these employees, and the results can be very costly. Investments in the exiting employee (i.e., hiring, training, and salary costs) and performance losses (e.g., downtime, increased hours for other employees) occur when high-performing, newly trained, or key employees leave the organization. Although we hinted earlier that some areas of voluntary turnover are often preventable, involuntary turnover can also reveal important trends that require intervention to prevent organizational loss.

Importance of Defining Terms

Organizations typically use turnover measurement and its changes over time to analyze aspects of employment. Therefore, it is important to standardize a definition within the organization that provides the information needed. When deciding how to define the calculation of turnover, diversity practitioners must think broadly about what the organization needs or wants to know about turnover. It may be very important to the organization to compare internal turnover rates to a published industry standard. Comparison to a standard measurement requires that internal turnover be calculated exactly the same as the standard. For example, if the published standard being used as a baseline measurement does not include part-time employees, that group cannot be included in the organization measurement or the comparison will be misleading; however, the organization may have a large number of part-time employees and find it important to include them in the turnover calculation. If so, comparison to the standard may be less meaningful than comparison to other organizations or units that also include part-time employees in the calculation. Depending on what the organization is trying to determine from turnover analysis, needs may dictate that diversity practitioners deviate from the standard to provide meaningful information.

The Bureau of National Affairs (BNA) provides a definition of turnover, and its calculation has become the standard by which the diversity profession can *generally* measure turnover as an aggregate; however, the BNA does not break this turnover number down by demographic group. National quarterly data from the BNA provide a standard measurement to compare turnover among organizations and within industries. To use the BNA data to compare organizations, turnover must be measured by using the exact method employed by the BNA. The BNA defines *turnover* as all permanent separations of employees, whether voluntary or involuntary. The definition seems clear-cut; however, unless we know the meaning of the terms used in the definition, we could make misleading comparisons of the organization to this published standard.

Separations is defined as permanent disassociations from the group, such as termination, resignation, and retirement. It does not include temporary separations such as employees placed on temporary or indefinite layoff or employees who are on temporary leaves of absence. *Employees* is defined as regular employees and does not include temporary help, part-time employees, or interns (BNA, 2001).

The calculation for turnover is the number of separations from the group being analyzed divided by the average number of employees in the group. For an organization, the calculation is:

(Number of permanent separations for the month ÷

Average number of employees on payroll for the month)

× 100 = Turnover percentage rate

The following scenario illustrates the calculation. An organization had an average of 100 employees last month. Nine employees resigned for reasons such as better opportunity, more money, and closer to home. One employee retired. Five employees were terminated because of poor performance, on-the-job altercation, third written warning for absences, and so on. Five more employees were terminated for failing to report to work for three days without calling in. One employee left for a 30-day personal leave of absence. Hence, 20 permanent separations occurred last month. The employee on leave of absence is not included because that person is expected to return after 30 days.

According to the BNA turnover formula, the number of permanent separations for the month (20) is divided by the average employees for the month (100). Thus, the turnover rate for last month is 20 percent. Although the BNA measurement is a widely accepted standard that provides a means of comparison among organizations and industries, diversity practitioners may need to further refine the definition to analyze the data and provide information needed by the organization, especially breaking these turnover numbers down by demographic group and length of service. Following is an example of how the definition of terms for the calculation of turnover affects the outcome of the measurement.

Is it best to measure voluntary versus involuntary turnover or preventable versus nonpreventable turnover in a particular organization? Within that organization, what types of separations are voluntary? Resignations and retirements are generally voluntary; if an organization really wants to measure preventable turnover, however, including retirements in the calculation will overstate the resulting rate. Conversely, excluding employees who do not come to work and do not call in to explain their absence (commonly called three-day no-call, no-shows) may understate preventable turnover. In many organizations, terminations of employees who fail to follow an attendance policy may be considered involuntary turnover; however, if the organization decides that those employees have resigned without notice, such terminations may be considered voluntary or preventable turnover. It is important to decide exactly what the organization needs to measure. Doing so helps define what does or does not go into the calculation and what the measurement is telling the organization (Fleming and Wilson, 2001).

In the example described previously, if only the nine official resignations and the one retirement are included in the calculation, the rate would be

$$\frac{10 \text{ voluntary permanent separations}}{100 \text{ employees (average)}} = .10 \times 100 = 10\%$$

The organization might be comfortable with 10 percent voluntary turnover, but five employees were terminated because they stopped coming to work. If those employees are considered voluntary separations (resigned without notice) for turnover calculation purposes, the voluntary rate would be

$$\frac{15 \text{ voluntary permanent separations}}{100 \text{ employees (average)}} = .15 \times 100 = 15\%$$

The organization may or may not be comfortable with 15 percent voluntary turnover; however, if the no-call, no-shows had not been included in the calculation, voluntary turnover in the organization would be understated. The organization may really want to know how much preventable turnover there was. If the organization considers the no-call, no-shows voluntary resignations and considers all nonretirement resignations preventable, only the nine resignations and the five no-call, no-shows would have been included. In this case, the result is a more accurate preventable turnover percentage rate of 14 percent.

From a diversity standpoint, what if of the nine resignations, 80 percent were women or minorities leaving the organization. The combined turnover rate overall is still 14 percent, but this suggests that the actions taken to prevent turnover of this kind in the future may heavily require a diversity management solution instead of a general management approach.

These types of issues need to be decided when defining what, how, and why the organization will measure turnover. Defining exactly what is to be measured and deciding what is or is not to be included in the calculation are important not only in the calculation itself, but also in the analysis and presentation of the results. People interpret turnover measurement in different ways. If different people are providing measurements from different units to contribute to an overall organizational measure, each person needs to fully understand what to include in the calculation. Users of the data also need to fully understand what is included in order to draw accurate conclusions from the data.

Typical Critical Success Factor Areas

As stated in the previous chapter, a critical success factor (CSF) area is an important must-achieve, make-or-break performance category for the organization. They typically focus on the organization's outputs and/or intended outcomes for success in that area. The workforce profile area requires that the diversity practitioner have an accurate profile or picture of the organization's human resources and key themes, patterns, and trends that are affecting that profile. In general, a sample set of critical success factor areas in the diverse workforce profile area might include outcomes such as the following:

- ☐ Workforce demographic representation
- ☐ Workforce turnover
- ☐ Workforce profile of women
- ☐ Workforce profile of minorities
- ☐ Recruitment impact
- ☐ Cost per hire
- ☐ Workforce retention
- ☐ Workforce stability
- ☐ Workforce profile of people with disabilities
- ☐ Workforce profile of new hires

This is just a brief list of the critical success factor areas that can be included in the diverse workforce profile perspective of the diversity scorecard. Each critical success factor area reflects a wide range of analysis tracks that can be undertaken to assess the strength of the organization's diverse workforce profile.

Sample Measures to Drive the Index

Table 9-5 provides a starter set of metrics that can be used in the diverse workforce profile section of a diversity scorecard. Ideally, the choices made should provide a basic yet thorough look at the investment and utilization levels of human capital assets within the organization.

ANALYZING DATA

Once an organization decides exactly what is needed in the measurement of its diverse workforce profile, diversity practitioners can dig even deeper into the analysis of each metric. For example, turnover rates compare organizations or groups within different parts of the organization. The diversity organization can track these rates over time to determine cyclical trends in turnover or if certain events contribute to sudden changes in the rate. The data in Table 9-6 bring several questions to mind.

What looks like a significant change in the turnover rate occurred in August and December. What could be causing the changes? Is the

Table 9-5. Potential Diverse Workforce Profile Measures

☐ Percentage new hires by demographic group	☐ Recruitment adjusted gain percentage
☐ Diversity hit rate	☐ Percentage people of color by demographic group
☐ Time-to-fill rate	
☐ Percentage minorities as officials and managers	☐ Percentage women as officials and managers
☐ Percentage diversity survival and loss rate	☐ Percentage diversity stability factor and instability factor
☐ Percentage turnover by length of service	☐ Percentage people with disabilities by demographic group
☐ Percentage absenteeism by demographic group	☐ Number returning from leave by demographic group
☐ Number of employee referrals by	☐ Average tenure by demographic group
☐ demographic group	
☐ Percentage voluntary turnover: exempt and nonexempt	☐ Percentage involuntary turnover: exempt and nonexempt
☐ Number of offers to interviewees	☐ Percentage hired versus applicant flow
☐ Cost per hire	

Source: Hubbard MDR Stat Pak Diversity Measurement "Calculate and Go" Software.

Table 9-6. Example of
Cyclical Trends in Turnover

June	8%
July	6%
August	12%
September	8%
October	7%
November	5%
December	2%

organization unknowingly hiring students who had intentions of working only for the summer? Possibly, a new policy or program was implemented in July that affected turnover for August. A decrease in turnover may be a normal phenomenon because employees tend to stick it out for holiday spending needs or to obtain the organization's holiday bonus.

Determining what organizational units or employee groups are most vulnerable to high turnover can help concentrate diversity intervention efforts. Conversely, knowing which groups are experiencing less turnover may help determine whether some intraorganizational best practices for diversity could be expanded to other areas. Turnover analysis, in conjunction with exit interviews, which ask "Why are you leaving?", and retention interviews, which ask "Why are you staying?", can help the diversity organization determine not only what's wrong but also what's working within the organization.

Analysis of Other Types of Turnover

Different types of turnover and characteristics of separated employees can also be analyzed in order to provide information about who is leaving the organization and what might prevent turnover. Knowing the overall turnover rate helps compare organizations. Knowing the proportion of voluntary to involuntary turnover by demographic group may also be helpful. An overall rate of 20 percent, compared to an industry average of 25 percent, may be acceptable to an organization, but some of that turnover may be preventable. Additional analysis may help diversity practitioners determine whether some of the turnover could have been avoided. Of the 20 employees who permanently separated, maybe only six employees left because of involuntary termination and the other 14 employees voluntarily resigned because of poor diversity management.

In such a case, the total separations constitute the divisor and the preventable separations the numerator:

$$\frac{14 \text{ preventable separations}}{20 \text{ total separations}} = .7 \times 100 = 70\%$$

According to the calculation, 70 percent of the diverse workforce turnover might have been prevented! If it had been prevented, the overall rate would have been only 6 percent (6 employees of the 100 average employees for the month left the organization). Rather than being comfortable with having a turnover rate below the industry average, the organization might have been considered an employer of choice.

To find out when employees tend to leave an organization, diversity practitioners would again look at only the group of employees who have left the organization. Pertinent data list the employees and their length of service, as shown in Table 9-7.

According to these data, the average length of service of the employees who have left the organization can be calculated at about 16 months. That figure may or may not be helpful information for the organization. Diversity practitioners may wish to look for patterns within the length of service. For example, five of the employees (50%) had between 19 and 21 months of service, four employees (40%) had 1.5 months or less, and one had 5 years of service. A pattern emerges when analyzing data in this manner. Employees seem to be experiencing decision points at around 30 days, 18 months, and 5 years of service. Further analysis may determine what happens to employees at those points in their service. The diversity organization may create and implement some initiatives targeted to address those points. In addition, practitioners may add other

Table 9-7. Example of Employee Length of Service

Employee A	19.0 months
Employee B	20.0 months
Employee C	60.0 months
Employee D	19.0 months
Employee E	21.0 months
Employee F	20.0 months
Employee G	1.0 months
Employee H	1.5 months
Employee I	0.5 months
Employee J	1.0 months

Table 9-8. Demographic Groups of Employees

Employee A	19.0 months	Black
Employee B	20.0 months	Black
Employee C	60.0 months	White
Employee D	19.0 months	Black
Employee E	21.0 months	Black
Employee F	20.0 months	Black
Employee G	1.0 months	Hispanic
Employee H	1.5 months	Hispanic
Employee I	0.5 months	Hispanic
Employee J	1.0 months	Hispanic

data points to further refine the analysis. For example, looking at the demographic group that the employees belong to may provide additional valuable information, as shown in Table 9-8.

Analyzing the turnover data can provide some valuable insights for diversity practitioners. They can determine not only the length of service of those employees who left, but also what proportions of employees were from what racial groups. Five of the 10 separations (50 percent) are Black or African American, and these employees who are leaving are doing so soon after the 18-month mark. The organization has some phenomenon that sets in at about 18 months. It could be the end of a training period. If so, the organization may suggest implementation of further retention bonuses, a pay-back clause in a training agreement, or improvement in the selection process for job assignments after the training program. Or, it could be an organizational climate issue that begins to surface for this group after that timeframe.

Conversely, in the Hispanic employee population, where 40 percent of the turnover occurred, the length of service of those employees who have left the organization is much shorter. Perhaps there is a need in that department for a realistic job preview or for improved orientation and training programs that are diversity friendly. Armed with this information, diversity practitioners may decide to create or strengthen retention programs and re-recruitment efforts aimed at the employees who are about to reach length-of-service milestones. Continued analysis of the data after implementation of improvements may provide additional data showing the effectiveness of the turnover intervention.

Diversity practitioners should be open to unexpected results. For example, you may be surprised to find, contrary to assumptions, that women and minorities on the night shifts did not have higher turnover rates than those employees on day shifts. This finding would help an organization change its assumptions and cause it to look deeper into the data to find out what was different about the night shifts.

REPORTING DATA

Today's presentation, spreadsheet, and graphing software makes it easy to create highly professional presentations of diverse workforce profile data such as turnover data. As diversity practitioners are increasingly called to the table as strategic partners, it is more important for all diversity practitioners to become comfortable with software tools. Most introductory courses in spreadsheet software will include the basics of graphing. Once you are comfortable with navigating the software, experimenting with the different options is an extremely valuable learning activity that can be applied in diversity work immediately.

Determining what purpose turnover analysis is used for within the organization will help dictate how the information is best presented to users of the data. If the organization measures the effect of managerial performance on diverse workforce turnover, analyzing by manager or department is important and may be reported with bar or column graphs as well as time-series analysis. If the organization is concerned with the number of employees it loses from its workforce because of EEO or AA concerns, or if a certain benefit such as day care will help retain workers, the organization may want to use pie charts to analyze and report by employee demographic characteristics (Fleming and Wilson, 2001). Although it is always important to know the needs and preferences of the audience (e.g., some managers prefer tabled data versus charts or vice versa), some simple guidelines can help the diversity practitioner focus the audience on the desired objectives of the presentation.

Written Reports

Generally, it is helpful to give a snapshot of how things are, show changes from the last report, and discuss possible contributing factors and solutions. A written report should begin with a summary page that includes definitions of terms and shows comparison data. Busy executives appreciate concise information and often prefer to see basic information at a glance. A table format with comparison and summary data can provide very good information in a small amount of space and allow the user to draw overview conclusions, such as turnover is decreasing. This type of

Table 9-9. Summary Page

Measure	This Period	Last Period	% Change
Overall Rate	12%	14%	+16.7%
Voluntary Rate	7%	5%	–28.6%
Involuntary Rate	5%	9%	+80%

overview invites users to dig in to the details at their convenience (see Table 9-9).

In the example in Table 9-9, definitions of *overall, voluntary,* and *involuntary* would appear on the summary page to accompany the table. Later pages of the report include text and discussion regarding observations of trends, recent changes in the organization that may or may not have influenced the results, and any plans that may be under development for addressing the issues. A table of contents or an index of graphs included in the report allows the user to pinpoint where particular information can be found in the report. Graphic presentations can be included within the body of the report or as appendices.

Charts

Generally, a line graph is effective for showing trends over time. A timeline can represent monthly, quarterly, or annual periods. It may be helpful to report time-based measurements in ways similar to other departments within the organization. For example, quarterly reporting might be the norm in an organization. From the example of monthly rates in Figure 9-1, the diversity practitioner might graph a timeline such as the one shown in Figure 9-2.

For comparisons of turnover among groups, a standard column chart is helpful, such as the one in Figure 9-3.

For proportions or characteristics of subgroups (e.g., preventable separations only), a pie chart or a stacked column graph can be helpful. For example, using a pie chart to show reasons given by the employees who have voluntarily left the organization helps the audience see not only the big picture but also the separate components (see Figures 9-4 and 9-5).

Tips for Effective Presentation

Titles for graphs are extremely important. The time period and group that the chart or graph describes should always be included. For example, a

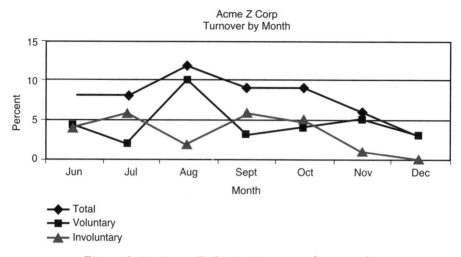

Figure 9-1. Acme Z Corp. Turnover by month.

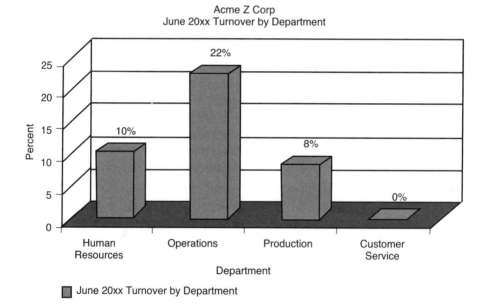

Figure 9-2. Acme Z Corp. Turnover by department.

chart showing voluntary turnover for a specific department for a specific month should have a descriptive title such as "Operations Department Voluntary Turnover, June, 20xx." Or if the chart shows turnover by the same department over several months, it may have a title of "20xx Operations Department Voluntary Turnover by Month."

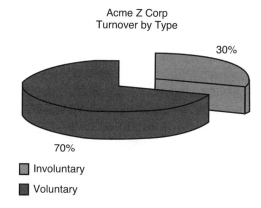

Figure 9-3. *Acme Z Corp. Turnover by type.*

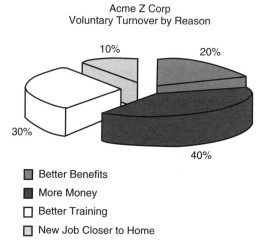

Figure 9-4. *Acme Z Corp. Voluntary turnover by reason.*

Having definitions of terms in the chart is also very helpful to the user. For example, a chart of voluntary turnover should include the organization's definition of the term, such as "Voluntary turnover is defined as the number of permanent employee-initiated separations but does not include temporary or part-time employees, interns, retirements or temporary absences." The text box feature of most spreadsheet software can be used to add the definition directly to the chart, or the definition can be added to the margin footer (Fleming and Wilson, 2001).

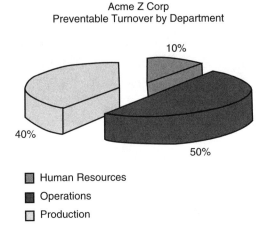

Figure 9-5. Acme Z Corp. Preventable turnover by department.

Consistency in Reporting

Periodic reporting of diverse workforce profile data is highly recommended. Audiences usually find it helpful to have the presentation appear in a standard format each period. Such standardization helps the audience concentrate on the trends rather than on figuring out the legend keys. For example, in a line graph that compares overall, voluntary, and involuntary timelines, the person creating the graphics should use the same color for each line each time the data are reported. The overall timeline could always appear in red, the voluntary in green, and the involuntary in yellow. For black-and-white presentations, solid, dotted, and dashed lines can be used.

FINAL THOUGHTS

The diverse workforce profile perspective plays an important role in the diversity scorecard that helps the organization understand critical aspects of its workforce. Using statistical analysis, this perspective requires an assessment of workforce personnel by race, gender, ethnicity, length of service, voluntary/involuntary turnover, organizational level, and sometimes by age and physical ability. It is critical to examine how people are attracted to the organization and the degree to which they are retained once hired. If the organization is having difficulty attracting and retaining women, people of color, or other diverse groups, building a workforce profile will help create a big picture to analyze what is needed to improve the organization's performance.

In the next chapter, we will learn what is needed to effectively analyze the organization's workplace culture and systems. It will provide insights into employee perceptions of diversity management practices and the level of diversity-friendliness in the organization's policies, procedures, and processes.

REFERENCES

Bureau of National Affairs. *BNA Quarterly Report on Employee Turnover.* Washington, DC: BNA, 2001.

Fleming, Maureen J., and Jennifer B. Wilson. *Effective HR Measurement Techniques.* Alexandria, VA: Society for Human Resource Management, 2001.

Hubbard, Edward E. *How to Calculate Diversity Return on Investment.* Petaluma, CA: Global Insights, 1999.

Hubbard, Edward E. *Measuring Diversity Results (MDR) Stat Pak 1: Diversity Scorecard Startup Metrics.* Petaluma, CA: Global Insights, 2000.

Hubbard, Edward E. *The Manager's Pocket Guide to Diversity Management.* Amherst, MA: HRD Press, 2003.

Judy, Richard W., and Carol D'Amico. *Workforce 2000.* Indianapolis: Hudson Institute, 1987.

Judy, Richard W., and Carol D'Amico. *Workforce 2020: Work and Workers in the 21st Century.* Indianapolis: Hudson Institute, 1997.

Kennedy, Debbe. *Assessment: Defining Current Realities.* San Francisco: Berrett-Koehler, 2000.

Kennedy, Debbe. *Achievement: Measuring Progress, Celebrating Success.* San Francisco: Berrett-Koehler, 2000.

Mercer, W. *Turning Your Human Resources Department into a Profit Center.* New York: American Management Association, 1989.

Swanson R., and E. Holton. *Human Resource Development Research Handbook: Linking Research and Practice.* San Francisco: Berrett-Kohler, 1997.

Williams, R.W. "Head off Turnover at the Selection Pass." *Employment Management Today,* 4(4):1999, 22–26.

FURTHER READING

Baytos, Lawrence M. *Designing & Implementing Successful Diversity Programs.* Englewood Cliffs, NJ: Prentice Hall, 1995.

Bloch F. *Statistics for Non-Statisticians.* Washington, DC: Equal Employment Advisory Council, 1997.

Fernandez, John P. *Race, Gender & Rhetoric.* New York: McGraw-Hill, 1999.

Fitz-enz, J. *How to Measure Human Resources Management.* New York: McGraw-Hill, 1995.

Fitz-enz, J. *The ROI of Human Capital.* New York: AMACOM, 2000.

Henry, Pamela K. *Diversity and the Bottomline: Prospering in the Global Economy.* Austin, TX: TurnKey Press, 2002.

Loden, Marilyn. *Implementing Diversity*, Chicago: Irwin, 1996.

CHAPTER 10

Workplace Culture/Climate Perspective

DEFINITION

The diverse workplace culture/climate profile perspective reflects a statistical summary of employee perceptions of the workplace and its systems sorted by key demographic groups. This perspective often includes an analysis of the workplace in terms of employee satisfaction and commitment, perceptions of climate and culture, grievances and complaints, perceptions of leadership and management practices, and the like. This information is typically tracked to determine if the organization's workplace is inclusive with key diversity management processes and systems in place to sustain the diversity strategic change process.

Many organizations conduct attitude surveys, which reflect the degree to which employees feel satisfied with the organization, their jobs, their supervisors, their co-workers, and a host of other issues. From a diversity standpoint, data is sorted via cross-tab correlations to gauge diverse workforce perceptions. Employee job satisfaction is closely correlated with absenteeism and turnover, both of which are often linked to the rationale for conducting specific diversity initiatives. Some workplace attitude survey items focus on issues directly related to diversity, such as satisfaction with the ability of leaders, managers, and supervisors to operate in a multicultural environment.

Attitude survey data are usually linked to diversity initiative results when specific issues on the survey relate to diversity or a problem or issue is being assessed. For example, when a new pay plan is implemented for all employees, the annual attitude survey contained five questions directly tied to perceptions and attitudes influenced by the new plan as seen by various diverse groups. Or, if access to career development or training was previously blocked for some demographic groups, the survey may ask questions related to access and analyze the scores by demographic group to see if these perceptions still exist.

Because attitude surveys are usually taken annually, the results may not be in sync with the timing of the initiative's implementation. When job satisfaction is one of the initiative objectives, some organizations conduct surveys at a prescribed timeframe after the diversity initiative is implemented and design the survey instrument around issues related to diversity. This approach, however, can cost more than an annual survey.

ORGANIZATIONAL COMMITMENT

Measuring organizational commitment is perhaps a more important method for understanding the motivational state of a diverse workforce and their perceptions of the culture/climate. Similar to attitude surveys, organizational commitment instruments reflect the degree to which employees align with company goals, values, philosophy, and practices. High levels of organizational commitment often correlate with high levels of productivity and performance; therefore, organizational commitment is an important intangible diversity measure. Changes in diverse workplace survey data may reflect the success of a diversity initiative in improving organizational commitment. The difficulty with this intangible measure is that it is not routinely measured in organizations.

Climate Survey Data

Some organizations conduct climate surveys, which reflect work climate changes such as variances in communication, openness, trust, and quality of feedback. Climate surveys are similar to attitude surveys but are more general and often focus on a range of workplace issues and environmental enablers and inhibitors. Climate surveys conducted before and after the implementation of diversity initiatives may reflect the extent to which the diversity initiative changes these intangible measures.

Cultural Audit Data

Diversity cultural audits are among the best-known survey approaches that measure diverse employee perceptions about the traits, practices, and processes that reinforce a set of specific behaviors (called behavioral norms) that an organization's members believe are expected of them if they are to fit in and survive. These behavioral norms lead to patterns of behaviors and attitudes that guide the way a diverse workforce approaches its work and how organizational members interact. These consistent patterns of behavior become known as the organization's culture.

Cultural audit data help provide a picture of the operating cultures of the organization in terms of how things are done at that company and what is expected of its members. These patterns can be positive and productive or negative and destructive. Getting to know the organization's culture helps determine if cultural norms present in the workplace support or detract from high performance. Most important, assessing the culture brings to light opportunities for change and improvement that can nurture and sustain a diverse, high-performing atmosphere over time.

Cultural audits are also conducted before and after the implementation of a diversity initiative to reflect the extent to which the diversity initiative changes these behavioral (normative) measures. Some of the perceptions and outcomes of the cultural audit may be more qualitative and anecdotal and therefore are reported as intangibles.

Employee Complaints

Some organizations record and report specific employee complaints. A reduction of employee complaints sometimes directly relates to diversity initiatives, such as a building diverse work teams initiative. Consequently, the level of complaints is used as a measure of a workplace climate initiative's success and is sometimes reported as an intangible measure when aspects of the impact are more qualitative than quantitative.

Grievances

In both union and nonunion organizations, grievances often reflect the level of dissatisfaction or disenchantment with a variety of factors in the organization. Sometimes, diversity initiatives that focus on building labor management cooperation are designed to reduce an excessive number of grievances. An improvement in the grievance level reflects the success of the diversity initiative. This measure may be converted to a monetary value; however, it may also be reported as an intangible measure.

Discrimination Complaints

Employee dissatisfaction shows up in different types of discrimination complaints, ranging from informal complaints to external charges and even litigation. New HR and diversity policies and initiatives may be designed to prevent complaints or to reduce the current level of complaint activity. The result of the policies and programs, in terms of complaint reduction, sometimes is not converted to monetary values because of the various assumptions and estimations involved in the process. When this is the case, these measures are reported as intangible benefits.

Stress Reduction

Occasionally, diversity initiatives reduce work-related stress by showing participants how to work with others who are different from them to improve the way they accomplish their jobs, accomplish more in a workday, and relieve tension and anxiety. The subsequent reduction in stress may be directly linked to the diversity initiative and therefore drive diverse workplace climate and culture perceptions that are reflected in the diversity scorecard results.

As mentioned in an earlier chapter, making a commitment to diversity means more than striving for immediate results such as improved demographics. Employees must feel welcomed and supported as part of the organization's climate and culture. They need to know that the organization has systems, processes, and people in place to help give them the best possible chance for success and allow them to build an invigorating career.

COLLECTING DATA

Collecting data for the workplace culture/climate index requires examining a variety of sources that will shed light on the organization's culture and climate. These sources can include some of the following:

- ☐ Level of organizational commitment from employees
- ☐ Aspects of climate
- ☐ Aspects of culture
- ☐ Employee complaints
- ☐ Number of grievances
- ☐ Types of discrimination
- ☐ Work life initiatives and balance

☐ Leadership behaviors and practices
☐ Diversity work team interactions

Let's examine a few of these sources in more detail. *Organizational culture* is "the set of shared, taken-for-granted implicit assumptions that a group holds and that determines how it perceives, thinks about, and reacts to its various environments" (Schein, 1996). This definition highlights two important characteristics of organizational culture: (1) it influences our behavior at work; and (2) it operates on two levels, which vary in terms of outward visibility and resistance to change.

At the less visible level, culture reflects the values shared among organizational members. At Healthco, a UK-based international pharmaceuticals company, the difference between the two levels became very clear when a corporate culture change was implemented. The first part of the change process, focused on behavior (e.g., teamwork, innovation), is extremely well embedded within the organization. The second stage, the issue of a values statement, became far less integrated in the company's culture (Hope and Hendry, 1995). At the more visible level, culture represents the normative behavior patterns accepted by organizational members. These patterns are passed on to others through the socialization process. Culture is more susceptible to change at this level. Each level of culture influences the other.

For example, if an organization truly values providing high-quality service to ethnic markets, employees are more likely to adopt the behavior of responding faster to emerging-market customer complaints. When British Airways began moving toward privatization, a top priority was changing a culture of indifference to a culture of service. Without a culture of service it would not be able to compete in a global marketplace (Egan, 1994). Similarly, causality can flow in the other direction. Employees can come to value high-quality service based on their experiences as they interact with customers. To improve their customer-oriented philosophy, a Dutch leisure group specializing in holiday villages has introduced a job rotation system. Four times a year people change jobs for one day. This way, people get acquainted with their diverse co-workers and their colleagues' jobs. In addition, they learn the clients' needs and wishes at every spot in the customer interaction process.

Understanding Culture Formation

To gain a better understanding of how organizational culture is formed and used by employees, this section discusses data collection by reviewing the manifestations of organizational culture, a model for interpreting organizational culture, the four functions of organizational culture, and the research on organizational cultures.

Manifestations of Culture

When is an organization's culture most apparent? One theory suggests that cultural assumptions assert themselves through socialization of new employees, subculture clashes, and top management behavior. Consider these three situations:

☐ **Situation 1:** A newly hired Hispanic employee who shows up late for an important meeting is told a story about someone who was fired for repeated tardiness.

☐ **Situation 2:** Conflict between product design engineers who emphasize a product's function and marketing specialists who demand a more stylish product reveals an underlying clash of subculture values.

☐ **Situation 3:** Top managers, through the behavior they model and the administrative and reward systems they create, prompt a significant improvement in the quality of a company's products.

Each of these situations highlights the makings of workplace culture whose impact must be measured to determine its application and effects on diverse groups throughout the organization.

Vijay Sathe, a Harvard Researcher, developed a useful model for observing and interpreting organizational culture (see Figure 10-1).

This model highlights four general manifestations or evidence of workplace culture that include shared things (objects), shared sayings (talk), shared doings (behavior), and shared feelings (emotion). The diversity practitioner can begin collecting cultural information within the workplace by asking, observing, reading, and feeling (experiencing) the culture.

An organization's culture also fulfils four functions. To help bring these four functions to life, let us consider how each of them has taken shape at 3M (Jacobs, 1995; Anfuso, 1995). This 3M example is particularly helpful in understanding these four functions because the company has a long history of being innovative—it was founded in 1902—and it was ranked as the 11th most admired company in the United States by *Fortune* in 1996, partly due to its strong and distinctive culture.

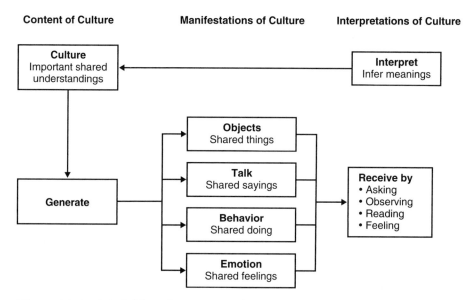

Figure 10-1. Model for observing and interpreting organizational culture. (Source: Adapted from Sathe, V. "Implications of Corporate Culture: A Manager's Guide to Action," Organizational Dynamics, *Autumn 1983.)*

1. *Give members an organizational identity.* 3M is known as being an innovative company that relentlessly pursues new-product development. The organization's top management, for example, decreed that 30 percent of sales must come from products introduced within the past four years. The old standard was 25 percent in five years. Creating rewards that reinforce innovation reinforces this identity. For example, 3M has its version of a Nobel Prize for innovative employees. The prize is the Golden Step award, whose trophy is a winged foot. Several Golden Steps are given out each year to employees whose new products have reached significant revenue and profit levels.

2. *Facilitate collective commitment.* One of 3M's corporate values is to be a company that a diverse workforce is proud to be a part of. People who like 3M's culture tend to stay employed there for long periods. This collective commitment results in a turnover rate of less than 3 percent among salaried personnel. Consider the commitment and pride expressed by Kathleen Stanislawski, a staffing manager. "I'm a 27-year 3Mer because, quite frankly, there's no reason to leave. I've had great opportunities to do different jobs and to grow a career. It's just a great company."

3. *Promote social system stability.* Social system stability reflects the extent to which the work environment is perceived as positive and reinforcing, and conflict and change are managed effectively. This stability is reinforced within 3M through a promote-from-within culture, a strategic hiring policy that ensures that a diverse group of capable college graduates are hired in a timely manner, and a layoff policy that provides displaced workers with six months to find another job at 3M before being terminated. Executives also attempt to reduce resistance to change by continually communicating the company's quest for new-product development and continuous improvement of internal processes.

4. *Shape behavior by helping members make sense of their surroundings.* This function of culture helps employees understand why the organization does what it does and how it intends to accomplish its long-term goals. 3M sets expectations for innovation in a variety of ways. For example, the company employs an internship and coop program. In 1994, for instance, 30 percent of 3M's college hires came through an internship or coop program. 3M also shapes expectations and behavior by providing detailed career feedback to its employees. New staff members are measured and evaluated against a career growth standard during their first six months to three years of employment.

Thus, the data you collect to assess workplace culture/climate will be generated from both the manifestations of culture in the organization as well as its functions.

Typical Critical Success Factor Areas

A sample set of critical success factor areas in the diverse workplace culture/climate perspective might include outcome areas such as the following:

☐ Employee commitment
☐ Organizational flexibility
☐ Employee complaints
☐ Grievances
☐ Discrimination
☐ Work life balance
☐ Leadership behaviors and practices
☐ Teamwork

☐ Employee satisfaction
☐ Openness to change

This is just a brief list of the critical success factor areas that can be included in the diverse workplace culture/climate perspective of the diversity scorecard. Each critical success factor area reflects a wide range of analysis tracks that can be undertaken to assess the quality of the organization's diverse workplace environment.

Sample Measures to Drive the Index

Table 10-1 provides a starter set of metrics that can be used in the diverse workplace culture/climate section of a diversity scorecard. Ideally, the choices made should provide a basic yet thorough look at the level of

Table 10-1. Potential Diverse Workplace Culture/Climate Measures

☐ Percentage favorable ratings on cultural audit demographic group
☐ "Employer of Choice" ratings versus top 5 to 10 competitors
☐ Retention rates of critical human capital
☐ Number of lawsuits by demographic group
☐ Perception of consistent and equitable treatment of all employees
☐ Diversity tied to management compensation
☐ Number and type of policies and procedures assessed for diverse workforce impact
☐ Number and type of policies and procedures changed for diversity impact
☐ Absence rate
☐ Dollar cost of lawsuits by demographic group
☐ Percentage diversity initiatives fully implemented

☐ Percentage favorable ratings on climate surveys by demographic group
☐ Average time for dispute resolution
☐ Cost per grievance
☐ Employee referral rate by demographic group
☐ Percentage absenteeism by demographic group
☐ Absenteeism cost
☐ Average hourly rate
☐ Percentage gender-based pay differential
☐ Effect of absenteeism on labor utilization
☐ Diversity performance appraisal metrics by demographic group
☐ Percentage work life benefits utilized
☐ Organization "openness" ratings
☐ Workplace flexibility index ratings
☐ Workplace health index ratings
☐ Percentage managers receiving diversity-related incentives by department

Source: Hubbard MDR Stat Pak Diversity Measurement *Calculate and Go* Software.

inclusion and key diversity management processes and systems in place to sustain the diversity strategic change process.

ANALYZING DATA

Researchers have attempted to identify and measure various types of organizational culture in order to study the relationship between types of culture and organizational effectiveness. This pursuit was motivated by the possibility that certain cultures were more effective than others. What they found was that workplace culture is a complex phenomenon to evaluate. Although there is not a uniformly agreed-upon method to assess culture, several cultural surveys and interviewing protocols have been recommended (Dennison, 1996). Let's take a look at what we have learned to date.

First, John Kotter and James Heskett tried to determine if organizational culture was related to a firm's long-term financial performance. They studied 207 companies from 22 industries for the period 1977 to 1988. After correlating results from a cultural survey and three different measures of economic performance, results uncovered a significant relationship between culture and financial performance (Kotter and Heskett, 1992). A similar finding was obtained on a longitudinal sample of 11 U.S. insurance companies from the period 1981 to 1987. More recently, a team of researchers sent a survey measuring workplace culture and subjective and objective indexes of profitability, quality, sales growth, satisfaction, and overall performance to 764 companies. Culture was significantly related to all of these organizational outcomes (Gordon and DiTomaso, 1992). Second, studies of mergers indicated that they frequently failed because of incompatible cultures (Tully, 1996). Third, several studies demonstrated that organizational culture was significantly correlated with employee behavior and attitudes.

For example, culture was associated with (1) the performance and voluntary turnover for a sample of 904 accountants; (2) the organizational commitment of 80 Australian manufacturing employees; and (3) the innovativeness, work avoidance, and voluntary turnover of a sample of 4,890 employees working in a variety of organizations (Sheridan, 1992). Finally, results from several studies revealed that the congruence between an individual's values and the organization's values was significantly correlated with organizational commitment, job satisfaction, intention to quit, and turnover (Harris and Mossholder, 1996).

These research results underscore the significance of diverse workplace culture and the need to measure it. They also reinforce the need to learn more about the process of cultivating and changing an organization's culture. An organization's culture is not determined by fate. It is formed and shaped by the combination and integration of everyone who works in the organization. As a case in point, a recent longitudinal study of 322 employees working in a governmental organization revealed that managerial intervention successfully shifted the workplace culture toward greater participation and employee involvement. This change in workplace culture was associated with improved job satisfaction and communication across all hierarchical levels and types of employees (Zamanou and Glaser, 1994). This study further highlights the interplay between workplace culture and organizational change. Successful organizational change is highly dependent on an organization's culture. A change-resistant culture, for instance, can undermine the effectiveness of any type of workplace culture/climate change. Although it is not an easy task to change an organization's culture, we will take a preliminary look at how this might be done. Implied in the process are methods and areas of analysis that are critical to evaluating diversity scorecard results.

High-Performance Cultures

An organization's workplace culture may be strong or weak, depending on variables such as cohesiveness, value consensus, and individual commitment among its diverse members to collective goals. Contrary to what might be suspected, a strong culture is not necessarily a good thing. The nature of the culture's central values is more important than its strength. For example, a strong but change-resistant culture may be worse, from the standpoint of profitability and competitiveness, than a weak but innovative culture. IBM is a prime example: Its strong culture, coupled with a dogged determination to continually pursue a strategic plan that was out of step with the market, led to its failure to maintain its leadership in the personal computer market. This strategy ultimately cost the company about $97 billion (Byrne, 1996). Similarly, an organization that is out of step with the demographic changes in the diverse workforce and ethnic customer markets will find itself at a loss in staying competitive in the long run.

Three perspectives have been proposed to explain the type of workplace cultures that enhance an organization's economic performance. They are referred to as the strength, fit, and adaptive perspectives, respectively:

1. The *strength perspective* predicts a significant relationship between strength of corporate culture and long-term financial performance.

The idea is that strong cultures create goal alignment, employee motivation, and needed structure and controls to improve organizational performance. This perspective assumes that the strength of the workplace culture is related to the organization's financial performance.

2. The *fit perspective* is based on the premise that an organization's workplace culture must align with its business or strategic context. Accordingly, there is no one best culture. A culture is predicted to facilitate economic performance only if it fits its context. This perspective assumes that a workplace culture must align with its business or strategic context.

3. The *adaptive perspective* assumes that good cultures help organizations anticipate and adapt to environmental changes. This proactive adaptability is expected to enhance long-term financial performance. This perspective assumes that adaptive cultures enhance an organization's financial performance.

The study by John Kotter and James Heskett partially supported the strength and fit perspectives; findings were completely consistent with the adaptive culture perspective. Long-term financial performance was highest for organizations with an adaptive culture. The characteristics of an adaptive culture are also completely consistent with producing a high-performing, inclusive work environment. By implementing high-performance culture strategies, the organization is building a workplace that is conducive for diversity success.

Developing an Adaptive Culture

Figure 10-2 illustrates the process of developing and preserving an adaptive culture. The process begins with leadership (i.e., leaders must create and implement a business vision and associated strategies that fit the organizational context). A vision represents a long-term goal that describes what an organization wants to become; however, the existence of an organizational vision does not guarantee success. A vision held only by its leadership is not enough to create any real change.

To ensure success, management must continuously and creatively articulate the organization's vision and goals. This is achieved through open communication systems that encourage diverse workforce feedback and facilitate a two-way flow of information. Because the organization's ultimate goal must be to satisfy the organization's constituents, it is imperative that employees understand what is expected of them as well

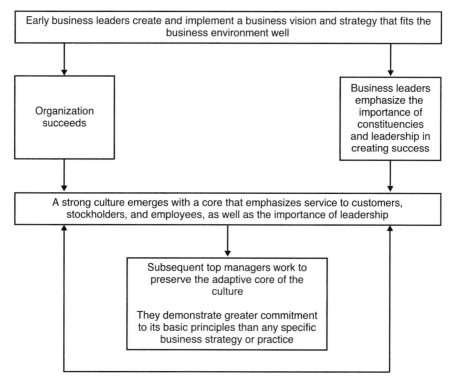

Figure 10-2. Process for developing and preserving an adaptive culture. (Source: Kotter, J.C., and J.L. Heskett. Corporate Culture and Performance, The Free Press, New York, 1992.)

as their responsibility for working together effectively, regardless of demographic differences to achieve results.

Adaptiveness is promoted over time by a combination of organizational success and a specific leadership focus. Leaders must get employees to buy into a timeless philosophy or set of values that emphasizes effectiveness with the organization's key constituents—customers, stockholders, and employees—and also emphasizes the improvement of leadership. An infrastructure must then be created to preserve the organization's adaptiveness. Management does this by consistently reinforcing and supporting the organization's core philosophy or values of satisfying constituency needs and improving leadership. This is precisely what Herb Kelleher, CEO of Southwest Airlines, has done.

Southwest Airlines has grown from a startup company 25 years ago to one of the most consistently profitable airlines by creating a strong or widely shared belief in a constituency-oriented culture. Long before *empowerment* became a management buzzword, Ms. Barrett (the number-two executive at Southwest) was giving employees freedom from centralized policies. She constantly reinforces the company's workplace message that employees should be treated like customers and continually celebrates workers who go above and beyond the call of duty. When she sensed that the carrier was outgrowing its personality-kid-among-the-impersonal-giants image, she created a culture committee of employees charged with preserving Southwest's spirit. Southwest employees are well-paid compared with their counterparts at other airlines. Celebrations are an important part of work, from spontaneous fun sessions to Christmas parties beginning in September to a lavish annual awards banquet, where the individual's contribution to the whole is glorified. At the same time, employees work like crazy between festivities. With that formula, the airline has avoided the bureaucracy and mediocrity that infect other companies when they outgrow their entrepreneurial roots (McCartney, 1996).

Avoiding Analysis Paralysis

A diversity research survey based on the metrics in the diversity scorecard perspectives will often produce findings on 25 to 75 questions and perhaps more. Furthermore, the data may have been cut into perhaps 8 to 16 different race and gender groups. Additional data breakouts may be made by position (exempt, nonexempt, and hourly), age or service breakdowns, and so on. Perhaps additional data cuts have been made by organization (e.g., headquarters and field departments). The data displays alone might require several hundred pages.

In addition to the numerical data, you may also have several pages of employee write-in comments from the written survey. Moderator reports on focus groups might generate additional dozens or hundreds of pages of text depending on the level of detail reported. All of this information coming in at once can bring the process to a stop while everyone gets comfortable with the data.

Considering Competing Constituencies

The data will typically show several areas where there is a commonality of interest; however, there will also be some aspects of change strongly desired by some groups (e.g., training and career development for nonexempt employees, dependent care assistance) that are of no consequence to others. The concern for spreading around the goodies to meet a wide variety of needs complicates the planning process, especially if it is being done in an environment of profit pressures and strict budget controls (Baytos, 1995).

Each organization has its own style for action planning and implementation. Some organizations that are analytical and cautious will sift, sort, and savor the data for months. On the other end of the spectrum is the intuitive, impatient organization that is comfortable with the "Ready, fire, aim!" approach. The diversity professional must be able to sort through all of the data, priorities, agendas, and the like to help create the best possible outcome for the organization.

REPORTING DATA

There are a wide variety of ways to display and report your diverse workplace culture/climate data. This data can be presented in tables, graphs, narratives, pictograms, and so on. For example, when you look at a completed analysis for a survey project, you will likely see a report consisting of some general text about the process and recommendations, figures such as tables, bar graphs, and pie charts, and within those figures, some statistics. In general, workplace survey data reporting requires that you consider at least three basic levels of analysis:

1. How many people said what?
2. Are there differences between questions or respondent subsets?
3. Are the differences significant? If so, at what level?

How deeply you go into these analyses and reporting levels depends on the diverse workplace culture/climate survey initiative objectives. You may analyze and report some questions at the top levels and only delve deeply into a few. The relevant issue is whether the deeper level will produce new information that is useful in answering your research questions and therefore your organization's diversity problems and/or issues. The most effective approach suggests that you always do just the analysis and reporting that makes sense for the organization's strategic objectives and then take action.

Reporting on Employee Experiences/Perceptions

In your diverse workplace scorecard research process it will be extremely helpful to ask and report on some rather direct questions regarding perceptions about the workplace. Perceptions do not necessarily equal the reality because the responses may be strongly influenced by cultural preconditioning; however, people will act on their perceptions as if they are real. Nevertheless, the data can be both useful and surprising. Tables 10-2, 10-3, and 10-4 provide an example to illustrate questions that might be posed and how some employees responded in a sampling of companies that have not had exceptional diversity progress.

Data in Table 10-2 would indicate that jokes and comments of a sexual nature are common among exempt employees because less than half agree with the statement; however, the 63 to 64 percent approval rating given by the nonexempt females seems to indicate that they are more likely to be spared jokes and comments of a sexual nature.

The perceptions of minority employees about ethnic jokes and comments shown in Table 10-3 are somewhat lower than for the white respondents for two of the groupings.

Table 10-2. Sample Survey Report by Racial Group and Level
Statement: Jokes and comments of a sexual nature
are not tolerated in my department

	% Who Strongly Agree/Tend to Agree	
Race/Level	Male	Female
White Exempt	50%	47
Minority Exempt	43%	53
White Nonexempt	*	64
Minority Nonexempt	*	63

* Insufficient number of responses in this category.

Table 10-3. Sample Survey Report by Gender and Level
Statement: Jokes and comments of a sexual nature
are not tolerated in my work area

	% Who Strongly Agree/Tend to Agree	
Gender/Level	White	Minority
Male Exempt	54%	35%
Female Exempt	60%	57%
Female Nonexempt	66%	49%

Table 10-4. Sample Data Patterns

Statement: The manner in which this company's employees are treated is not influenced by their gender, ethnic background (age, sexual preference, disability, etc.)

	% Who Strongly Agree/Tend to Agree		
Race/Level	Male Exempt	Female Exempt	Female Nonexempt
White	59%	36%	47%
Minority	36%	22%	22%

The last set of data, in Table 10-4, demonstrates a pattern that is sometimes found (i.e., females give lower ratings than their male counterparts, and minorities give lower ratings than nonminorities).

Managers often express surprise and disappointment about their data. Perhaps they have assumed that the relatively small number of formal EEO charges or open complaints indicates the true feelings of employees; however, the number of formal discrimination charges may bear only a slight resemblance to employee feelings. Filing a charge is a last resort, and even if the charging employee wins, he or she recognizes the possibility of losing more in the long run by coming forward.

Managers are often distressed to see data such as that shown in Tables 10-2 through 10-4. In most cases they feel strongly that they are doing a better job than the data would indicate. In fact, some evidence in employee feedback suggests that the situation is not as bad as it would appear. Perhaps employees are simply using the opportunity to send a clear message to management. While they are disappointed, their overall support of the organization may be stronger than one would assume from the data alone (Baytos, 1995).

Mobilize Current Employees to Move Ahead

If you want to report on the improvement of diversity performance in the organization, one of the best places to start is to harness the energies and goodwill of those already on board. Testimony from a like person about the workplace culture/climate will be taken more seriously by a potential recruit than trite statements in the organization's recruiting brochure. To help track an overall perspective of satisfaction of your diverse employee groups, you can include several questions in your scorecard research to report on which call for some summary judgments on the desirability of the employer, such as shown in Tables 10-5 and 10-6.

Table 10-5. Survey Questions Related to Minority Satisfaction Level
Statement: I would recommend this organization
as a good employer for minorities

Race/Level	% Who Strongly Agree/Tend to Agree		
	Male Exempt	Female Exempt	Female Nonexempt
White	64%	52%	52%
Minority	30%	27%	35%

Table 10-6. Survey Questions Related to Women's Satisfaction Level
Statement: I would recommend this organization
as a good employer for women

Race/Level	% Who Strongly Agree/Tend to Agree	
	Male	Female
White Exempt	65%	47%
Minority Exempt	47%	37%
White Nonexempt	*	51%
Minority Nonexempt	*	33%

*Insufficient number of responses in this category.

The typical spread in evaluations between white respondents and others is again demonstrated in Table 10-5. The low approval rating given by minority employees poses a challenge when enlisting their aid in helping to attract other minorities to the organization. As the data in Table 10-6 indicates, the female employees are not happy with the environment they perceive to exist.

In total, the data in Tables 10-2 through 10-6 suggest that female and minority employees (in particular) may view the environment with ambivalence. Less than one-third of the minorities would recommend the organization as a place for other minorities to work. Less than half the females would recommend their employer to other females. The organization has some work to do to build credibility before it can count on employees to help recruit their ethnic/gender counterparts into the workplace. It is a workplace culture/climate in need of a diversity makeover to transform it into one equipped with effective diversity management capability and inclusion processes.

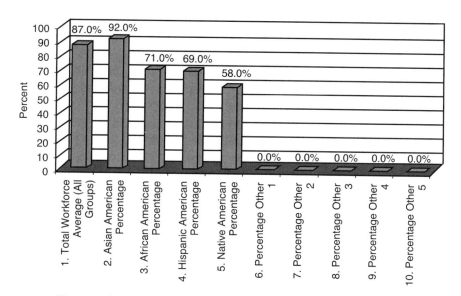

Figure 10-3. Workplace Culture/Climate Rating by Group

Your diverse workplace culture/climate reporting can include the type of graphics shown from the Hubbard Measuring Diversity Results (MDR) Stat Pak Software line of products. For example, a variety of reporting charts are predesigned for each set of metrics included in MDR Stat Pak 1: Diversity Scorecard Startup Metrics. A sample chart is shown in Figure 10-3 (Hubbard, 2000).

Reporting on this aspect of the diversity scorecard must reflect more than just the numbers. It should help paint a picture for the audience that displays and conveys what it is like to be an employee working in the organization's environment.

FINAL THOUGHTS

The diverse workplace culture/climate perspective allows the organization to get a glimpse of employee perceptions of the workplace and its systems. It is important for this perspective to include an analysis of the workplace in terms of employee satisfaction and commitment, perceptions of climate and culture, grievances and complaints, perceptions of leadership and management practices, and the like. The information gathered will help determine if the organization's workplace is inclusive and viable to support diversity.

In the next chapter, we will explore the learning and growth perspective of the diversity scorecard. It will help the organization determine the level of effectiveness of its diverse workforce development and utilization systems.

REFERENCES

Anfuso, D. "3M Staffing Strategy Promotes Productivity and Pride." *Personnel Journal*, February 1995, 28–34.

Baytos, Lawrence M. *Designing and Implementing Successful Diversity Programs*. Englewood Cliffs, NJ: Prentice Hall, 1995.

Byrne, J.A. "Strategic Planning." *Business Week*, August 26, 1996, 46–52.

Dennison, D.R. "What IS the Difference Between Organizational Culture and Organizational Climate? A Native's Point of View on a Decade of Paradigm Wars." *Academy of Management Review*, July 1996, 619–654.

Egan, G. "Cultivate your Culture." *Management Today*, April 1994, 39–42.

Gordon, G., and N. DiTomaso. "Predicting Corporate Performance and Organizational Culture." *Journal of Management Studies*, November 1992, 783–798.

Harris, S.G., and K.W. Mossholder. "The Affective Implications of Perceived Congruence with Culture Dimensions during Organizational Transformation." *Journal of Management*, 1996, 527–548.

Hope, V., and J. Hendry. "Corporate Culture Change: Is It Relevant for the Organizations of the 1990s." *Human Resources Management Journal*, 1995, 61–73.

Hubbard, Edward E. *Measuring Diversity Results (MDR) Stat Pak 1: Diversity Scorecard Startup Metrics*. Petaluma, CA: Global Insights, 2000.

Jacobs, R. "Corporate Reputations: The Winners Chart a Course of Constant Renewal and Work to Sustain Cultures that Produce the Very Best Products and People." *Fortune*, March 6, 1995, 54–64.

Kotter, John P., and James L. Heskett. *Corporate Culture and Performance*. New York: Free Press, 1992.

McCartney, S. "Airline Industry's Top-Ranked Woman Keeps Southwest's Small-Fry Spirit Alive." *The Wall Street Journal*, November 30, 1996, B1, B11.

Sathe, Vijay. "Implications of Corporate Culture: A Manager's Guide to Action." *Organizational Dynamics*, Autumn 1983.

Schein, E.H. "Culture: The Missing Concept in Organization Studies." *Administrative Science Quarterly*, June 1996, 236.

Sheridan, James E. "Organizational Culture and Employee Retention." *Academy of Management Journal*, December 1992, 1036–1056.

Tully, S. "Northwest and KLM: The Alliance From Hell." *Fortune*, June 24, 1996, 64–72.

Zamanou, S., and S.R. Glaser. "Moving towards Participation and Involvement." *Group and Organization Management*, December 1994, 475–502.

CHAPTER 11

Learning and Growth Perspective

DEFINITION

The diversity learning and growth perspective reflects a statistical summary of the organization's ability to maintain and enhance the capability of its diverse intellectual assets. It includes priorities to create a climate that supports organizational change, innovation, and growth. It enables the organization to ensure its capacity for long-term renewal by effectively developing and utilizing its diverse workforce for improved performance, a prerequisite for survival in the long run. In this perspective the organization should consider not only what it must do to maintain and develop the know-how required for understanding and utilizing its diverse workforce, but also determining what's needed to build a long-term sustaining infrastructure to enhance its core competency base. By doing so, the organization will be in a much better strategic position to satisfy its employee and customer needs as well as to sustain the necessary efficiency and productivity of its processes, which create financial value.

Intense global competition requires that organizations continually improve their capabilities for delivering value to customers and shareholders. Organizational learning and growth come from three principal sources: people, systems, and organizational procedures. Scorecards typically reveal large gaps between the existing capabilities of people, systems, and procedures and what is required to achieve breakthrough performance. To close these gaps, businesses have to invest in reskilling employees, enhancing information technology and systems, and aligning organizational procedures and routines (Kaplan and Norton, 1996).

Because know-how, to an ever-growing degree, is a perishable commodity, it will become increasingly important to decide which core competencies (Hamel and Prahalad, 1994) the organization should cultivate as a basis for its future development. It requires that the organization identifies its strategic direction for the future and builds rapport with its diverse employee audience to maintain and increase retention. An innovative idea or core competency skill level does not have a race, color, creed, or specific ethnicity. It simply reflects someone with this level of competency or skill. Depending on the organization's ability to manage diversity and to create an environment where people can do their absolute personal best work, employees will either stay or leave. The degree to which the organization is willing to invest in all employees through its training, career planning, mentoring, and succession planning efforts to build core capabilities and the like will heavily influence the employee's perception of the workplace and the organization's ability to meet its competitive challenges.

In addition, as a consequence of these strategic choices, the organization will also have to determine how to obtain the know-how and skill, which it will still need in areas where it has decided not to have its core competence. This must be done to protect itself in areas of vulnerability and to create an early warning system if the need for capability in these areas become more acute. This forces the organization into an analysis of a "make" or "buy" decision. In essence addressing the question: "Do we want to grow our core competency talent or buy it?" Regardless of the answer, the organization's workplace climate, training and development systems, and its culture must be diversity-friendly because the marketplace will reflect the changing demographic diversity composition.

In arriving at an appropriate competence strategy, which specifies those areas in which the company will invest to develop its own competence from within and those in which it will resort to collaboration and contacts with outside parties, the following questions may prove helpful:

☐ What does the competence consist of?
☐ For what should it be used?
☐ How does it affect value for our employees?
☐ How does it affect value for our customers?
☐ How specialized is it?
☐ How does it change over time?
☐ How frequently is it used?
☐ How is it affected by the organization as a whole?
☐ How does our competitive marketplace affect it?

Another model, which has proved useful in developing competence strategies, is the competence matrix of Hamel and Prahalad (1994), shown in Table 11-1.

Table 11-1. Hamel and Prahalad's Competence Matrix

| | | Market | |
		Existing	New
Core Competence	New	What new core competencies will we need to build to protect and extend our franchise in current markets?	What new core competencies will we need to build to participate in the most exciting emerging markets of the future?
	Existing	What is the opportunity to improve our position in existing markets by better leveraging our existing competence from all of our diverse groups?	What new products or services could we create by imaginatively redeploying or recombining our current competence fully utilizing the diverse workgroup and other assets we possess?

Adapted from Hamel and Prahalad's competence matrix ("Establishing the Core Competence Agenda"). Hamel and Prahalad, 1994.

In addition to developing competence strategies as discussed previously, the organization should also describe its internal infrastructure for transmission of information and the process of decision making in general terms. In other words, it should describe the structure and the conditions that exist for developing a learning organization utilizing diverse workforce assets that are necessary for the unrelenting defense of its competitive market position (i.e., a structure conducive to developing and sustaining a high degree of workforce motivation and a proper focus on a common mission for success).

Some organizations decide to focus only on financial and operational measures and choose not to include learning and growth measures because they feel that "that stuff's going to happen anyway." The adverse long-term consequences of consistent failure to enhance employee, systems, and organizational capabilities will not show up in the short run, and when they do, some organizations and managers reason, it may be on somebody else's watch. Wrong! It can show up sooner than the organization thinks, and it is not going to just happen. There must be a concerted effort to ensure that it does. If the organization does not have a planned implementation for its learning and growth initiatives, it will never really have a balanced diversity scorecard or derive the benefits of a full scorecard system. The value-creation process in today's organization is overwhelmingly dominated by the influence of human capital. People, and their knowledge and means of sharing it, are what drives value in the new global economy. Describing the activities that drive this value is the purview of the organization's learning and growth perspective.

The measures of the learning and growth perspective are really the enablers of the other perspectives. Motivated employees with the right mix of skills and tools operating in an organizational climate designed for sustaining improvements are the key ingredients in driving process improvements, meeting customer expectations, and ultimately driving financial returns. Kaplan and Norton have noted that people often object to the placement of this perspective in scorecard diagrams. They ask: Doesn't placing it at the bottom minimize its importance? Quite the contrary, the scorecard architects say. It is at the bottom because it acts as the foundation for everything else above it. Scorecard designer Bob Kaplan describes the learning and growth perspective as the roots of a powerful tree, which are the sources of support and nourishment leading to the blossoms of financial returns (Nivens, 2002).

In case you are still not convinced of the importance of the soft measures, here are a couple of real-life examples that might influence your thinking on the subject:

> *The Service-Profit Chain at Sears.* Using econometric modeling techniques, Sears has quantified the linkage between employee satisfaction and financial performance. The company can now predict that for every 5 percent increase in employee satisfaction, it will see a corresponding 1.3 percent increase in customer loyalty three months into the future. This spike in loyalty drives a 0.5 percent increase in revenue another three months down the road. In 1997, Sears predicted and achieved an incremental $200 million in revenues based on a 4 percent improvement in employee satisfaction (Heskett et al., 1996).
>
> *Maister Makes a Point.* David Maister has chronicled the link between satisfied employees and financial returns in his book *Practice What You Preach* (2001). He was convinced that happy employees really do drive financial success and set about to find the actual proof of his suspicions. In 1999 he surveyed 5,500 employees of a large advertising and media conglomerate who were dispersed among 139 offices in 15 countries. His study found that a company could boost its financial performance by as much as 42 percent by raising employee satisfaction by 20 percent.

These stories illustrate the unequivocal link between employee performance and financial returns. Not only do the measures in the employee learning and growth perspective lead to improved financial results for the organization, but through these indicators we also pave the way for sustaining that success over the long term. As the business environment inevitably changes, the enablers of future success described in this perspective will allow your organization to maintain flexibility and adapt to changing conditions.

Several prerequisites must be met if members of your diverse workforce are to positively contribute to organizational strategy. First, they must possess certain capabilities the organization deems critical to success. Second, employees must have the ability to manipulate knowledge through the use of physical and nonphysical tools. Finally, all employees must be motivated and acting in alignment with overall firm goals. Let's look at these areas in more detail.

MEASURING CAPABILITIES

Peter Drucker has suggested that any business can be as good as any other business. The only distinction is how it develops its own people. Suggestions for developing your most precious resource include the following (Niven, 2002):

> *Use core competencies to measure skill development.* As mentioned earlier, the term *core competence* was coined by Gary Hamel and C.K. Prahalad in their immensely successful book *Competing For the Future* (1994). Over time, the phrase has evolved and now is described as "an attribute or behavior that individual managers and employees must demonstrate to succeed at their particular company" (Gendron, 1996). The first step in the core competence process is identifying the differentiating competencies you need to achieve your strategy. Experts agree that the best way of doing this is to involve as many people as possible from all levels of the organization. Focus groups and interviews can be used to assess company needs and competence gaps. If you have not gone through this competence inventory process, it could represent a good first-year metric for this aspect of your diversity scorecard. After all, you cannot evaluate your current staff against desired skills until you have catalogued those skills you deem as necessary to create a competitive advantage.

Use Personal Development Planning (PDP) to boost competence holders. Many organizations have introduced the idea of personal development planning (or sometimes referred to as Individual Development Plans or IDPs) to assist employees in generating goals. This is certainly an admirable effort; however, certain criteria must be stressed if PDP or IDPs are to prove beneficial to the employee or the organization. The principal issue is alignment to organizational strategic goals. Most personal goals in the plan should help the employee influence the achievement of the organization's strategy. Goals in the plan should also be measurable and include specific action steps.

Once you have identified the core competencies you need to be a leader in your industry and your employees have developed plans that signal their contribution to your goals, you are ready to begin measuring. Track the percentage of employees who meet their personal development plan goals. Don't make it an annual measure. To motivate action on this important task, ask employees for quarterly or even monthly progress updates. You can also measure your competency coverage ratio, which tracks the percentage of necessary skills you currently possess throughout your workforce. In other words, how many qualified employees do you have to meet your anticipated needs?

Encourage healthy lifestyles. Experts suggest that more than 50 percent of all mortality is related to lifestyle choices. Many organizations will include occupational health and safety measures in the learning and growth perspective, such as lost time accidents, workers' compensation claims, and injury frequency rates; however, enlightened organizations are moving beyond these lagging indicators and attempting to offer employees an environment that facilitates and encourages them to adopt better lifestyles. Organizations pursuing this "health promotion" philosophy are attempting to create a win-win environment in which employees take responsibility for their own well-being and employers reap the benefits of lower lifestyle-related costs. Simple and low-cost solutions such as lunchtime walking clubs, weight-control programs, and health fairs have enabled one Southern Ontario auto parts company to institute a health promotion program for more than 450 employees at a cost of only $30 per employee per year (Downey, 2001). You can measure your health promotion initiatives by tracking the number of employees who take advantage of the program or by gauging employee attitudes regarding lifestyle choices.

These measures may also be considered leading indicators of other popular culture/climate and learning and growth measures such as absenteeism, morale, and productivity per employee.

Measure diversity and other training initiatives. Virtually every organization will have at least one performance measure relating to diversity training initiatives. And why not? Through training the organization gets better skilled workers who are more versatile, while employees learn new skills and gain new ways of interacting with others and seeing their work and how it affects overall organizational success. The mistake most organizations make with diversity and other training metrics is that they simply look at the raw amount of training offered (e.g., number of training hours per employee). For diversity and other training to prove effective, it must be linked to organizational goals and objectives, and organizations should measure results of the training (i.e., the demonstration of new behaviors or skills, not just attendance). You should also encourage trained employees to share their new-found knowledge with their peers, affinity groups, and networks in the organization. Some experts refer to this as *third-person teaching* and suggest that it offers many benefits to both the student and the trainer. For example, knowing they will have to share what they are learning will motivate most people to pay greater attention and capture more of the information they are receiving.

Determine actual employee productivity. Investing in overall personal and diversity competency development and planning should yield results in the form of greater productivity, and many organizations will measure just that. The problem with this measure, at least in its traditional form, is that it divides the organization's revenue by the number of employees. It is fairly easy to manipulate this ratio by reducing the number of employees, outsourcing entire functions, or increasing revenue in possibly unprofitable segments. Similar to the financial metric of economic value added, you should attempt to determine the value added per employee by deducting externally purchased materials from your numerator. Utilizing productivity metrics pioneered by Jac Fitz-enz and used in the Hubbard *MDR Stat Pak Software Series* such as Human Capital Revenue Factor (HCRF), Human Economic Value Added (HEVA), Human Capital Cost Factor (HCCF), Human Capital Value Added (HCVA), and the like help address these issues to obtain a more accurate reflection of the productivity impact (Fitz-enz, 1995; Hubbard, 2000; 2003).

Capabilities are a must for success in the new economy, but to achieve your goals employees must have access to certain physical and intangible tools to get their jobs done. Some of these tools, and how their impact on results might be measured, include the following (Nivens, 2002):

> *The instruments of business.* Employees in this day and time must have access to at least the basic tools of business. Some employees do not have access to or do not have computers on their desks; in fact, some do not have voice mail on their phones. A diversity scorecard can be developed for them, but many benefits of initiatives such as real-time reporting of changing diverse markets, diverse customer needs, and so on and using decision-support systems to make informed choices would be very limited given this technology-deprived state. This may sound like an oversimplified performance measure to assess the level of technology, but it is important to ensure that employees have up-to-date and modern equipment if the organization hopes to compete in today's global, multicultural economy.

> *Access to information.* For those associates fortunate enough to have the necessary equipment, you need to make certain they can also retrieve the right information. What percentage of customer-facing staff have the ability to access detailed diverse customer information within 30 seconds of a customer interaction to utilize key differences in needs during their interaction? You should determine what information is critical to diverse workforce decision making and develop a performance measure that tracks the percentage of employees who have this information available to them.

Motivation and Alignment

All the training and sharing of information in the world will accomplish little if employees are not motivated to perform their best or aligned with organizational goals. To some extent, this was discussed in the section dealing with the workplace culture/climate perspective. Motivation and having a climate that supports diversity is even more essential if learning is to take place. Considerations when measuring motivation and alignment include the following:

> *Employee satisfaction.* Perhaps the most common employee learning and growth measure is the employee satisfaction rating. Most organizations attempt to take the pulse of their organizations

through annual surveys and use the findings to design better ways to do things. At least that's how it is supposed to work. Unfortunately, many employees believe the annual survey is a sham and waste of money, with the results gathering dust on a shelf and never acted upon. Calculating levels of satisfaction is a valuable metric. It is critical that the organization use the data appropriately by swiftly acknowledging areas requiring improvement and developing action steps to improve them. You should also consider using the many technological tools at your disposal to gauge the mood of your employees on a more frequent basis. Corporate intranets and e-mail systems can be used to gather feedback from employees semiannually or quarterly. Given the pace of change in today's environment, you need the most up-to-date information from the front line if you expect to react quickly.

Alignment. Your diversity scorecard should capture your strategy through the objectives and measures that make up your individual story. In addition, these objectives and measures must link to the organization's goals and objectives. In the early stages of balanced scorecard implementation, a good alignment measure was simply the number of scorecards produced within the organization. Once the performance management discipline became more mature, it became mandatory to refine the measure by analyzing individual scorecards and assessing their degree of alignment (i.e., the percentage of measures directly relating to your strategic goals) (Niven, 2002). Obviously, the target should be 100 percent. This is a great way to perform a diagnostic check on cascaded diversity scorecards.

COLLECTING DATA

Collecting data for the learning and growth index requires examining a variety of sources that will shed light on the organization's human asset development infrastructure and its ability to integrate a diverse group of intellectual assets for organizational performance. These data collection areas and sources can include some of the following:

- ☐ Career development policies and procedures
- ☐ Training and development systems including classroom, distance learning, e-learning, and the like
- ☐ Human Resource Planning (HRP) systems
- ☐ Business technology systems

☐ Technology policies and procedures
☐ Productivity enhancement systems
☐ Work life benefit policies and procedures
☐ Processes used to build morale

Let's examine a few of these sources in more detail. Career development policies and procedures are a good data collection source in the organization. Using them, it is important to check to see if the following questions regarding career development have been addressed:

☐ Have criteria been established for managing people in support of a diverse workforce?
☐ Have current position descriptions for mid- and senior-level managers been evaluated to see if the descriptions reflect what is needed to effectively manage people and support a diverse workforce?
☐ Does the organization take a more proactive approach to placing women, minorities, and people with disabilities in positions that will break stereotypical behavior?
☐ Does the organization encourage and reward those who take rotational/exchange assignments? Do they even exist?
☐ Are managers and supervisors trained in how to coach employees to support career development?
☐ Has the organization seriously considered and evaluated the benefits of shadowing assignments for women, minorities, and people with disabilities?
☐ Does the organization determine and publicize the number and percentage of women and minority candidates considered and chosen for senior-level vacancies and first-line managerial positions on a yearly basis.
☐ Does the organization reward or give special recognition to employees whose actions or recommendations are instrumental in removing or reducing career development barriers for people with disabilities?

These are just a few of the questions that must be answered to collect data in the career development scorecard measurement area.

Your first step in evaluating diversity training is to determine your major evaluation questions. The second step is to use the relevant diversity measurement information and strategies to plan and conduct the appropriate level of training evaluation. The decision table in Table 11-2 is helpful in identifying some of the major questions and methods that

Table 11-2. Major Questions and Evaluation Techniques

Major Questions	Evaluation Technique
How satisfied are the participants with the course?	Level 1: Reaction evaluation
Do the participants believe they learned the values and skills the course was intended to teach?	Level 2: Learning evaluation. Use the learning self-assessment evaluation tool.
Can the participants demonstrate the values, knowledge, and skills that are taught in the course?	Level 2: Learning evaluation. Use the short-answer evaluation tool.
Do the participants report that they are using their diversity values, knowledge, and skills on the job?	Level 3: Behavior evaluation. Use the post-training survey for course participants.
Do the managers of the participants have the impression that the participants are using their diversity values, knowledge, and skills on the job?	Level 3: Behavior evaluation. Use the post-training survey for managers of participants. For example, the manager fills out a survey based on general impressions of the participant.
Do the managers actually observe and report that participants are using their diversity values, knowledge, and skills on the job?	Level 3: Behavior evaluation. Use the diversity behavior checklist. For example, the manager keeps a record of observations for one month.
Do managers believe that the organization is benefiting from diversity training?	Level 4: Results evaluation. Use the organizational results questionnaire tool.
Does the organization experience specific benefits (financial and nonfinancial) as a result of the diversity training program?	Level 5: Return-on-investment evaluation. Use the diversity cost and benefit formulas and calculations.

Source: *Measuring Diversity Results, 1997.*

can be addressed to get you started with this data collection process for diversity training.

To get a better sense of the data collection involved, let's examine some of the issues around Level 1 training evaluation. The purpose of Level 1 evaluation of participants' reactions is to find out how the learners feel about their newly learned awareness and skills from training. It provides a measure of satisfaction that is useful for determining whether learners have a positive attitude toward the course and how to improve it if they do not.

The intent of this initial level of evaluation is to measure participant's attitudes and feelings toward the following:

- ☐ Interest and usefulness of the content
- ☐ Effectiveness of the instructor
- ☐ Quality of the materials
- ☐ Their planned actions

This level of evaluation does not tell how much participants learned (the learning level does this); however, this level is important because it provides continuous feedback for quality improvement. It also provides a forum for participants to air their suggestions, and it helps produce a course that is satisfying and effective (Hubbard, 1997).

Level 1 evaluation is used for almost every training event. A Level 1 questionnaire can be given to the participants at several different times:

- ☐ *End of course.* Having participants fill out the Level 1 measure at the end of the training session while they are still in the classroom is the most common approach.
- ☐ *During the course.* It can also be given at the end of each day during a multiple-day program. This gives the instructor and course manager valuable information that can be used to confirm that the course is on the right track or to determine what changes to make the next day. Daily evaluations are useful if you have more than one instructor or speaker. They allow the participants to respond while their reactions are still fresh.
- ☐ *Shortly after the course.* If it is not feasible to do a Level 1 evaluation while participants are still in the classroom, they can do it within a short time after the course and return it by mail or e-mail. This method is less desirable, however, because of uncontrollable factors that can influence responses, and some participants usually do not return questionnaires.

Like all data collection processes, it is important to have a well-crafted strategy that identifies what objectives your data collection should achieve.

Typical Critical Success Factor Areas

A sample set of critical success factor areas in the learning and growth perspective might include outcome areas such as the following:

- ☐ Career development
- ☐ Level diversity competency
- ☐ Diversity training
- ☐ Competency coverage
- ☐ Affinity group performance
- ☐ Productivity
- ☐ Morale
- ☐ Learning gain
- ☐ Technology access
- ☐ Technology utilization
- ☐ Innovation

This is just a brief list of the critical success factor areas that can be included in the learning and growth perspective of the diversity scorecard. Each critical success factor area reflects a wide range of analysis tracks that can be undertaken to build core and diversity management capabilities to effectively develop and utilize the organization's intellectual assets. Table 11-3 presents sample measures to drive the index.

Table 11-3. Potential Learning and Growth Measures

☐ Number and percentage of diversity-competent employees	☐ Training investment per customer by demographic group
☐ Percentage of employees with advanced degrees by demographic group	☐ Number of cross-trained employees by demographic group
☐ Employee suggestions	☐ Participation in stock ownership plans
☐ Value per employee	☐ Motivation index
☐ Empowerment index	☐ Personal goal achievement
☐ Health promotion	☐ Number of employees with computers
☐ Timely completion of performance appraisals by demographic group	☐ Competency coverage ratio
☐ Knowledge management	☐ Cross-functional assignments
☐ Ethic violations	☐ Innovation index

Source: Edward E. Hubbard, *Measuring Diversity Stat Pak Software Series*. Petaluma, CA: Global Insights, 2000.

ANALYZING DATA

Analyzing data in the learning and growth perspective enables the organization to look at itself through the eyes of its own employees and to determine what is needed to build core competency and capacity for effectively managing the diversity of its workforce. This entails assessing the organization's systems for career development, cross-training, sharing knowledge, fostering innovation, increasing information access, and developing new skills and capabilities. By doing this, the organization gains insights and a deeper understanding to see what is working and what learning and growth systems need changing.

In the diversity training and development arena, evaluation of this area can provide several levels of analysis. For example, when analyzing diversity training at Level 1, there are at least two approaches diversity professionals can use: one for rating scales and one for open-ended questions.

> *Rating scales.* For each question, you can add the individual responses and divide by the total number of responses to find the average. This is the most common and useful statistic.

$$\text{Average} = \frac{\text{\# individual responses}}{\text{total responses}}$$

> If you want more detail, you can add the total number of each type of response (how many people answered "1"; how many answered "2", etc.). This is called a *frequency distribution,* and it gives you a picture of how similar or different people's attitudes are. Other statistics can be computed as well, and they are described in other technical books and materials on evaluation. The two described here are sufficient for most purposes. The scores from the rating scale provide a quantitative measure that is easy to use for making comparisons between individuals or courses. Each item has a scale ranging from 1 for Poor to 5 for Excellent. There are also short-answer questions that ask about major strengths, suggestions for improvement, and general comments.

> The advantages of this type of analysis tool is that it can be administered quickly; the process of analyzing participant responses can be automated by using scanning equipment and statistical software packages; and you can compare the results of one course to another. The disadvantage is that it does not give you very

much information about the specifics of the course content, goals, instructor, or materials.

Open-ended questions. To analyze the results, you will summarize the answers that participants have given. If it is a small class and the answers are short, you can simply list them in your summary of class activity. When the class is large or the answers are long, the procedure is to read them and sort them into groups of similar comments or themes. For each group of similar comments, write a comment or paragraph that captures the key points. You can then list a few of the actual comments or excerpts as examples.

Participant Reactions: Rating Scale
Reactions to Diversity Training

Instructions: For each, circle the number that represents your opinion.

Pre-course Preparation
1. My level of understanding of the objectives and job relevance of this course before attending it
1-Poor　　2-Fair　　3-Good　　4-Very Good　　5-Excellent

Overall Course
2. Level of difficulty of the course
1-Poor　　2-Fair　　3-Good　　4-Very Good　　5-Excellent

3. The degree to which the course met my expectations
1-Poor　　2-Fair　　3-Good　　4-Very Good　　5-Excellent

Expectation for Job Transfer
1. Relevancy of the course to my job
1-Poor　　2-Fair　　3-Good　　4-Very Good　　5-Excellent

Materials/Media
1. The degree to which materials and media were consistent with course objectives
1-Poor　　2-Fair　　3-Good　　4-Very Good　　5-Excellent

Instructor Effectiveness
1. InstructorÕs ability to deal with conßict in a productive manner
1-Poor　　2-Fair　　3-Good　　4-Very Good　　5-Excellent

2. InstructorÕs ability to deal with emotional issues
1-Poor　　2-Fair　　3-Good　　4-Very Good　　5-Excellent

Short Answer
1. The most beneficial part of the course was:

2. The least beneficial part of the course was:

Figure 11-1. Participants' reactions rating scale.

The second Level 1 tool contains items that ask about overall course and materials, instructor effectiveness, potential applications after training, and suggestions for improvement. Most of the items are open-ended, but a few have rating scales.

Variations. You can modify both of these tools by changing the contents to include the topics of most interest to you and to fit the time allocated for this evaluation. You can also modify the format of the tools by changing open-ended questions to rating scales and vice versa. It all depends on the amount and type of information you want to receive (Hubbard, 1997). Figures 11-1 and 11-2 illustrate examples of a rating scale and open-ended measurement tool.

Participant Reactions: Open-Ended Course Evaluation

Instructions: For those question items that use a rating scale, circle the number that best represents your opinion. For all other question items, write your response in the space provided.

Overall Course and Materials
1. Overall, this workshop was:
1-Poor   2-Fair   3-Good   4-Very Good   5-Excellent

2. What aspects of the training, if any, were distracting or inhibited your learning?

_____

3. What did the training provide that you did not anticipate?

_____

Instructor Effectiveness
1. Overall, the instructor was:
1-Poor   2-Fair   3-Good   4-Very Good   5-Excellent

Application After Training
1. What aspects of this workshop were most relevant to your work?

_____

2. How will you use what you have learned when you return to the job?

_____

Figure 11-2. Participants' reactions open-ended measurement tool.

REPORTING DATA

There are a wide variety of ways to display and report your learning and growth data. This data can be presented in tables, graphs, narratives, pictograms, and so on. For example, when you look at a completed analysis for a training initiative, you will likely see a report consisting of some general text about the training session, figures such as tables, bar graphs, and pie charts, and within those figures, some statistics. Figures 11-2, 11-3, and 11-4 present examples of key learning and growth measures that can be reported to organizational stakeholders.

Reporting the results of the learning and growth perspective is essential to building a diverse workforce that has the core capability and competency to meet the requirements of a global marketplace. If any organization desires to become an employer of choice, a primary characteristic and driver of its attraction in the marketplace will be the state and

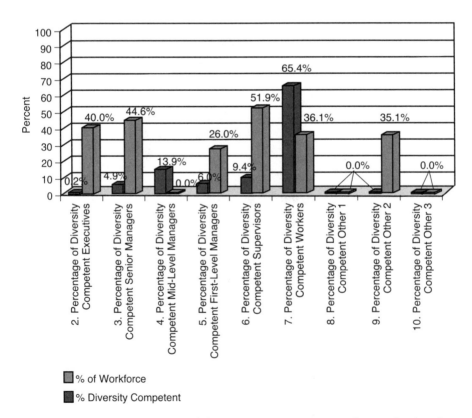

Figure 11-3. Percentage of diversity competent employees by level.

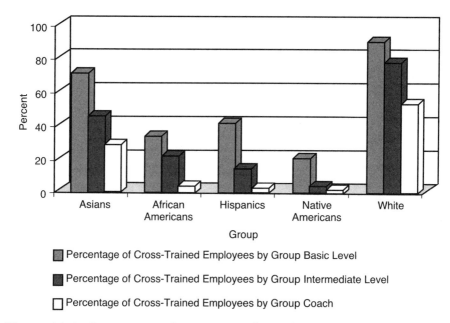

Figure 11-4. Percentage of cross-trained employees by group. (Source: Edward E. Hubbard Diversity Scorecard Stat Pak–Diversity Measurement "Calculate and Go" Software Series. Petaluma, CA: Global Insights Publishing, 2002.)

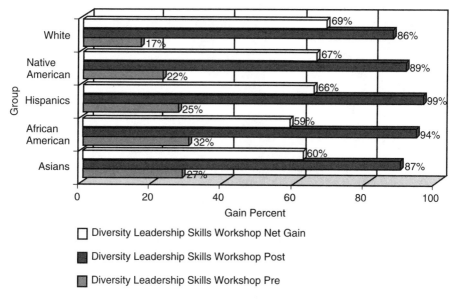

Figure 11-5. Diversity leadership skills results by net learning gain. (Source: Edward E. Hubbard Diversity Scorecard Stat Pak–Diversity Measurement "Calculate and Go" Software Series. Petaluma, CA: Global Insights Publishing, 2002.)

effectiveness of its learning and growth infrastructure to meet workforce and business needs.

FINAL THOUGHTS

Learning and growth are critical elements for organizational renewal and progress. If an organization seeks to build an effective, high-performing diverse workforce, then employee-centered systems, processes, and procedures must be in place to build, maintain, and/or enhance organizational learning. This suggests a well-crafted set of diversity performance objectives and clear goals. Performance objectives are concise statements that describe the specific things you must perform well if you are to successfully implement your organizational and diversity strategy.

If you hope to achieve substantial gains for customers and shareholders and improve internal processes, it requires keen attention to the processes that generate improved capability. Measures in the employee learning and growth perspective are really the enablers of other perspectives. These indicators ensure that you have employees who possess the right skills, can access the appropriate information, and are motivated and aligned with organizational goals. Effective employee learning and growth measures help sustain your ability to grow and improve as the business environment inevitably changes.

REFERENCES

Downey, Angela M. "Promoting Health on the Job." *CMA Management,* May 2001, 24.

Gendron, Marie. "Competencies and What They Mean to You." *Harvard Management Update,* September 1996.

Hamel, G., and C. K. Prahalad. *Competing for the Future.* Boston: Harvard Business School Press, 1994.

Heskett, James L., Thomas O. Jones, Gary W. Loveman, Earl W. Sasser, Jr., and Leonard A. Schlesinger. "Putting the Service-Profit Chain to Work." *Harvard Business Review,* March/April 1996, 164–174.

Hubbard, Edward E. *Measuring Diversity Stat Pak Software Series.* Petaluma, CA: Global Insights, 2000.

Kaplan, Robert S., and David P. Norton. *The Balanced Scorecard.* Boston: Harvard Business School Press, 1996.

Maister, David. *Practice What You Preach: What Managers Must Do to Create a High Achievement Culture*. New York: Free Press, 2001.

Nivens, Paul R. *Balanced Scorecard*. New York: John Wiley & Sons, 2002.

FURTHER READING

Fitz-enz, Jac. *How to Measure Human Resources Management*, 2nd ed. New York: McGraw-Hill, 1995.

Hubbard, Edward E. *The Diversity Scorecard Fieldbook*. Petaluma, CA: Global Insights, 2003.

Hubbard, Edward E. *The Manager's Pocket Guide to Diversity Management*. Amherst, MA: HRD Press, 2003.

Hubbard, Edward E. *A Casebook in Diversity Measurement and Diversity Management*. Petaluma, CA: Global Insights, 2003.

CHAPTER 12

Diverse Customer/Community Partnership Perspective

DEFINITION

The diverse customer/community partnership perspective reflects a statistical summary of the organization's ability to connect with and leverage emerging demographic changes in the global marketplace and its ability to play a significant role in supporting its local and the broader world community. This perspective often includes an analysis of the organization's relationship with Asians, African Americans, Hispanics, Native Americans, women, people with disabilities, gays and lesbians, and many other groups in terms of products and services, responsiveness, specialized needs, and the like. In addition, it includes an analysis of procurement and contracting behavior, philanthropy level by community, and so on. This information is typically tracked to determine if the organization is in tune and in touch with the changing economics of its marketplace, aware of the needs of its community, and if it has access to the rich database of diverse resources that are available.

This perspective describes the ways in which value is to be created for diverse customers, how diverse customer demand for this value is to be satisfied, and why emerging-market customers will be willing to pay for it. It also describes how the organization addresses the needs of the communities it serves. It answers the question: "Is the organization a good corporate citizen?" As a result, this perspective should be a major driver of the organization's internal processes and development efforts.

Much of the effort is directed at determining how to increase and ensure diverse customer loyalty. To understand what must be done, we must become thoroughly acquainted with every aspect of ethnic markets and the purchasing process or its customers. We have to develop an exact picture of what the product/service means to them. If our customer is an industrial or institutional customer (e.g., where you sell to other institutions and not directly to a consumer), we should ask whether our product or service is an essential element of their process of creating added value for their share of the ethnic customer market. How important is price to these customers compared to other values, such as quality, functionality, delivery time, image, relationships, and so on. Not until we have familiarized ourselves with these details can we decide on our basic strategies in relation to ethnic customers and markets and then go on to the other perspectives. It is also important that these analyses rely as much as possible on what ethnic customers in fact appreciate and not, as is so often the case, on the conventional wisdom at our own organization (Niven, 2002).

Any organization that would like to expand into ethnic marketing should think about entering this new market in the same way it would think about entering a new market abroad. You begin by asking three strategic questions:

1. What are the relevant market segments (size and defining attributes)?
2. What is your unique value proposition to these segments? How well do your products fit the needs of the target consumers?
3. What are the optimal channels to fulfill the requirements of the target segments?

Suppose you decided to sell your products in Vietnam. How should you undertake your marketing efforts? You would not simply go there with your products, place advertisements in Vietnamese electronic media and magazines, and expect to succeed. You would begin by asking the three key strategic questions.

Yet many American businesses approach ethnic markets *without* asking these same strategic questions. These businesses proceed by spending money and time placing ads. They view ethnic markets as only a *downstream tactical initiative*. Over and over again, mid-level marketing and brand managers are charged with making decisions about the ethnic markets, although they lack clear knowledge on how to approach them. These managers have defaulted to hiring ethnic advertising agencies and placing ads in what the agencies have defined as culturally relevant media. Creative content in the ad is typically an African-, Asian-, or

Hispanic-American face. In most instances, these may be the same ads used in the mainstream media. And they think the job is done.

This approach reflects the prevalent attitude that ethnic marketing is really an afterthought, something that comes after your mainstream marketing efforts. The result? Nonstrategic, uncoordinated efforts that get very little incremental revenues or fail to build lasting diverse customer loyalty.

Let's reconsider how you would go into Vietnam and try to achieve market success there. (The same questions might be asked about China, Eastern Europe, or any emerging market.) If you followed the current practice—hiring an ethnic-oriented agency and placing some ads—you would sell some product because there is always latent demand in any market for products that meet the needs of consumers. But are these sales the true potential of the product? Would these practices get the sales and diversity return-on-investment (DROI) you should expect from growing markets? To achieve success, you must find answers to the questions mentioned earlier:

1. *What are the relevant market segments (size and defining attributes)?* Remember, not every Vietnamese person will buy your product. It's more likely that a target segment, perhaps two million Vietnamese, will potentially buy what you have to sell. They are your relevant market segment. Taking things further, you can divide the potential two million target consumers. You may determine that within that group there is a segment that will buy your premium product and another segment that will buy your best-value product.

2. *What is your unique value proposition to these segments?* How well do your products fit the needs of the target consumers? What products will these consumers want? Keep in mind that the desired products may be somewhat different from those you have in your current portfolio. Back to our example, in Vietnam, you might identify two unique customer segments to target: upscale consumers and more general, value-oriented consumers. You would not view the Vietnamese population as monolithic. Yet here in America, some corporations market to African, Asian, or Hispanic Americans through a monolithic lens. Suppose you are a manufacturer of fine dinnerware entering the Vietnamese marketplace. There may exist a consumer segment, which will desire high-end, premium dinnerware. You might look at your product portfolio and say, "What product do I have in my portfolio that is high-end fine china?"

Then you might say, "Okay, I have some elegant gold-encrusted patterns that might meet the needs of the consumer." Or you might do even better and say, "The patterns that will sell best must be unique and culturally relevant to that population. I can't position something in my existing lineup as what they want." So you can take the product and make incremental changes so that it is relevant to the high-end Vietnamese customer segment. This is all about ensuring optimum fit between your products and the target customer.

3. *What are the optimal channels to fulfill the requirements of the target segments?* In order to sell product, you must make it available where the target customer will most likely seek it. In our example, high-end Vietnamese consumers will seek the product in the high-end channels (e.g., fine department stores). Similarly, those seeking your best-value product would look for it at the mass-market retailers. This same principle applies to ethnic markets. The key for corporations is understanding that multicultural marketing is not simply taking existing products and advertising them to your target consumers through appropriate media; you must determine the appropriate products and place them in the relevant channels and markets.

In the past, companies could concentrate on their internal capabilities, emphasizing product performance and technology innovation. But companies that did not understand their customers' needs eventually found that competitors could make inroads by offering products or services that were better aligned to their customers' preferences. In many cases, customers in ethnic markets were all but ignored. Many were forced to select their products from the market-at-large. Companies had little regard for adjusting their product and/or service offerings to meet the specific needs of ethnic consumers; however, as more organizations begin to recognize the tremendous financial potential of these markets and the impact of changing demographics in general, ethnic markets are becoming a major force for enhancing revenue and other objectives. Thus, companies are now shifting their focus externally, to customers. Mission and vision statements routinely declare their goal to be "number one in delivering value to our customers" and to become "the number one supplier to our customers." Apart from the general impossibility of all companies being the number-one supplier to their customers, we cannot quarrel with inspirational statements that focus all employees on satisfying customer needs. Clearly, if business units are to achieve long-run superior financial performance, they must create and deliver products and services that are valued by customers.

Beyond aspiring to satisfying and delighting customers, business unit managers must, in the customer perspective, translate their mission and strategy statements into specific market- and customer-based objectives. Companies that try to be everything to everybody usually end up being nothing to anyone. Businesses must identify the market segments in their existing and potential customer populations and then select the segments in which they choose to compete. Identifying the value propositions that will be delivered to targeted segments becomes the key to developing objectives and measures for the customer perspective. Thus, the customer perspective of the scorecard translates an organization's mission and strategy into specific objectives about targeted customers and market segments that can be communicated throughout the organization (Kaplan and Norton, 1996).

According to *Women and Diversity WOW Facts 2000*, published by Edie Fraser's Diversity Best Practices Organization and the Business Women's Network, emerging ethnic markets will be a major factor for an organization's future (Business Women's Network, 2002). They cite the following:

☐ The total collective buying power of Hispanic Americans, Asian Americans, African Americans, American Indians, gays and lesbians, and people with disabilities totaled $2.789 trillion in 2001. That is a 64.7 percent faster rate than the overall U.S. buying power. *(Selig Center for Economic Growth at the University of Georgia, Santiago and Valdes Solutions)*

☐ Of the more than 281 million total population of the United States, ethnic segments represent about 30 percent. Hispanics now account for 12.5 percent, Asian Americans for 3.6 percent, African Americans for 12.3 percent, American Indians for 0.7 percent, gays and lesbians for 10 percent, and people with disabilities for 10 to 35 percent. *(Santiago and Valdes Solutions, U.S. Small Business Administration and Golden Hills Organization, Greenfield Research, and Kinsey Report)*

☐ 2000 Census data confirms that multicultural segments are the fastest growing in the population. *(U.S. Census data)*

Growth of Minority Purchases (Between 1990 and 2001)

☐ Hispanic buying power has increased 118 percent.
☐ Asian-American buying power has increased 124.80 percent.

☐ African-American buying power has increased 85 percent.
☐ American Indian buying power has increased 81 percent.

(Selig Center for Economic Growth at the University of Georgia)

U.S. Current Buying Power: Diversity Constituents

☐ Hispanic Americans $550 billion
☐ Asian Americans $253.8 billion
☐ African Americans $500 billion
☐ Native Americans $34.8 billion
☐ Gay and lesbian $450 billion
☐ People with disabilities $1 trillion

(Santiago and Valdes Solutions, U.S. Pan Asian American Chamber of Commerce Datamonite, Selig Center for Economic Growth at the University of Georgia, Diversityinc.com, National Organization on Disability, and EmployAbility)

Paying attention to changes in ethnic market buying power is essential today and for the future, especially for organizations that interact with customers on a retail and services basis. These organizations must develop a level of customer intimacy and relationship that immerses them firmly in the customer's needs and cultural sensitivities that improves their ability to be successful in each market segment.

SUPPLIER DIVERSITY

No matter what type of business you are in, chances are you have heard a lot about improving your supply-chain practices. This rapidly growing field has gone from the back room of most organizations to the executive suite, where leaders use the latest techniques to gain cost, quality, and service advantages over their competition. While ultra-efficient supply-chain processes are the bread and butter of the operationally excellent company, every business organization can benefit greatly from measuring and improving this vital process.

According to *Women and Diversity WOW Facts 2002*, organizations now have access to a wider range of minority suppliers to help improve their service delivery to ethnic as well as other mainstream customers. They cite the following:

☐ Minority-owned businesses are growing four times faster than the national average for small businesses. They employ 4.5 million workers and generate $591 billion in annual revenues. *(U.S. Census Bureau)*

☐ Minorities owned 15 percent of all private U.S. firms in 2002. *(USA Today)*

☐ According to the 2000 Census, Latinos owned 1.4 million businesses, Asian Americans owned 900,000, African Americans owned 880,000, and Native Americans owned 200,000 businesses *(U.S. Census Bureau)*

☐ The number of non-minority-owned businesses are increasing at 7 percent per year, whereas minority-owned businesses are increasing at the following rates:

> Hispanic-owned firms increased 12.8 percent, with a sales growth of 24.11 percent per year.
>
> African-American firms increased 7.9 percent, with a sales growth of 10.25 percent per year.
>
> Asian-American-owned firms increased 10 percent, with a sales growth of 23.98 percent per year.
>
> Native-American-owned firms increased 37 percent, with a sales growth of 55 percent per year.

(Minority Business Development Agency, U.S. Department of Commerce)

Despite the burgeoning growth, minority business owners are still underrepresented. Minority firms make up 12 percent of our nation's businesses.

☐ African Americans: 13 percent of population, 3.6 percent of firms
☐ Latinos: 13 percent of population, 5 percent of firms
☐ Asian Americans: 4 percent of population, 3.5 percent of firms
☐ Native Americans: 0.02 percent of population, 0.9 percent of firms
☐ Women: 50 percent of population, 33 percent of firms

(U.S. Census data 2000; Minority Business Development Agency and Milken Institute)

☐ Minority-owned businesses have $1.3 trillion in purchasing power, 20 percent of all U.S. disposable income. This is expected to increase three to four times to $4.5 to $6 trillion in the next 50 years, when it will represent 32 to 45 percent of all disposable income.

(U.S. Department of Commerce)

A *supply chain* may be defined as "a set of three or more organizations directly linked by one or more of the upstream and downstream flows of products, services, finances, and information from a source to a customer" (Mentzer et al., 1999). Many people think of a supply chain as comprising three main processes: (1) sourcing and procurement, (2) order fulfillment, and (3) planning, forecasting, and scheduling. In industry after industry, supplier diversity management practices are becoming the key basis of competition, and little wonder since the stakes are significant.

Some organizations are already enhancing their supply-chain impact through the use of diverse suppliers. For example, the Commercial Airplanes Group of Aerospace leader Boeing is using their balanced scorecard to support a unique program designed to increase procurement of goods and services from minority- and women-owned businesses. Under the business direction perspective of the scorecard are two items. The first measures the percentage of subcontracting dollars to small businesses, small minority-owned businesses, and small women-owned businesses. The second tracks growth in the number of small and minority-owned and women-owned small business suppliers. Each line item receives a color corresponding to performance. Green means the procurement director is meeting the plan, yellow indicates caution, and red signals a plan not being achieved. If the measure score is either yellow or red, the procurement director meets with Boeing management to discuss what happened and how they can move the needle back to green performance (Kooker, 2001).

Boeing awards about $15 billion in annual contracts to more than 3,000 suppliers. In 2001, their goal in the Commercial Airplane Group is to spend about 2 percent with minority-owned suppliers, 2 percent with women-owned suppliers, and 20 percent with small businesses. Before the launch of this initiative, which supporters call cutting edge, there was no common set of performance metrics procurement directors could use to track their progress (Kooker, 2001).

Unfortunately, performance measurement in the supply-chain field has not kept pace with today's world of diverse, interdependent business relationships. In fact, many organizations focus on the optimization of particular supply-chain functions, often to the detriment of the overall process. The use of diverse suppliers must become a critical element in the upstream and downstream flow of products, services, finances, and information.

COLLECTING DATA

Collecting data for the diverse customer/community partnership index requires examining a variety of sources that will shed light on the organization's ability to meet the diverse needs of its customers, use a variety of sources of supply to create the best solution, and enhance its ability to operate as a good corporate citizen. The data collection strategies chosen should be based on an analysis of key customer areas as mentioned previously. In general, diverse customer/community partnership data collection will focus on the following:

- ☐ The level of ethnic group market share
- ☐ The degree of customer loyalty, measured for instance by frequency of new purchases by group
- ☐ Inflow of new customers
- ☐ Diverse customer satisfaction with the organization's product/service
- ☐ Profitability by diverse customer group
- ☐ The level of philanthropy
- ☐ The level of organizational interaction with the community
- ☐ Brand recognition and image

It is also important to learn at an early stage about any changes in customer preferences and behavior. One method, among others, would be by timely interviews to investigate possible changes in underlying customer values suggested by a diverse customer-satisfaction index. Furthermore, the organization should watch for any changes in quality, delivery time, delivery capability, frequency of returns, and so on. Preferably it should react before suffering a significant loss of ethnic customer loyalty and thus any major financial damage; in other words, it should be alert to minor changes and tendencies and capable of responding promptly. Moreover, the company should not become overly attached to its existing customers and products. It may have the potential, including employee competence, to attract new diverse market customers and offer new products.

Typical Critical Success Factor Areas

A sample set of critical success factor areas in the diverse customer/community partnership perspective might include outcome areas such as the following:

- ☐ Ethnic group market share
- ☐ Customer loyalty

☐ New customers
☐ Diverse customer satisfaction
☐ Profitability
☐ Philanthropy
☐ Community interaction
☐ Corporate citizenship
☐ Brand recognition
☐ Brand image
☐ Customer intimacy

This is just a brief list of the critical success factor areas that can be included in the diverse customer/community partnership perspective of the diversity scorecard. Each critical success factor area reflects a wide range of analysis tracks that can be undertaken to build core capabilities to meet customer intimacy needs to build effective relationships.

By providing an unparalleled mixture of superior services that offer a total solution for emerging markets, the customer-intimate organization is able to move beyond simply providing a product or service to cultivating a lasting relationship with its diverse clientele. Access to key diverse customer information is a driving force in this endeavor. The more information the customer-intimate firm has about its diverse customer base, the better able it is to personalize, anticipate, and even predict customer patterns. A strong information foundation paves the way for this to occur. The information must provide users with a total view of the customer, be integrated from all sources, be meaningful and actionable, and be user friendly.

Organizations offering total solutions to their diverse clients through unmatched knowledge must focus on a holistic view of the processes involved, such as marketing, selling, delivery, and service. Every customer "touch point" should have supporting diversity performance measures that complement the entire process. For example, focusing only on diverse customer marketing without a counterbalancing measure of post-sale service may lead to more customers, but a lack of attention to service could also lead to more frustrated customers and increased defections. Armed with a base of diverse customer information to work from, it is now possible for the customer-intimate organization to measure critical supporting activities, such as its ability to develop total solutions for diverse markets and offering strategic advice to create change.

Sample Measures to Drive the Index

Most organizations have little difficulty in generating a multitude of customer measures. They usually focus on a combination of the following metrics in their diverse customer perspective: market share, customer profitability, acquisition, retention, loyalty, and that old standby, customer satisfaction. Although satisfaction may be the most popular metric suggested for this perspective, it has come under criticism by many and should be carefully defined and crafted before making an appearance on your diversity scorecard.

Some people argue that satisfaction metrics were born in an era of poor quality when so many customers were dissatisfied that virtually any improvement in quality meant a boost to the bottom line. But as quality has improved, the link between satisfaction and the bottom line has become less clear (Hochman, 1999).

A better proxy in today's environment may be the measurement of customer value, the market's evaluation of all the costs and benefits of using a particular product as compared to its alternatives. This is referred to as *pulse calls,* or measuring the pulse of customers. Ford-owned Kwikfit exemplifies this approach—their call center agents, unprompted, call thousands of customers every night and say, "You had your car serviced with us today. Do you have a minute to tell me how the experience was for you? Is there anything we could have done better?" (Dourado, 2001).

For diverse customers, the issue went beyond getting quality. In some cases, just getting any product or service that addressed their needs would have been a good start. Customers in ethnic markets often have to deal with poor or no products and services that are uniquely designed for their marketplace; however, this is changing, even to the point where adhesive bandages are now designed to match all types of skin colors!

Despite the drawbacks, customer satisfaction is still an important and valuable component of any customer perspective. Organizations need to know whether the value proposition they have worked so hard to perfect and measure with leading indicators is actually leading to happier customers who will return and do business with them once again. The key is tightly defining your satisfaction metric so that anyone evaluating your score can quickly identify its determinants and make appropriate decisions based on the results presented. Embassy Suites Hotels, the first all-suite upscale brand to enter the industry, carefully tracks customer satisfaction at each of its more than 150 hotels. Each location is judged on a guest satisfaction rating system in the form of surveys sent to customers from an outside survey company. Randomly selected past guests are asked to rate various aspects of their experience, including reservations, checkout, room service, quality of food, and overall service. These scores are an important component of the company's scorecard, and locations achieving great success on satisfaction scores are publicly acknowledged.

Measures for Customer Intimacy

Customer-intimate organizations recognize that their clients have needs beyond which their product alone can satisfy. They offer their customers a total solution that encompasses a unique range of superior services so that customers get the greatest benefit from the products offered. Attributes of customer-intimate organizations and the measures that may be used to track success include the following:

> *Diverse customer knowledge.* To succeed, every customer-intimate organization requires a deep and detailed knowledge of its customers, cultural norms, and their buying habits. To gauge staff knowledge, they may measure training hours on multiethnic products. Sharing of knowledge is critical to the customer-intimate firm, and this metric also ensures that staff has the latest information available.
>
> *Solutions offered.* Customer-intimate firms also realize that customers are not turning to them for low cost or the latest product—it's the unmatched total solution they offer. To measure this attribute, the customer-intimate firm will measure total number of solutions offered per client.
>
> *Penetration.* At the height of IBM's success, customer intimacy assured their good fortune. The critical objective IBM legend Thomas Watson put forth to his staff was customer penetration or share of targeted customer spending. The customer-intimate organization aims to provide complete solutions for its entire customer base and needs to ensure that these efforts are achieving success by deep penetration of accounts.
>
> *Customer data.* To offer the solutions only they can, these organizations also require abundant and rich data on their diverse customers. Percentage of employees with access to diverse customer information may be measured to track this key differentiator of success.
>
> *Culture of driving client success.* Employees of customer-intimate organizations feel they have succeeded when the customer has attained success; this is deeply rooted in their culture. An award

from a cherished client as proof of their contribution is the greatest prize a customer-intimate company can receive. The number of diverse customer awards received helps track this goal.

Relationships for the long term. Customer-intimate organizations do not take a short view of any client relationships. Their goal is to build long-lasting unions during which they can increase their share of the client's business by providing unparalleled levels of knowledge and solutions. The relationship does not end when the sale is made, but is in fact just beginning. Some organizations even have personnel located at the client's site. The number of staff at client locations could be a measure of the deep relationship these organizations maintain with their clients.

If you choose a customer-intimate strategy, the focus in your diverse customer/community partnership perspective will be on measures gauging your level of service to diverse customers and the relationship you are attempting to cultivate with them. In addition to the measures noted previously, hours spent with diverse customers to track service and number of referrals received from existing ethnic customers can be used as an indicator of the strength of your ethnic market relationship.

Measures of Good Citizenship

All organizations have important stakeholders and constituents beyond their four walls. Regulated industries such as utilities and telecommunications must maintain positive relationships with regulators and other governmental officials and adhere to environmental regulations. Additionally, all organizations must strive to be good corporate citizens in the communities in which they operate. Organizations are beginning to realize that this is not only the right thing to do, but it makes good business sense. A study by the Conference Board of Canada found that 80 percent of Canadian managers feel that their company's good reputation goes a long way in recruiting and keeping good employees (Nivens, 2002).

Those organizations required to follow guidelines regarding environmental or health and safety issues have a wonderful opportunity to use the diversity scorecard as a tool for moving from strict compliance to leadership. For example, Nova Scotia Power Inc. (NSPI), a regulated utility, must adhere to many environmental and health and safety guidelines enforced by various government agencies. They used the scorecard not simply to measure compliance with environmental regulations, but they challenged themselves to develop a measure and corresponding target that would establish them as environmental and safety leaders in the Canadian utility industry. An environmental performance index comprising several leading environmental indicators was constructed, which would guide NSPI's decisions on this carefully monitored aspect of their business. By including the index on the scorecard, NSPI management signaled to the entire organization the importance of environmental stewardship and created a challenge for all employees to conduct their jobs in a manner that would positively affect this important indicator.

To prove successful over time, a company both contributes to, and relies heavily on, the prosperity of the community. Although organizations are not solely responsible for the welfare of their surrounding communities, it is incumbent upon them, and in their best interests, to monitor community success and ensure that they are contributing to their area's ongoing prosperity. Bob Nelson expresses this point in his book, *1001 Ways to Energize Employees.* Nelson says: "These days the best organizations are involved in and contribute to their communities. ... It all boils down to helping find ways to make their communities better places to live, work, and do business through the sharing of resources, the labor of their employees, or just plain old-fashioned cash" (Nelson, 1997).

He chronicles several leading-edge organizations that have taken community involvement to a new level. One such company is Maryland spice manufacturer McCormick and Company. They open their plant one Saturday each year for Charity Day. Employees work their normal shifts, but all wages are directed to the charity of the employee's choice. In the spirit of community caring, McCormick donates twice the employee's daily wage to the charity. You can monitor your community involvement by tracking donations to various charities, logging the number of hours employees spend volunteering (on company time), or counting the number of community-related partnerships you enter. Table 12-1 highlights some potential diverse customer/community partnership measures you can use.

The measures shown are generic but will provide some guidance. Your challenge is to identify the unique processes that drive the diverse customer value proposition in your organization, and define specific measures that tell your particular story. You will also discover that unlike traditional performance management systems, which focus on the incremental improvement of existing processes, the diversity scorecard and corresponding measures in your financial and diverse customer perspectives may lead you to entirely new processes necessary to achieve your strategic aims. Uncovering these *missing measurements,* as Kaplan and

Table 12-1. Potential Diverse Customer/Community Partnership Measures

- ☐ Percentage subcontracting dollars to minority businesses
- ☐ Percentage subcontracting dollars to women-owned businesses
- ☐ Dollars given to community by group
- ☐ Percentage customer retention by group
- ☐ Total number of solutions offered per client by group
- ☐ Level of access to ethnic group customer information
- ☐ Number of hours spent with diverse customers
- ☐ Awards received from the community
- ☐ Percentage on-time delivery rating by diverse group
- ☐ Number of sponsored community events
- ☐ Number of countries, cultures, languages by customer vs. your workforce representation
- ☐ Percentage ethnic market share penetration
- ☐ Percentage customer loyalty
- ☐ Number and percentage of new ethnic group customers
- ☐ Percentage diverse customer satisfaction
- ☐ Profitability by diverse customer group
- ☐ Percentage brand recognition
- ☐ Level of diverse customer knowledge
- ☐ Percentage target customer group spending
- ☐ Number of diverse customer awards received
- ☐ Number of staff at client locations
- ☐ Number of referrals received from ethnic existing customers
- ☐ Number and percentage of customer complaints by issue by group
- ☐ Percentage change customer demographics
- ☐ Number and percentage of diverse customers by group vs. number and percentage of workforce representation by group

Source: Edward E. Hubbard, *Measuring Diversity Stat Pak Software Series*. Petaluma, CA: Global Insights, 2000.

Norton term them, is often one of the most gratifying aspects of the scorecard development process (Niven, 2002).

Other Sources of Customer Measures

Choosing your value proposition and identifying your target ethnic customer segments will greatly enhance your efforts in developing measures for the diverse customer/community partnership customer perspective; however, they are not your only options. Other sources that can lead to measures you may wish to track include the following:

Customer objectives and measures that drive financial performance. Do not forget that the diversity scorecard should tell the story of your strategy from financial measures through the customer, processes, and employee capabilities you will need to achieve success. Once you have developed financial objectives and measures, ask yourself how they translate into customer requirements. For example, if you have a financial target of double-digit revenue growth, you may require greater ethnic customer loyalty or ambitious new customer acquisition policies to achieve that goal (Niven, 2002).

The customer's voice. The Internet is an incredibly powerful medium for spreading customer perceptions about your products and services, whether good or bad. Message boards and targeted sites across the vast universe of the web likely contain a host of references to your company and its offerings. Take advantage of this opportunity by listening to what your diverse customers have to say about you and then proactively defining yourself.

Moments of truth. Any point at which a customer comes in contact with a business defines a moment of truth. The interaction can be either favorable or unfavorable and have a great impact on future business. Mapping these moments of truth provides you with an opportunity to isolate the differentiating features you offer and design metrics to track your success (Carlzon, 1987).

Work from the customer experience. Many people start their day with a trip to Starbucks or their favorite coffee purveyor and shell out anywhere from $2 to $5 for the pleasure. The company that harvested the beans probably received the equivalent of about one or two cents, but you just paid about 200 times that. Why? Because of the pleasurable experience the restaurant or coffee shop provided. Look at the experience you are designing for your diverse customers, and you will be sure to unearth critical measures of success for the customer and all other perspectives of the diversity scorecard.

ANALYZING DATA

Analyzing data in the diverse customer/community partnership perspective enables the organization to examine its ability to affect the processes and systems that touch the customer and the community. This entails assessing the organization's effectiveness in attracting, servicing, and retaining diverse customers and meeting the needs of the community. By doing this, the organization gains insights and a deeper understanding of differing customer and community needs by group.

How is success evaluated? Of course, the organization can monitor sales and see what happens. Or people can be polled to see how their attitude toward the organization or its products has changed. Fortunately, more sophisticated and useful new approaches have evolved. The ideal method is to engage in not just a DROI analysis, but what can be called a closed-loop process, meaning that at the end of a marketing effort the organization tries to understand the effect of what it has done and then apply that knowledge to its next efforts on behalf of the customer. When an organization understands the effect of the decisions it has made, the organization is able to arrive at a statistical framework that allows it to go back to the beginning of the process and make better decisions the next time (Schreiber, 2001). So in effect, the organization is engaged in a process of back-end DROI analysis that loops back and becomes part of its front-end planning the next time around. Ideally, this should create a continuous learning process.

Making Optimal Use of New Information Sources

One of the things marketers are doing with increasing sophistication is classic mix modeling, a statistical technique that has been used in the marketing world, primarily by packaged-goods marketers, for more than 10 years. This technique monitors not just sales and other basics but also goes deeper and establishes statistical understanding of just what each piece of the marketing mix produces for the organization, and furthermore, how all the parts of the mix coordinate statistically. Because of computing power, new techniques, and a variety of other factors, including the sophistication of both suppliers and clients, the mix-marketing approach has become more widespread and pervasive in its application. It provides a sophisticated level of diverse customer ROI modeling.

Thanks to the growing sophistication of marketing data available, it has become increasingly possible to statistically isolate the tangible business contributions of the different elements of a marketing mix. The elements can be viewed either in terms of big pieces, such as advertising versus sales versus pricing, or data considered at granular levels. For example, what is the difference in return between a 15-second television commercial and a 30-second television commercial in terms of creating tangible results or sales? Now formulas can accurately describe the different contributions of the mix elements. With the new research tools, an organization can compare the efficacy of each dollar spent in the general market to what that dollar would return in the targeted ethnic marketing (Schreiber, 2001).

Establishing Baseline Criteria

To analyze the data, we could go into many hows and whens of research, but perhaps it is time to pose a more fundamental and far simpler question: What would your position be in the marketplace? How much would you be selling if you were undertaking no marketing activity at all? Think about it. Most brands and most companies, after all, coast along on momentum, be it from the sales generated at point of sale, from residual brand awareness, or even from momentum that remains from advertising and marketing efforts undertaken in the past. We do know that advertising has a residual value; sometimes, even years after a dollar has been spent on advertising, a company can continue to receive payback in increased sales and brand awareness. So, how do you arrive at your baseline measurement? This is a complex issue.

Obtaining data is more difficult than simply looking at point-of-sale data or reviewing profit-and-loss statements. Understanding your baseline data requires a near-artistic sense of how some of these different factors affect customer activity regarding your product, including elements such as the following:

- ☐ Pricing
- ☐ The products and marketing activities of your competitors
- ☐ Seasonality
- ☐ Sales efforts
- ☐ Local and regional economic conditions
- ☐ Trade promotions
- ☐ Weather
- ☐ Advertising generated on behalf of your products by retailers

The goal in establishing a baseline is to understand the profits you generate as a fundamental point of measurement, separated from what you might normally obtain from advertising. In other words, your baseline should answer the question, "How well would we be doing if we were conducting no advertising or marketing at all?" (Schreiber, 2001). Once your baseline figures are established, and they can include the general marketplace as well as specific ethnic segments, the organization will be in a position to evaluate the results and returns of its marketing efforts.

Analyzing the Mix

What marketing statisticians are able to do through measuring and analysis is answer questions that were not even possible only 15 years ago, such as the following:

☐ How much of your total sales is attributable to print advertising? To radio? To TV ads?

☐ If you have print and TV ads running at the same time, how much more effective is their combined contribution than the sum of just print plus TV?

☐ If you are running newspaper ads to support an event you are staging, what is their statistical contribution to event attendance and the bigger picture of generating sales in key ethnic markets?

Such complex and elusive information can be obtained today because of the many sources of data available: from Nielsen ratings to point-of-sale retail data to detailed information from radio stations on total listenership when your ad is played. In sum, mix analysis can be a strategic tool for organizations that desire to better understand the specific contributions of each element of their overall marketing program, and it might just be an excellent step as organizations begin to add ethnic marketing to their mix.

Unfortunately, that information could take up several books on its own. And doing it well really does require the expertise and knowledge of someone who understands the many variables at hand, the sources of information, as well as the many causalities at work in analyzing and understanding so much raw, interconnected data. Analyzing supplier diversity data is much more straightforward in that much of the analysis can be performed with a comprehensive mixture of comparative analysis for key elements of the supplier diversity plan and specific ratios. In summary, remarkable results can be achieved in the diverse customer/community partnership perspective when the right questions are asked and the right plans and methodologies are put in place.

REPORTING DATA

There are a wide variety of ways to display and report your diverse customer/community partnership data. This data can be presented in tables, graphs, narratives, pictograms, and so on. For example, when you examine a completed analysis for a customer impact study, or a supplier diversity Minority and Women Business Enterprise (MWBE) analysis, you will likely see a report consisting of some general text about the process and recommendations, figures such as tables, bar graphs, and pie charts, and within those figures, some statistics. In general, these surveys will have data reporting requirements that include answers to the following questions:

☐ How many people said what?
☐ Are there differences between questions or respondent subsets?
☐ Are the differences significant? If so, at what level?
☐ What is the overall trend?
☐ What is the cost of losing our ethnic market share?
☐ What is impact on our brand in the community?

How deeply you go into these analyses and reporting levels depends on the diverse customer/community partnership initiative objectives. You may analyze and report some questions at the top levels and only delve deeply into a few. The relevant issue is whether the deeper level will produce new information that is useful in answering your research questions and therefore your organization's diversity challenges and/or issues. The most effective approach suggests that you always do just the analysis and reporting that makes sense for the organization's strategic marketing objectives and then take action. Figures 12-1 and 12-2 present examples of diverse customer/community partnership measurements that can be reported to organizational stakeholders.

Figures 12-3, 12-4, and 12-5 can be used in combination to show the changes in the diverse customer demographics over a period of time.

Reporting the results of the diverse customer/community partnership perspective is essential to stay in touch with the pulse of customer and community needs. By charting and reviewing progress to date, organizations can make informed choices about their next strategic move for improved customer and revenue performance.

FINAL THOUGHTS

Today's marketplace is faced with changing customer and community demographics and increased competition on a global scale. Thus, no organization can afford to sit back and rely on customer and community marketplace strategies of the past. Customers and community members are different and require different approaches that go beyond one-size-fits-all. It will take competence and skill to form new customer and community relationships with people who have unique needs that do not necessarily conform to traditional selling and buying patterns. To be effective, organizations will need to make changes, develop ethnic customer relationship strategies, and measure their performance in a variety of new ways to meet customer and community requirements now and in the future.

In the next chapter, we will explore measures that reflect the financial impact of our diversity efforts on the bottom line.

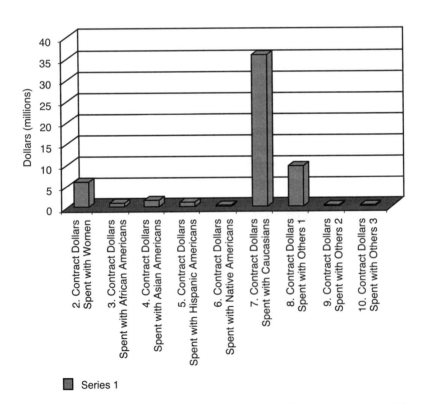

Figure 12-1. Dollars spent with MWBE suppliers. (Source: Edward E. Hubbard Diversity Scorecard Stat Pak–Diversity Measurement "Calculate and Go" Software Series. Petaluma, CA: Global Insights Publishing, 2002.)

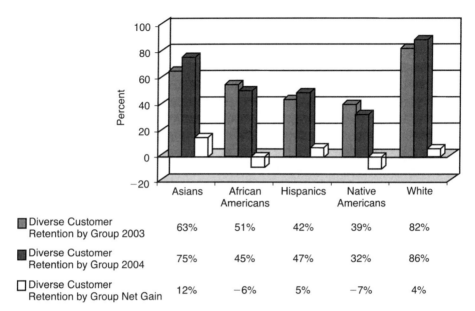

	Asians	African Americans	Hispanics	Native Americans	White
■ Diverse Customer Retention by Group 2003	63%	51%	42%	39%	82%
■ Diverse Customer Retention by Group 2004	75%	45%	47%	32%	86%
☐ Diverse Customer Retention by Group Net Gain	12%	−6%	5%	−7%	4%

Figure 12-2. Diverse customer retention by group. (Source: Edward E. Hubbard Diversity Scorecard Stat Pak–Diversity Measurement "Calculate and Go" Software Series. Petaluma, CA: Global Insights Publishing, 2002.)

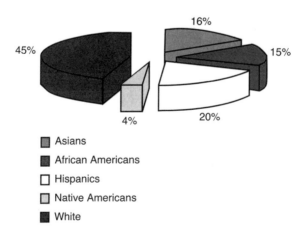

■ Asians
■ African Americans
☐ Hispanics
▧ Native Americans
■ White

Figure 12-3. Percentage diverse customer market share 2003. (Source: Edward E. Hubbard Diversity Scorecard Stat Pak–Diversity Measurement "Calculate and Go" Software Series. Petaluma, CA: Global Insights Publishing, 2002.)

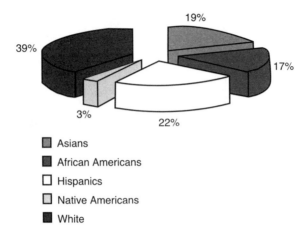

Figure 12-4. Percentage diverse customer market share 2004. (Source: Edward E. Hubbard Diversity Scorecard Stat Pak–Diversity Measurement "Calculate and Go" Software Series. Petaluma, CA: Global Insights Publishing, 2002.)

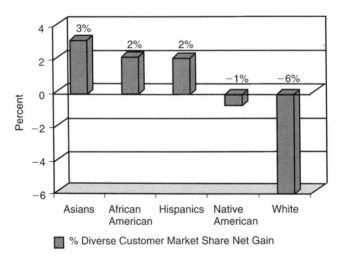

Figure 12-5. Percentage diverse customer market share net gain. (Source: Edward E. Hubbard Diversity Scorecard Stat Pak–Diversity Measurement "Calculate and Go" Software Series. Petaluma, CA: Global Insights Publishing, 2002.)

REFERENCES

Carlzon, Jan. *Moments of Truth*. Cambridge, MA: Ballinger, 1987.

Dourado, T. "Ten Steps to World-Class." *Management Services*, March 2001, 14–16.

Hochman, Mark. "Customer Satisfaction Measurements: An Answer to Yesterday's Problems?" *Harvard Management Update*, August 1999, 10.

Hubbard, Edward E. Diversity Scorecard Stat Pak–Diversity Measurement "Calculate and Go" Software Series. Petaluma, CA: Global Insights Publishing, 2002.

Kaplan, Robert S., and David P. Norton. *The Balanced Scorecard*. Boston: Harvard Business School Press, 1996.

Kooker, Naomi R. "Boeing Takes the Initiative." *Purchasing*, February 2001, 45.

Mentzer, J.T., W. De Witt, J.S. Keebler, S. Min, N.W. Nix, C.D. Smith, and Z.G. Zacharia. *A United Definition of Supply Chain Management*, Working Paper, University of Tennessee, 1999.

Nelson, Bob. *1001 Ways to Energize Employees*. New York: Workman, 1997.

Nivens, Paul R. *Balanced Scorecard*. New York: John Wiley & Sons, 2002.

Schreiber, Alfred L. *Multicultural Marketing*. Chicago: NTC Business Books, 2001.

Women and Diversity WOW Facts 2002. Washington, DC: Business Women's Network, 2002.

FURTHER READING

Henry, Pamela. *Diversity and the Bottom Line*. Austin, TX: TurnKey Press, 2002.

Hubbard, Edward E. *Measuring Diversity Stat Pak Software Series*. Petaluma, CA: Global Insights, 2000.

Hubbard, Edward E. *A Casebook in Diversity Measurement and Diversity Management*. Petaluma, CA: Global Insights, 2003.

Hubbard, Edward E. *The Diversity Scorecard Fieldbook*. Petaluma, CA: Global Insights, 2003.

Hubbard, Edward E. *The Manager's Pocket Guide to Diversity Management*. Amherst, MA: HRD Press, 2003.

Olve, Nils-Goran, Jan Roy, and Magnus Wetter. *Performance Drivers: A Practical Guide to Using the Balanced Scorecard*. Chichester, UK: John Wiley & Sons, 2000.

Plummer, Deborah L. *Handbook of Diversity Management*. Lanham, MD: University Press of America, 2003.

CHAPTER 13

Financial Impact Perspective

DEFINITION

The financial impact perspective reflects a statistical summary of the organization's diversity efforts' influence on its financial performance. This perspective often includes an analysis of dollars saved as a result of diversity initiatives, reduced litigation and complaint costs, incremental increases in revenue resulting from successful penetration into emerging markets, and the like. This index perspective is typically tracked to determine if the organization has experienced direct and indirect financial effects caused by implementing its diversity strategy. This perspective should show the results of the strategic choices made in the other perspectives, while targeting several of the long-term goals. The financial impact perspective sets a large part of the general ground rules and premises for the other perspectives.

In an earlier chapter, the balanced diversity scorecard was introduced as a method any organization can turn to for overcoming their almost exclusive reliance on financial measures of performance as the prime indicator of a department's success. Several issues relating to financial measures were discussed (Niven, 2002):

☐ They are not consistent with today's business environment in which intangible assets create most of the value.
☐ Financial measures provide a great "rearview mirror" of the past but often lack predictive power.
☐ Consolidation of financial information tends to promote functional silos.
☐ Long-term, value-creating activities may be compromised by short-term financial metrics from activities such as employee reductions.

☐ Most high-level financial measures provide little in the way of guidance to lower-level employees in their day-to-day actions.

Despite their apparent shortcomings, a well-constructed balanced diversity scorecard is not complete without financial measures of performance. Scorecard practitioners recognize this fact, and most actually consider financial measures to represent the most important component of the scorecard. One recent study indicated that 49 percent of organizations give financial measures higher importance than any other indicators (Maisel, 2001). By using a balanced diversity scorecard, an organization has the opportunity to mitigate, if not eliminate entirely, many of the issues related to financial measures mentioned previously. For example, cascading your financial impact measures to lower levels of the organization provides an opportunity for all employees to demonstrate how their day-to-day utilization of diversity contributes to the organization's overall strategy and goals, ultimately influencing financial returns.

THE HIGH COST OF HUMAN ASSET MISMANAGEMENT

Mismanaging people can be expensive. Failure to treat employees with respect, with dignity, and with procedures that are seen as fair by all concerned parties can lead to a host of negative outcomes. Consider direct cash payments, negative publicity, and long-term damage to an organization's brand image as examples. Texaco (prior to the Chevron-Texaco merger), the big producer of oil and gas, refiner, and marketer of petroleum products, learned this lesson in a painful and expensive way.

In 1994, six African-American officials in the company's finance department filed a lawsuit alleging that white men in Texaco's "good-old-boy" network secured coveted promotions and the biggest raises and treated African-Americans dismissively. Initially, Texaco believed it stood a chance of winning the case in court, but its opinion changed when audiotape transcripts of managers belittling African-American employees' grievances became public. Texaco settled the lawsuit for $176.1 million, the largest sum (at that time) ever paid in the United States to resolve such a case. That represented about 68 cents per share of Texaco stock in 1996 ("Texaco to Pay," 1996).

Although the size of the monetary payout was enormous, the impact on the way Texaco did business at every level was even larger because the firm opened itself up to an exceptional level of outside scrutiny. As part of the settlement agreement, the company established a seven-member equality and tolerance task force with extraordinary powers. The task force was authorized to help shape HR policies and practices, and its recommendations were mandatory, unless Texaco could convince the federal judge supervising the settlement that to do so would be unsound business or technically unrealistic. The seven members of the task force included three members designated by Texaco and three by the plaintiffs in the suit. The seventh member was jointly named by both sides and served as chairperson. The overall objective of the task force was to ensure greater racial diversity within the 27,000-employee company. Said one energy industry analyst, "It's unprecedented that external forces ... play such a strong role" ("Texaco to Pay," 1996).

As another example, consider the results of a six-month *Business Week* investigation of Astra USA, Inc., the American arm of Swedish pharmaceutical company Astra. The investigation revealed a bizarre case of abuse of power, where a 15-year pattern of sexual harassment emanated from the president's office and worked its way down through the ranks of the organization. According to the federal Equal Employment Opportunity Commission (EEOC), Astra USA's president routinely replaced mothers and older female employees with attractive, young, single women who were pressured into having sex with company executives, including the president. The president was fired in 1996, accused by Astra of spending company cash on home repairs, vacations, and prostitutes. Astra then sued him for $15 million to recover costs related to the EEOC investigation (Miller, 1998).

The results? Terrible publicity for the company, payments in the millions of dollars to the victims, and a 21-month prison term without parole for the president of the U.S. subsidiary (for failing to report more than $1 million in income on his federal tax returns). The firm agreed to pay almost $10 million to 79 women and one man who said he was punished for speaking out (Bildman, 1998; *Business Week*, 1997). Indirect costs included lowered productivity among surviving employees, poor morale, increased voluntary turnover, and difficulty in attracting new employees to work for the company. Who needs that? (Casio, 2000).

These cases are not isolated instances. In 1993, Shoney's paid $132 million in another race-based case. Lucky Stores and State Farm Insurance settled sex discrimination suits for $107 million and $250 million, respectively (Seligman, 1999). Every year, thousands of complaints of unlawful discrimination are filed with local, state, and federal enforcement agencies. In 1997 alone, the EEOC received more than 80,000 such complaints, and the number of employment lawsuits is increasing by more than 20 percent annually (Sharf and Jones, in press). Other cases that have brought our attention to the financial implications of these issues include major bias settlements such as the following:

☐ Coca-Cola $192 million
☐ Home Depot $110 million
☐ Publix $82 million
☐ Denny's $54 million

Pending cases include the following:

☐ Metlife
☐ Allstate
☐ Salomon Smith Barney
☐ Morgan Stanley
☐ JP Morgan Chase
☐ Wal-Mart
☐ Johnson & Johnson
☐ Bell South

These cases have also generated increased Office of Federal Contract Compliance (OFCCP) enforcement and compliance activities as well as a rash of law firms that are actively monitoring organizations and employees for potential class action work. Not to mention a tremendous impact on an organization's brand image and ability to attract and retain employees and customers.

Civil rights complaints by job applicants or employees may allege unfair discrimination on the basis of age, race, ethnic group, gender, religion, or disability. What happens after a complaint is filed? As an example, consider that once it receives a complaint of discrimination, the EEOC, a main enforcement agency for civil rights complaints, follows a three-step process: investigation, voluntary reconciliation, and (if that does not work) litigation. In response to work-related complaints, companies do their own internal investigations, and when sued, they prepare for litigation.

Everyone knows that litigation is an expensive process, but investigation is costly, too. Recall that Astra sued its former president for $15 million to recover costs related to an extensive EEOC investigation. It has often been said that litigation is a luxury that few can afford. Too often, organizations that do not truly value and utilize diversity inevitably get to see just how expensive that luxury really is (Casio, 2000).

Financial measures should be part of any diversity scorecard, whether a private enterprise or not-for-profit or public-sector organization. Let's take a minute to explore some implications of assessing financial impact in the not-for-profit or public sector.

APPLICATIONS OF FINANCIAL IMPACT IN THE PUBLIC AND NOT-FOR-PROFIT SECTORS

In public and not-for-profit sector diversity scorecard models, financial measures can best be seen as either enablers of customer success or constraints within which the group must operate. The ultimate goal of a government agency, for example, is to fulfill its mission and customer requirements, not achieve financial success; however, financial metrics still have an important place in the overall framework.

Working efficiently and creating value at lowest cost will be of critical importance in any organization, regardless of its status. Determining the costs of services rendered can lead to important conclusions and dramatically affect funding decisions. Government organizations, like their colleagues in the private sector, are increasingly looking to activity-based management techniques to assist them in establishing the true drivers of costs and how best to minimize total outflows in the future; however, applying disciplined cost control methods and tracking detailed financial metrics can be a particularly stressful undertaking for many public-sector managers.

Consider those working in the field of human services, such as adoption or family services. They will suggest, with merit, that you cannot put a price on placing a child in a supportive and loving home or reuniting a child with parents who have successfully completed a counseling program and show tremendous promise for the future. Skillful scorecard practitioners must coach the reluctant managers to see that financial measures are not necessarily at odds with their nonfinancial goals but are intended to balance the ultimate goal of serving customers with fiscal accountability and responsibility (Niven, 2002).

Neither public-sector nor not-for-profit organizations look to financial rewards as their ultimate show of success. Instead, they seek to achieve lofty missions aimed at improving society. As mission-focused organizations, they must change the architecture of the diversity scorecard, elevating the role of the mission and customers, and reducing the influence of financial indicators. Public-sector and not-for-profit scorecards will differ in their application of the financial impact perspective versus their private industry counterparts. The diversity scorecard has found a home in many not-for-profit and government agencies, but the task has not always been easy. Several implementation challenges await managers looking to institute a diversity scorecard solution. We will review several issues and offer advice on overcoming many of the associated pitfalls of applying a scorecard in these areas. A growing number of agencies have overcome the difficulties of developing a diversity scorecard in the public and not-for-profit sectors and are using the tool to align all employees with the diversity strategy. We will examine some of these techniques and share a few secrets of those who have made strides toward this strategic objective.

PERFORMANCE MEASUREMENT IN THE PUBLIC SECTOR

Niven (2000) chronicled the roadmap of performance measurements in the public sector that began to pave the way for the use of scorecards. He points out that President Clinton wasted little time shaking things up in the federal government. On August 3, 1993, he signed into law the Government Performance and Results Act (GPRA). The act required that federally funded agencies develop and implement an accountability system based on performance measurement, including setting goals and objectives and measuring progress toward achieving them. But more than that, it sought to effect a fundamental transformation in the way government was managed by placing greater emphasis on what was being accomplished as opposed to what was being spent. As radical a departure as this seemed to represent, it was not without precedent.

Back in the 1960s the Program Planning and Budgeting System (PPBS) was introduced to the government as an extension of a successful Department of Defense application. Zero-based budgeting and management by objectives (MBO) replaced PPBS as the programs du jour of the 1970s, and the 1980s saw the rise of productivity improvement and quality management. In 1988, a President's Quality Award was established. The new program was closely aligned with the Malcolm Baldrige National Quality Award and focused on customer-driven quality, continuous improvement and learning, and employee participation and development, among a host of criteria. Once President Clinton assumed control of the oval office in 1993, he was anxious to leverage the new focus on quality with the performance improvement ethic he championed during his tenure as governor of Arkansas in the 1980s.

In March 1993, he appointed Vice President Al Gore to head a six-month study on what had to be done to further improve government performance. *Creating a Government that Works Better and Costs Less* was the resulting report, which eventually led to the development of the National Partnership for Reinventing Government. All of which leads us back to August 1993 and the signing of the GPRA. Under the new act, all federal agencies are required to develop mission statements, overall outcome-related goals, internal performance goals and objectives, and measures to be used to evaluate progress toward those goals and objectives (Thor, 2000).

The goals and ideals embodied in the GPRA are noble and make great sense, but movements of the past had similar objectives and soon faded from sight. The question is: Would the GPRA go the way of previous governmental attempts at results-oriented operations? Several pieces of evidence suggest things are different this time. A critical difference between the GPRA and earlier ancestors is the fact that it is a *law*, a creation of both the president and Congress. Unlike presidential directives that tend to begin and end with the term of the current president, the GPRA is meant to endure. In fact, current President George W. Bush has already sent signals that his administration will focus on making government results-oriented. In April 2001, the Bush administration announced that agencies will be required to submit performance-based budgets for selected programs during the fiscal 2003 budget cycle. This is the first time agencies have been forced to tie spending to performance goals.

Another pillar of GPRA and performance measurement strength is the changing tide of public funding. For many decades funding was stable or even growing, but today budgets are shrinking and programs must clearly display the value they create. With the advent of mass communication, today's citizenry is better informed than at any other point in history. Knowledge possessed by constituents equates to a demand of accountability on the part of government. More than ever, people want to know how their hard-earned dollars are being spent and whether the allocation of funds is helping to promote wide-ranging social benefits. Perhaps the key difference between earlier attempts at measuring public-sector performance and today's programs is the recent rise of the performance management discipline in the private sector.

Since Kaplan and Norton's first Balanced Scorecard article appeared in a 1992 edition of the *Harvard Business Review,* thousands of organizations across the globe have turned to this dynamic and effective method of gauging organizational success. The tidal wave of information available at the click of a mouse has also led to the swift and efficient dissemination of information on emerging practices in performance management. Public-sector managers have practically unlimited resources from which to draw when researching best practices on the latest performance management techniques. Since the mid-1990s, Performance Measurement in Government publications, resources, and conferences have sprung up around the country (Niven, 2002).

The U.S. Department of Commerce and Vice President Al Gore's National Partnership for Reinventing Government (NPR) sponsored a Best Practices in Achieving Workforce Diversity benchmarking study. The study identified best practices used by leading organizations to achieve workforce diversity. To build skills for the diversity strategic planning, diversity metrics, accountability, and assessment portion of the study, the NPR Study Director and a subset of the NPR Study advisors were trained by Dr. Edward E. Hubbard and the Hubbard Diversity Measurement and Productivity Institute (HDM&P) in diversity performance metrics processes to measure each benchmarking partner's diversity results and learned methods to create measurable diversity strategic plans. This training helped enhance the framework for collecting data during the process.

The NPR study team identified the following critical success factors to evaluate best practices:

1. Leadership and management commitment
2. Employee involvement
3. Strategic planning
4. Sustained investment
5. Diversity indicators
6. Accountability, measurement, and evaluation
7. Linkage to organizational goals and objectives

The practices that are included in the report are not identified by specific organization in order to preserve the organization's confidentiality.

The study team reviewed a wide range of diversity literature and identified more than 600 companies and organizations, both public and private, which were recognized for their efforts in achieving workforce diversity. The study team conducted an additional screening procedure to identify organizations whose exemplary practices in achieving workforce diversity were truly world class based on the identified critical success factors. As a result, 65 organizations were selected for more detailed analysis.

The study team developed a telephone survey that was administered to representatives of these organizations to gain additional insights on their current diversity practices. Based on survey results and availability considerations, nine benchmarking partners were ultimately selected for on-site visits. More than half of these partners had been featured in *Fortune* and *Next Step* magazine articles highlighting their cutting-edge diversity best practices (Ellison, 1999; Robinson and Hickman, 1999).

The team outlined the focus of their benchmarking efforts in the study's Executive Summary as follows:

Diversity Affects the World

Advances in technology and the advent of a global economy bring the people of the world closer together than ever before. Given this fact, businesses, educational systems and other entities are investigating ways to better serve their constituents. This includes being able to attract and retain the best and most qualified workers. Organizations that can develop and employ the necessary policies and procedures to do this will maintain a competitive advantage among their counterparts and increase their effectiveness. The private sector competitive model may not squarely fit Federal departments and agencies, given the lack of profit motive as the reason for their existence. Yet, Federal organizations must compete to recruit and retain the best talent if they hope to achieve their bottom line, their statutory missions.

The changing demographics of our nation also affect the nation's businesses and in turn the nation's economy. For our government and businesses to continue to be effective and motivate citizens to contribute to building these institutions, our leaders must recognize and capitalize upon the diversity of the nation.

Why is this important?

To achieve success and maintain a competitive advantage, we must be able to draw on the most important resource—the skills of the workforce. With the increasing richness of diversity in the world and in the workforce, we need to expand our outlook and use creative strategies to be successful. Employees can provide this resource. This study identifies best practices that work in organizations that are doing just that. These practices can be adopted in any workplace.

Why should we pay attention?

Our partners have created communities of practice that achieve and value workforce diversity within their organizations. These practices reflect our partners' understanding that valuing and recognizing diversity is imperative in order to maintain a competitive advantage. They know that using these practices enhances productivity, effectiveness, and sustained competitiveness.

How is this different?

Frequently, diversity is viewed in a limited fashion, primarily addressing issues of race, ethnic or gender differences, and linked to the laws providing protected status to certain groups. We have used a very broad definition of diversity, to encompass most characteristics that individuals possess that affect the way they think and do things. This is critical. This study describes tested ways to draw on all the varied skills of our workforce.

What did we learn?

This study emphasizes the most valuable information that the best practices organizations have to offer. Our critical findings focus on the following information because we can use it to further and strengthen the U.S. government's efforts to achieve diversity in the workplace.

☐ **Organizations Benefit from Diversity**
   Organizations that promote and achieve a diverse workplace will attract and retain quality employees and increase customer loyalty. For public organizations, it also translates into effective delivery of essential services to communities with diverse needs.

☐ **Leaders and Managers are Responsible for Diversity**
   Leaders and managers within organizations are primarily responsible for the success of diversity policies because they must ensure that the policies are effective.

☐ **Leaders and Managers Must Create a Strategic Plan to Develop Diversity Initiatives Throughout the Organization**
   Leaders and managers within organizations must incorporate diversity policies into every aspect of the organization's functions and purpose.

☐ **Employees' Views and Involvement are Key to the Success of Diversity Initiatives**
   Organizations must view employee participation as a necessary part of the diversity initiative, in order to develop and maintain effective diversity policies.

The leaders of the best practices organizations understand that they must support their employees in learning how to effectively interact with and manage people in a diverse workplace. They recognize that they should encourage employees to continue to learn new skills in dealing with and managing people. They also recognize the impact that diverse clients will have upon the success or failure of an organization, as businesses must compete to satisfy these clients.

Our Key Finding
A key finding of this report is that diversity needs to be defined broadly and should encompass a wide range of initiatives that meet the changing needs of customers and workers. Leaders and employees should take active roles in implementing these diversity processes which, in order to succeed, should be fully aligned with core organizational goals and objectives. The findings in this report illustrate that the benefits of diversity are for everyone. Diversity is more than a moral imperative; it is a global necessity. Moreover, diversity is an essential component of any civil society (NPR, 2001).

This report and other studies clearly demonstrate that some organizations have successfully implemented programs and policies that foster diversity and inclusiveness in the workplace. There are common themes and elements among the organizations that have charted successful courses in this area. Through benchmarking studies such as this one, the federal civilian sector—which employs more than 1.6 million persons—has the opportunity to learn more about diversity from world-class organizations. The Department of Commerce and NPR recognize diversity as a key resource in fulfilling the goal of making government more efficient, productive, and responsive to the American citizenry. As a result, it is important that the federal sector view diversity as a process that influences work climates, organizational effectiveness, customer service, and ultimately, the way the government does business (NPR, 2001).

Results-based management certainly is not limited to the federal sector; it is finding its way into local government as well. Recent studies show that 34 percent of counties with populations over 50,000 and 38 percent of cities with populations over 25,000 use some type of performance measurement system (state and local governments that voluntarily embark on performance measurement systems are probably just staying slightly ahead of the curve). Many experts believe the Government Accounting Standards Board (GASB) will soon require these jurisdictions to provide "service efforts and accomplishments," which are tantamount to performance measures (Berman and Hu Wang, 2000).

This new way of managing in the public sector is just beginning to gain a critical mass and will most likely come into its own in the years ahead. Rather than bemoaning the radical new culture represented by performance measurement, public-sector managers are wise to embrace this movement and the many benefits it confers. Employing performance measurement techniques allows public-sector managers to clearly demonstrate to legislators and citizens alike the value their programs bring to constituents. Tracking that value comes from the development of meaningful, outcome-based indicators that can be used to gauge the effectiveness of program success.

In an age of declining budgets, those managers turning to performance measurement have the tools to clearly outline how the allocation of funds to their program will make a difference to the people ultimately affected by the service delivery. Public-sector employees are also beneficiaries of the performance measurement revolution. Like their private-sector brethren, these employees are now able to shift their focus from rote, non-strategic activities to the processes and initiatives that drive a meaningful contribution toward success. The knowledge and information sharing provided by the balanced diversity scorecard makes this possible. For these and many other reasons, early public-sector scorecard practitioners report that the results of developing a balanced scorecard are worth the effort. But—and this is a big but—they note there is a great deal of effort involved (Niven, 2002).

COLLECTING DATA

Collecting data for the financial impact index, for the most part, requires examining a variety of sources that will shed light on the organization's financial results derived from hard and soft assets. The data collection strategies chosen should be based on an analysis of key financial ratios that are used to track the organization's business results and the addition of current or new ratios that express the human resource impact in financial terms. In general, financial impact data collection will focus on collecting data for the following areas:

- ☐ Net profit numbers
- ☐ Voluntary and involuntary turnover costs
- ☐ Competency development expenses
- ☐ Dollars saved as a result of diversity initiatives
- ☐ Reduced litigation costs
- ☐ Incremental dollar increases generated from diverse market share penetration
- ☐ Human capital and the level of profitability generated by employees
- ☐ Accident costs related to diversity issues
- ☐ The percentage of the organization's budget allocated to diversity

If you had to pick at least one area of your organization's scorekeeping approach where you have good measures, the financial area would probably top the list. Chances are you have no shortage of financial data on the traditional measures: profit, ROI, income, expenses, cash flow, stock prices, accounts receivable, accounts payable, and so on. Every business is required to keep certain financial records for tax purposes, but does that mean that these are the right measures for running a business? Not necessarily. The problem with most organizations' approach to measuring financial performance is that they measure too many things, and too few of the measures are data that are useful in managing performance in the organization. And, if you are looking to see if the organization has any financial measures that reflect the impact of diversity performance, your search can be even harder. In other words, most financial reports do not contain the right amount or the right data that managers need to make good business decisions and effectively run the organization for all stakeholders (Brown, 1996).

Cyclical Process to Poor Performance

If there's one thing that American executives are good at, it's manipulating an organization's expenses to improve short-term profitability. A new executive comes in to take over a failing business unit. His or her first task is to remove costs from the business. Reducing head count normally does this because labor is one of the few variable-cost items that can be manipulated without directly impacting income. So, the new boss lays off 10 to 20 percent of the workforce, cuts overtime, and all of a sudden the bottom line starts improving. She or he reduces the cost of purchased goods and services by putting the squeeze on suppliers or finding new ones and reduces other big-ticket cost items like real estate by getting rid of offices. As a result of this cost cutting, profits really do improve, but often at the expense of quality, morale, and customer satisfaction.

Because organizations have been measuring financial performance in practically the same way for the last 30 years, executives have also learned to play games with the numbers to make their organizations look good. When $100,000 bonuses are at stake, there is a real incentive to make the numbers look good. Creative accounting techniques are often applied to ensure that executives still receive their big bonuses. All of this playing around with cost reduction and creative accounting usually results in a promotion for the executive. He or she moves on to a bigger and better job with a bigger salary, and someone new inherits the mess that was created when employee morale problems explode, or customers start buying from the competition because of poor quality, or diverse customers feel totally ignored.

However, the game continues with a new crop of executives who come in every few years and play around with the numbers again to make them look good. Not all of this is a charade. Many organizations do need to cut their head counts and expenses. Some of these reductions can result in the company being more efficient on a longer-term basis; however, cost cutting by itself will not secure an organization's future success (Brown, 1996).

There are also data collection challenges in the public and not-for-profit sector.

Challenges of Data Collection in the Public and Not-for-Profit Sector

As the old saying suggests, nothing worth having comes easy. So it is with developing a scorecard in the public sector. One of the best attributes of a scorecard is its simplicity. But remember, simple does not equal simplistic. Applying a sophisticated tool like the diversity scorecard requires rigor and discipline in any organizational structure, but the public sector offers some unique challenges. This section will explore a few of these issues and offer possible solutions to help you get the most from your diversity scorecard data collection effort. Think back to any performance data collection efforts you may have been involved in. Have you heard someone say the following?

What I do is not measurable. This is perhaps the most common lament of public-sector managers and employees alike. Health and social services agencies are the most vocal, and with good reason. Helping drug-addicted individuals get back on their feet, attempting to ensure that all poor children have health insurance, reducing disease rates, and reuniting troubled families are all outcomes that are subject to a wide variety of influences, making them difficult to measure. The key word in that last sentence is *outcomes.* Each of the examples cited is a long-range (usually) goal the government is working diligently to achieve. Many suggest that such outcomes are impossible to measure because they can take years to accomplish, involve a variety of contributors, and are subject to many variables out of the control of the public-sector agency. Trying to convince a dedicated social services manager that his or her work should be captured under the framework of a balanced scorecard can be one of the toughest tests to face even for the most tenacious diversity practitioner.

To overcome the challenge, public-sector agencies must distinguish between *outcomes* and *outputs.* Consider outputs the short- or medium-term substitutes for long-range outcomes the agency hopes to achieve. The hypothesis you are putting forth under this scenario suggests that short-term success on the outputs will eventually lead to long-term success on the outcomes (Niven, 2002).

For example, measuring the reduction of HIV rates in a community may be difficult and subject to myriad influences; however, as an output measure, tracking the number of high-risk individuals attending awareness presentations may over time help stem the growth of HIV rates. Not all substitute measures will be perfect surrogates for the outcome under question, but they will at least allow for a benchmark to be established and, more important, will stimulate conversation, information sharing, and learning among those involved in tracking the measure. After all, without measuring, how can you determine whether progress is being made in meeting social goals?

Public-sector agencies must begin to consider possible cause-and-effect relationships and start accumulating data that can be used to, at the very least, generate better questions, and at the most, lead to some insightful answers. As performance measurement systems in the public sector become increasingly sophisticated, creative managers are beginning to find ways to measure many things that were considered immeasurable. The city of Sunnyvale, California, has been a pioneer in the field of government performance measurement. They recently launched an initiative to measure perhaps the granddaddy of the immeasurable—quality of life. Their eight-point initiative focuses on performance measures encompassing community safety; high-quality education; a healthy and sustainable environment; efficient and safe transportation systems; quality, diverse, and affordable housing; community pride and involvement; a diverse and growing economy; and a community with diverse cultural opportunities (Niven, 2002).

Results will be used to punish. Many people who are unhappy in their current jobs have at least one thing in common. When they perform well there is usually no praise awaiting their achievements, but when things go wrong, the boss is on their back faster than a switch turning lights on in a room. Unfortunately, this negative conditioning tends to occur quite frequently in public-sector ranks and can be a huge issue in the successful implementation of a scorecard initiative. Two things need to happen in order to turn the tables on this problem. First, executives and managers have to be trained, coached, begged, pleaded, and coached some more about the dangers inherent in this practice. The scorecard introduces new practices, new performance measures, and new ways of thinking about the agency's business. It's all about a hypothesis of how what you do today will affect what happens tomorrow. Sometimes it does not play out exactly as planned, but that's life.

Poor performance results cannot be treated as defects but must be seen as opportunities for discussion and learning about the organization. The manager who enters a staff meeting declaring "Okay, we missed all our targets last quarter, what does that say about the way we are currently trying to create value utilizing diversity? What does this say about our strategy?" will go a long way toward cementing the diversity scorecard as an accepted business tool. Not only do executives and managers have to change their behaviors, but those affected by scorecard results must also start acting differently. It is incumbent upon them to turn the tables on their supervisors by using below-par performance results to demonstrate the need for support and requirements to generate improved approaches. Software tools such as MetricLINK (discussed earlier) provide a great resource for tracking diversity strategic objectives and tactics to measure and analyze the organization's performance. It provides a system for auditing your progress and defending performance by allowing commentaries to be entered regarding the organization's performance results on its diversity measures.

Ultimately, using the diversity scorecard results as a means for punishment, like so many of the issues we will discuss, is a cultural issue, and cultural issues cannot be solved overnight. The diversity scorecard is a communications tool, *not* a control tool. Cultural change will occur only through the persistent and sustained efforts of a committed group of executives, managers, and employees.

Typical Critical Success Factor Areas

A sample set of critical success factor areas in the financial impact perspective might include outcome and output areas such as the following:

- ☐ Profitability
- ☐ Diversity return-on-investment (DROI)
- ☐ Benefit generated
- ☐ Tracking the number of high-risk individuals attending HIV awareness presentations
- ☐ Market share of wallet
- ☐ Cost reduction
- ☐ Expense reduction
- ☐ Revenue improvement
- ☐ Litigation costs
- ☐ Troubled family caseload
- ☐ Human capital value

These are just a small sample of the broad range of critical success factor areas available to support the financial impact perspective.

Strategy remains at the core of the diversity scorecard system, regardless of whether it is a government agency, *Fortune* 500 company, or a mom and pop store; however, government organizations often have a difficult time cultivating a clear and concise strategy to define critical success factor areas. While many attempt to develop statements of strategy, in the government, they amount to little more than detailed lists of programs and initiatives used to secure dollars from legislative funding bodies. As a result, early governmental scorecard efforts focused primarily on internal measures of efficiency and quality with little regard to the ultimate goal of serving a diverse group of citizens. A review of the history books reveals some interesting trends.

As mentioned earlier, the 1980s and early 1990s saw a rise in prominence of the quality movement in government circles, the effects of which strongly influenced performance measurement. Clearly, public-sector organizations need to supplement the goals of strategy with higher-level objectives describing why they exist and ultimately what they hope to achieve. In other words, they need to describe their mission.

"Reducing illiteracy," "Decreasing the incidence of HIV," and "Increasing public safety," are all examples of goals we would expect public agencies to espouse, but they are not strategies. They are missions, providing the motivating force for action within the public-sector agency. These overarching objectives must be placed at the top of the government diversity scorecard to guide the development of performance measures that will lead to their fulfillment. With its position at the top of the scorecard, the mission clearly communicates to all why the organization exists and what it is striving to achieve (Niven, 2002).

A clear distinction between private and public sector scorecards is drawn as a result of placing the mission at the top of the framework. Flowing from the mission is a view of the organization's customers, not financial stakeholders. Achieving a mission does not equate with fiscal responsibility and stewardship; instead, the government or not-for-profit organization must determine who it aims to serve and how their requirements can best be met. In the profit-seeking world, companies are accountable to their capital providers (shareholders) for results, and they monitor this accountability through the results attained in the financial perspective of the scorecard.

Not so in the public sector. Here the focus is on customers and serving their needs in order to accomplish the mission. But the question of who is the customer is one of the most perplexing issues that government scorecard adopters face. In the public sector, unlike the for-profit world, different groups design the service, pay for the service, and ultimately benefit from the service. This web of relationships makes determining the customer a formidable challenge for many public-sector managers. Establishing the real customer in many ways depends on your perspective. The legislative body that provides funding is a logical choice, as is the group you serve; however, think about that group you serve. Would law enforcement agencies consider the criminals they arrest their customer? You could probably make a case for that. Conversely, many would argue that constituents are the ultimate beneficiaries of policing activities and are therefore the real customers.

Fortunately, scorecard technology does not force you to make this difficult decision. Including all customers is permissible and possible using the public-sector scorecard framework. Not only is it possible, it is desirable because meeting the mission will most likely entail satisfying disparate customer groups, each of whom figure in your success. Each group of customers identified will likely result in different measures appearing in the other perspectives of the diversity scorecard. Once public-sector executives and managers have made their way through

Table 13-1. Potential Financial Impact Measures

☐ Percentage diversity
  return-on-investment (DROI)
☐ Accident costs
☐ Benefits costs as a percentage *of*
  payroll *or* revenue
☐ Benefits costs/competitors'
  benefits costs ratio
☐ Diversity expense per employee
☐ Diversity expense/total expense
☐ Turnover costs
☐ Dollar incremental increase
  generated from diverse market
  share penetration
☐ Dollar expense reduction
☐ Cost per grievance

☐ Cost per hire
☐ Cost per trainee hour
☐ Diversity department budget as a
  percentage of sales
☐ Competency development
  expense per employee
☐ Dollars saved as a result of
  diversity initiatives
☐ Reduced litigation costs
☐ Human capital value added
☐ Cost reduction in troubled
  family caseload as a result of
  diversity improvement
☐ Dollar market share of wallet
☐ Dollar revenue improvement

Source: Edward E. Hubbard, *Measuring Diversity Stat Pak Software Series*. Petaluma, CA: Global Insights, 2000.

this tangled maze, the job of choosing performance measures in all perspectives becomes much simpler.

Sample Measures to Drive the Index

Most organizations have little difficulty in generating a multitude of financial impact measures. They usually focus on a combination of metrics in the financial impact perspective, such as those in Table 13-1.

The measures shown are generic but will provide you with some guidance. Your challenge is to identify the unique processes that drive the financial impact ratios in your organization, and define specific measures that tell your particular story.

ANALYZING DATA

Analyzing data in the financial impact perspective enables the organization to examine diversity's ability to affect the economic growth and stability of the organization. For many years, the general practice of matching human and financial variables at the corporate level has been confined to a single gross measure derived from the income statements of corporations. This metric is revenue per employee. It is simplistic, in that it does not separate the effects of human effort from the leverage of other assets.

For instance, we cannot see in revenue per employee the effects of automation, better inventory control, improved quality, training, effective marketing programs, monopolistic conditions, or anything else. All it yields is a general trend. Adherence to this single metric has driven the myth that the impact of human effort cannot be measured at the enterprise level. The fact is that several metrics can be applied to the relationship of human capital to corporate financials (Fitz-enz, 2000).

Human Capital Metrics and Corporate Financials

When organizations view their metrics, they are examining a result, not a cause. The same notion is true with corporate-level human capital metrics. It is the same as looking at gross sales or operating expense. These metrics are simply the end point of a large number of activities that occurred within the organization, many of which were affected by outside forces. For example, the gross sales metric does not indicate what activities within the sales and marketing function were the primary drivers of the result. It could have been the result of a cadre of great salespeople, a brilliant advertising campaign, having the best product, price discounting, or myriad other factors. It also could have occurred despite having a marginal sales force, based on great customer loyalty, a competitive advantage in delivery capability, or a series of competitor mistakes. In order to find causes, we have to break the corporate-level metric down and look at it from various angles over time. This segmented, longitudinal view will eventually indicate what drove the end result, be it good or bad. So, as the organization views several combinations of revenue, costs, and employees, it is important to keep in mind that the causes will be found later in the organization's processes, along with the way in which the firm or agency acquires and deploys its human capital (Fitz-enz, 2000).

A continuous series of events and reactions drives organizations. Many improvement programs, such as reengineering projects, start at a business unit process level with presumed but untested assumptions of some distant, vague value. This is a common, fundamentally flawed approach. Value can be added only if the goals of the enterprise are foremost. Everything starts there (Fitz-enz, 2000).

From the enterprise-wide financial, market, and human goals, the business units derive their service, quality, and productivity objectives. The objectives are achieved or not achieved through the actions of people, the human capital. In essence, everything in an organization oscillates across processes between corporate goals and human capital management. We need tactical-level metrics to measure improvements within the human resources–based functions and to monitor the human capital effects on business unit objectives. We need strategic-level metrics to show the effects of human capital on corporate goals. If the organization desires to demonstrate diversity's contribution to the bottom line, measures, strategies, and tactics must be linked and aligned to show "line of sight" to the organization's strategic goals and objectives.

A first step in looking at the human capital aspect of financials is to revise the traditional revenue per employee metric. Sales per employee is the standard measure used by the federal government and most business media. This equation is not only simplistic, it is out of date. In the days when management first began to look at sales or revenue per employee, the corporate landscape was considerably simpler than it is now. In other than seasonal businesses, most employees were hired to work full time. But in today's market, organizations employ human talent in several ways. In addition to the traditional full-time employee, many people work part-time. This changes the corporate denominator from employee to full-time equivalent (FTE). As a simple example, if 10 people work half-time, the FTE is five people, although the number of employees is 10. The number 10 represents what is commonly referred to as head count (Fitz-enz, 2000).

To further complicate matters, a growing percentage of the American workforce is what has come to be called *contingent*. These are often referred to as "rented" employees. According to government statistics, in 1998, contingent workers represented about 14 percent of the American workforce population. These people are not truly employees because they are not usually on the payroll. Nevertheless, their labor has to be accounted for in order to have a valid representation of the labor invested to produce a given amount of revenue.

The bottom line is that to calculate this human capital metric correctly, you must convert revenue per employee into what the Saratoga Institute reports as revenue factor, which is revenue per FTE (including full-time, part-time, and contingent labor hours). FTE is a surrogate for the total labor hours invested. It is a basic measure of human productivity, in that it conveys how much time is spent to generate a given amount of revenue. Although this is a better starting point than revenue per employee, it is still too simple. Organizations need more sophisticated metrics to understand the relationship of human capital to financial outcomes (Fitz-enz, 2000). Let's examine one such measure called human capital value added to illustrate this point.

Table 13-2. Financial Information

Financial Information	Amount
Revenue	$100,000,000
Expense	$80,000,000
Payroll and Benefits	$24,000,000
Contingents Cost	$3,750,000
Absence Cost	$200,000
Turnover Cost	$3,600,000
Employee (FTEs)	500
Contingents (FTEs)	100

Human Capital Value Added

The issue of human capital productivity was seen earlier in a simplistic form as revenue per employee; however, what if we wanted to improve the clarity of the organization's human capital impact picture by examining profitability per FTE? This could be accomplished using the formula shown as follows and a few hypothetical facts about the financial results of the organization.

Suppose the financial data given in Table 13-2 existed for the organization.

Using the following formula, human capital value added can be calculated:

$$\text{HCVA} = \frac{\text{Revenue} - (\text{Expenses} - \text{Pay and Benefits})}{\text{FTEs}}$$

In this example, we are looking at the profitability of the average employee. By subtracting all corporate expenses, except for pay and benefits, we obtain an adjusted profit figure. In effect, we have taken out nonhuman expenses. Then, when we divide the adjusted profit figure by FTEs, we produce an average profit per FTE. Note that this can be set up to include or exclude the cost of contingents, absence, and turnover. We will look at it both ways using the hypothetical figures—first, with only pay and benefits:

$$\text{HCVA} = \frac{\$100,000,000 - (\$80,000,000 - \$24,000,000)}{500}$$

$$HCVA = \frac{\$44,000,000}{500}$$

$$HCVA = \frac{\$88,000}{FTE}$$

If we include the cost of contingents, absence, and turnover, we would have an adjusted profit figure of $51,550,000. Calculated as

$$HCVA = \frac{\$100,000,000 - [\$80,000,000 - \$31,550,000]}{600}$$

$$HCVA = \frac{\$100,000,000 - \$48,450,000}{600}$$

$$HCVA = \frac{\$85,917}{FTE}$$

Note: The 600 FTEs include employees and contingents.

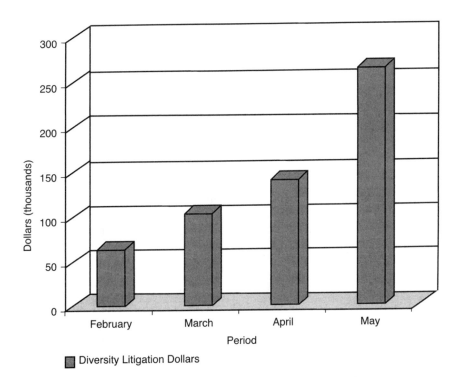

Figure 13-1. Diversity litigation costs over time.

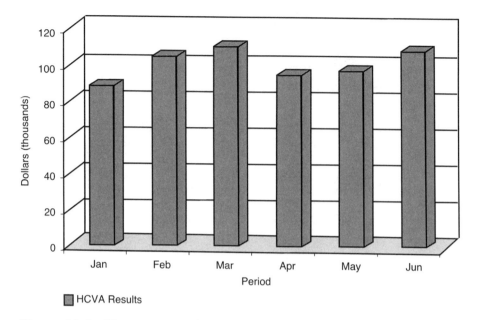

Figure 13-2. Human capital value-added results by periods. (Source: Hubbard, Edward E. *Diversity Scorecard Stat Pak Software Series.* Petaluma, CA: Global Insights Publishing, 2003.)

As can be seen with this example, with a minimum of effort an organization can gain an understanding of the effects of people on financials. To suggest there is no valid and consistent way to measure several financial aspects of human capital is tremendously shortsighted.

REPORTING DATA

There are a wide variety of ways to display and report your financial impact data. This data can be presented in tables, graphs, narratives, pictograms, and so on. For example, when you examine a completed analysis for a diversity financial impact study, you will likely see these measures appear on a separate scorecard report or integrated with standard organization financial reports. This report may consist of some general text about the diversity process, which influenced and/or drove the financial results, as well as recommendations, figures such as tables, bar graphs, and pie charts, and within those figures, some statistics. Sample graphics might include those presented in Figures 13-1, 13-2, and 13-3.

Reporting the results of the diversity financial impact perspective is an essential part of the organization's financial performance feedback

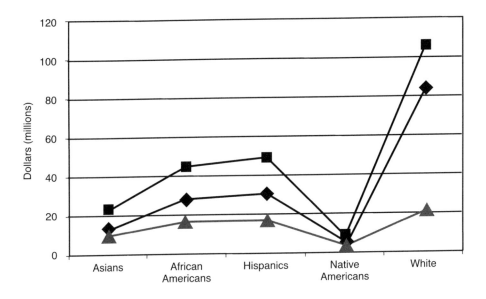

Figure 13-3. Period-to-period market share of wallet—consumer product division. (Source: Hubbard, Edward E. *Diversity Scorecard Stat Pak Software Series.* Petaluma, CA: Global Insights Publishing, 2003.)

system (like any other strategic portions of the business) to ensure that diversity-related changes implemented are providing value to the organization. By charting and reviewing progress to date, organizations can make informed choices about their next strategic move for improved organizational performance to meet the needs of its stakeholders and stockholders.

FINAL THOUGHTS

In a for-profit organization, the diversity financial impact perspective measures serve as the focus for the objectives and measures in all of the other scorecard perspectives. In public and not-for-profit sector diversity scorecard models, financial impact measures can best be seen as either enablers of customer success or constraints within which the group must operate. Every measure selected should be part of a link of cause-and-effect relationships that culminate in improving financial performance. This chapter highlighted some of the critical financial linkages that must be made to tie diversity back to business results in dollars and cents.

In the next chapter, we will bring all of the individual index perspectives together and create a sample diversity scorecard.

REFERENCES

Berman, Evan, and Xiao Hu Wang. "Performance Measurement in U.S. Counties: Capacity for Reform." *Public Administration Review*, September/October 2000, 3.

Best Practices in Achieving Workforce Diversity Report. Washington, DC: U.S. Department of Commerce and National Partnership for Reinventing (NPR) Government, 2001.

Bildman, Lars. "Go Directly to Jail." *Business Week*, February 9, 1998, 48.

Brown, Mark Graham. *Keeping Score*. New York: Quality Resources, 1996.

Casio, Wayne F. *Costing Human Resources*. Australia: South-Western, 2000.

Ellison, Keith. "The Next Step Diversity 100." *Next Step Magazine*, Spring 1999, 34.

Fitz-enz, Jac. *The ROI of Human Capital*. New York: AMACOM, 2000.

Hubbard, Edward E. *Measuring Diversity Stat Pak Software Series*. Petaluma, CA: Global Insights, 2000.

Maisel, Lawrence S. *Performance Measurements Survey*. American Institute of Certified Public Accountants, 2001.

Miller, L. "Workers Sex Suit Settled: Harassment Claims Net $9.85 Million." *The Wall Street Journal*, February 6, 1998, A3.

Niven, Paul R. *Balanced Scorecard: Step-by-Step: Maximizing Performance and Maintaining Results*. New York: John Wiley & Sons, 2002.

Robinson, Edward, and Jonathan Hickman. "The Diversity Elite." *Fortune*, July 1999, 62.

"Sex, Lies, and Home Improvements?" *Business Week*, March 31, 1997, 40.

Sharf, J.C., and D.P. Jones. "Employment Risk Management." In J. Kehoe (ed.), *Managing Selection in Today's Organizations*. San Francisco: Jossey-Bass (in press).

"Texaco to Pay $176.1 Million in Bias Suit." *The Wall Street Journal*, November 18, 1996, A3, A4.

Thor, Carl G. "The Evolution of Performance Measurement in Government." *Journal of Cost Management*, May/June 2000, 18–26.

Walters, Jonathan. *Measuring Up*. Washington, DC: Governing Books, 1998.

FURTHER READING

Casio, Wayne F. *Managing Human Resources: Productivity, Quality of Work Life, Profits*, 5th ed. Burr Ridge, IL: Irwin/McGraw-Hill, 1998.

Cox, Taylor H. Jr. *Cultural Diversity in Organizations: Theory, Research, and Practice*. San Francisco: Berrett-Koehler, 1993.

Henry, Pamela. *Diversity and the Bottom Line*. Austin, TX: TurnKey Press, 2002.

Hubbard, Edward E. *A Casebook in Diversity Measurement and Diversity Management*. Petaluma, CA: Global Insights, 2003.

Hubbard, Edward E. *The Diversity Scorecard Fieldbook*. Petaluma, CA: Global Insights, 2003.

CHAPTER 14

Building Your Diversity Scorecard

PREREQUISITES FOR SUCCESS

Constructing your organization's first diversity scorecard must be accomplished by implementing a systematic process that builds consensus and clarity about how to translate the organization's vision and strategy into diversity operational objectives and measures. Selecting the right diversity metrics or measures is actually much more than deciding what to measure. It is, in fact, a key part of your overall strategy for success. Select the wrong diversity performance metrics and you may help the organization go out of business, although all graphs indicate that you are healthy. Select the wrong metrics and your worst nightmare might come true—employees actually implement and perform well according to these wrong metrics (Brown, 1996)!

The concepts in this diversity scorecard book, in general, may appear straightforward. It is almost common sense that all organizations need a balanced diversity scorecard of some sort and that fewer measures are better than too many; however, coming up with a good, precise set of diversity metrics that actually predict your success and show causal relationships to performance is quite difficult. Doing so often requires extensive (and often expensive) research to settle in on the right index or metric that predicts your success in the marketplace. Some trial and error is also involved. It is critical that you have the training and expertise to design these measures effectively or that you hire a diversity metrics consultant with these diversity metric design skills to help you get off to a good start.

DIVERSITY MEASUREMENT IS A SPECIALIZED DISCIPLINE REQUIRING SPECIAL EXPERTISE

Measuring diversity results is a specialized discipline. Like finance, operations, marketing, and so on, diversity measurement design requires an expert with detailed learning, specialized diversity measurement skills, and the expertise to do it effectively and correctly. The importance of getting the organization's diversity metrics right initially is magnified by the number of people and processes its diversity initiatives will touch and the need to meet obligations to stakeholders and stockholders. Practitioners must approach work in the diversity metrics area, and others, with the utmost care and concerns, especially because key stakeholders will want to know what is the payoff and value-added by investing in diversity practices and processes.

Measuring the impact of diversity initiatives is often an afterthought. The Hubbard Diversity Measurement and Productivity (HDM&P) Institute research has shown that organizations rarely budget and/or plan for measurement processes ahead of time to evaluate the impact of their initiatives. They may have spent literally thousands and perhaps millions of dollars involving hundreds of employees in diversity awareness, skill building, work life, recruitment, and other initiatives and have little or no evidence to show the diversity return-on-investment and dollar benefit gained. Diversity measurement is often added at the end of the process when there are few dollars left to complete a comprehensive impact study. What if the organization is making tremendous progress and doesn't know it because of the lack of measurement practices? True diversity impact measurement must go beyond an end-of-course evaluation sheet. It must demonstrate learning as well as how that learning is applied. Where appropriate, diversity practitioners must analyze the initiative's business impact and its return-on-investment. Many organizations know diversity is the right thing to do. In addition, they also know that as organizational stewards, they must justify how much it cost to do the right thing and verify that it is the business thing to do!

All aspects related to building your diversity scorecard must be planned with adequate resources to forge the right measurement links to drive business performance. Selecting the right measures and indices for your scorecard will require a balanced mix of measures that are strategically linked to the organization's strategy. These measures cannot be a random collection of measures used simply because another respected organization happens to be tracking them. The diversity scorecard design team, with expert help, must make informed choices about what should be included in the scorecard. The project requires an architect who can frame and facilitate the process and collect relevant background information for constructing the scorecard. The diversity scorecard, however, should represent the collective wisdom and energies of the senior executive team's vision of diversity in the organization. Unless this senior team is fully engaged in the process, a successful outcome is unlikely. Without the active sponsorship and participation of the senior executives, a diversity scorecard project should not be initiated. It will surely fail without leadership and commitment at the top. The diversity scorecard initiative would most likely be seen as a staff-led initiative to provide a diversity measurement system, not to make fundamental changes in the way the organization viewed or managed itself.

The conceptual appeal of the diversity scorecard, however, is not a sufficient reason to embark on such an initiative. When the process is launched, the senior executive team should identify and agree on the principal purposes for the initiative. The initiative objectives will help to achieve the following:

☐ Guide the construction of objectives and measures for the diversity scorecard.
☐ Gain commitment among the initiative participants.
☐ Clarify the framework for implementation and management processes that must follow the construction of the initial diversity scorecard.

A diversity scorecard initiative is extremely valuable for an organization's success, and there are several reasons for constructing a scorecard, including the following (Kaplan and Norton, 1996):

☐ Obtain clarity and consensus about the diversity strategy.
☐ Achieve focus and direction.
☐ Identify the critical few drivers of organizational performance using diversity.
☐ Create a vehicle to set priorities.
☐ Achieve specific objectives of acknowledged strategic importance.
☐ Create operational consensus and teamwork.
☐ Eliminate non-value-added activities.
☐ Provide strategic intervention guidelines and rationale.

Implementing a diversity scorecard can bring clarity and purpose to the organization's diversity vision in a way that helps motivate and sustain the organization because it is linked to accomplishing the organization's objectives. It builds consensus around the role of diversity in the organizational landscape and helps provide concrete links to the way diversity will help create value-added performance. It helps eliminate non-value-added activities and processes and sets priorities for completing diversity objectives that are of acknowledged strategic importance in the organization. When needed, it helps provide direction for strategic interventions and outlines the guidelines and rationale for selection based on organizational performance needs and future goals.

In summary, the initial impetus for constructing a balanced diversity scorecard can arise from the need to achieve the following:

☐ Clarify and gain consensus about vision and strategy.
☐ Build a diversity management team.
☐ Communicate the diversity strategy.
☐ Link reward to achieving strategic objectives using diversity.
☐ Set strategic targets.
☐ Align resources and strategic initiatives.
☐ Sustain investment in intellectual and intangible assets.
☐ Provide a foundation for strategic learning.

Whether a diversity scorecard, marketing scorecard, operations scorecard, and the like, the above items offer value-added benefits to the organization.

THE DIVERSITY SCORECARD TEAM

Once agreement on the objectives and future role for the diversity scorecard has been reached, the organization should select the person who will serve as the architect, or project leader, for the diversity scorecard initiative. The architect will own and maintain the framework, philosophy, and methodology for designing and developing the scorecard. Of course, any good architect requires a client, which in this case is the senior management team. As in any building project, the client must be totally engaged in the development process because the client will assume ultimate ownership of the scorecard and will, along with the Chief Diversity Officer and/or others, lead the management processes associated with using it.

The architect guides the process, oversees the scheduling of meetings and interviews, ensures that adequate documentation, background readings, and market and competitive information are available to the project team, and, in general, keeps the process on track and on schedule. The architect, over the course of facilitating the construction of the initial diversity scorecard, must manage both a cognitive, analytic process—translating soft, general statements about strategy and intent into explicit, measurable objectives—and an interpersonal, even emotional, process of team building and conflict resolution.

The architect is usually a co-partnership of a senior staff manager and the Chief Diversity Officer in the organization. Experts like Robert Kaplan and David Norton have seen people from a broad range of backgrounds managing and facilitating the development process of a scorecard. They include the following (Kaplan and Norton, 1996):

☐ Vice president of strategic planning or business development
☐ Vice president of quality management
☐ Vice president of finance or divisional controller

Some organizations have used outside consultants to assist the internal architect for the scorecard development process. It is strongly recommended that, given the nature of diversity as an emerging theoretical and applied sciences discipline, the diversity scorecard team has a diversity metrics and measurement expert to assist in translating the organization's business strategies into diversity performance strategies and diversity metrics. The value these professionals can add to the process can be immeasurable.

BUILDING A DIVERSITY SCORECARD: THE PROCESS

Each organization is unique and will need to follow its own path for building a balanced diversity scorecard. It is possible, however, to describe a typical and systematic development plan that can be used to create a sample diversity scorecard with some of the basics. If executed properly, this process should encourage commitment to the scorecard among senior and mid-level managers and produce a good diversity scorecard that will help the organization utilize diversity for improved performance.

Action Step 1: The Organization Must Clearly Define Its Business Strategy

Senior leaders and the Chief Diversity Officer who sits at the business table as a strategic partner must provide an essential perspective that helps the organization craft its business strategy. By focusing on how to implement the strategy rather than solely on what the strategy consists of, they can facilitate a discussion about how to communicate the firm's goals throughout the organization. When strategic goals are not developed with an eye toward how they will be implemented and communicated throughout the organization, they tend to become very generic (e.g., maximize operating efficiency, or increase presence in ethnic markets, or improve productivity). These goals are so vague that individual employees simply cannot know how to take action to achieve them. Worse, employees cannot recognize them as unique to their organization.

You can test this theory using a process that Becker, Huselid, and Ulrich have found useful. They often run a simple experiment in their executive education classes. They ask participants to write down their organization's mission or vision statement, all of which are then retyped (removing any mention of the organization's name) and redistributed among the group. Next they ask participants to pick out their own mission and vision statements from this collection. These statements are so vague, and so similar, that most find it very difficult to do so (Becker, Huselid, and Ulrich, 2001).

Clarifying your organization's strategy in precise terms can take practice. The key thing is to state the organization's goals so that employees understand their role and the organization knows how it will measure success in achieving them.

Action Step 2: Build a Business Case for Diversity as a Strategic Asset

Once the larger organization clarifies its business strategy, diversity professionals need to build a clear business case for why and how diversity is linked to the business and how it can support that strategy. In making this business case, you have the benefit of a decade of systematic research to support your recommendations. While a comprehensive review of this research is beyond the scope of this book, some key results can be highlighted. First, evidence gathered from four national surveys and more than 2,800 organizations strongly suggests that a high-performance work system has a distinct, positive influence on an organization's financial performance (Becker, Huselid, and Ulrich, 2001). The results demonstrate that better people management matters, and it does so in terms that matter outside the human resources domain.

One study indicates that the ROI in a high-performance people management strategy are not linear. Organizations in the sample appear to have three distinct experiences as their people management systems become more focused on performance. First, organizations moving from the lowest percentile rankings to the twentieth percentile enjoy a significant improvement in organizational performance. At this point, the people management functions move from being an impediment to strategy implementation to having a neutral strategic influence. Said differently, by improving to the twentieth percentile, the Human Resource Management (HRM) system creates value simply by getting out of the way (Becker, Huselid, and Ulrich, 2001).

Second, for the broad middle range (twentieth to sixtieth percentile firms), improving the quality of a firm's people management system has little marginal impact on firm performance. This marks the consolidation of the transformation from a personnel to a professional focus in human resources. This approach does no damage, but HRM is still not really a strategic partner.

Finally, firms above the sixtieth percentile not only have adopted the appropriate HRM practices and implemented them effectively throughout the firm but also have begun to integrate the people management system into the strategic fabric of the firm. As a practical matter, above the sixtieth percentile, the marginal impact of people management on firm performance is the same as it is for those firms below the twentieth percentile, but for different reasons. The very best firms in the sample enjoy the payoffs from combining the appropriate people management policies and practices into an internally coherent system that is directly aligned with business priorities and operating initiatives most likely to create economic value. In essence, the study findings point to the significant financial returns available to organizations that dramatically increase the quality of their people management (HRM) systems (Becker, Huselid, and Ulrich, 2001).

Although these effects are financially significant, keep in mind that they do not represent a magic bullet. That is, simple changes in a people management practice will not immediately send an organization's stock price soaring. Remember that this study concentrates on measures that describe an entire human resource system. Changing this system by the magnitude required to enjoy these gains takes time, insight, and considerable effort. It is fair to say that it requires a transformation of the people management (Human Resource and Diversity) functions and organizational systems. If it could be done overnight, human resource, diversity, and organizational systems would be easily imitated and would quickly lose much of their strategic character (Becker, Huselid, and Ulrich, 2001).

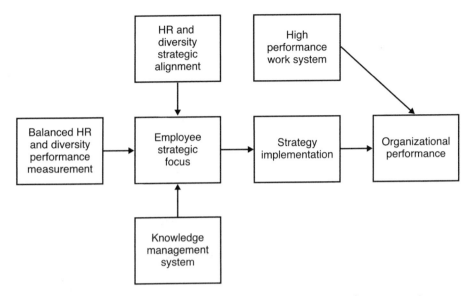

Figure 14-1. Model for a business case for strategic diversity. (Source: Adapted from Becker, B., M. Huselid, and D. Ulrich. The HR Scorecard. Boston, MA: Harvard Business School Press, 2001.)

The business case for a strategic diversity role must also incorporate diversity's key influence on strategy implementation and the role of strategically focused measurement systems. Becker, Huselid, and Ulrich describe a model for such a business case based on a recent survey of more than 400 firms. This model can also be applied to diversity management, as shown in Figure 14-1.

These results tell a simple but powerful story: Strategy implementation, rather than strategy content, differentiates successful from unsuccessful firms. It is simply much easier to choose an appropriate strategy than it is to implement it effectively. Moreover, successful strategy implementation is driven by employee strategic focus, HR strategic alignment, and a balanced HR and diversity performance measurement system. The linchpin of successful strategy implementation is a strategically focused workforce. It is the ultimate people management performance driver. Finally, a balanced performance measurement system, in tandem with an aligned people management system and effective knowledge management, is the foundation for a strategically focused organization.

Action Step 3: Create a Diversity Value Chain and Strategy Map

Clarifying your organization's strategy sets the stage for implementing that strategy, but it is just the first step. In most organizations, the value embodied in the organization's products and services is the result of a complex, cumulative process—what Michael Porter refers to as the organization's value chain. All organizations have a value chain—even those that have not articulated it—and the company's performance measurement system must account for every link in that chain (Becker, Huselid, and Ulrich, 2001). Diversity scorecard measures are a key part of that value chain for implementing change in an organization. As Figure 14-2 shows, this value chain is comprised of four basic components.

Generally speaking, all processes are begun to produce value. Any other purpose would be wasteful. One of our objectives should be to develop more effective ways to measure and evaluate changes in the organization's diversity improvement activities/processes, outcomes, impact, and resulting value. The scorecard development team must be able to construct the scorecard with an eye toward the value diversity creates for the organization. Table 14-1 shows some typical value chain examples.

For every use of resources to improve an organization using a diversity activity/process, there should be an improvement in result. We call the result an outcome. The difference between this outcome and the previous outcomes before the diversity process improvement was implemented is the impact. The dollar improvement represented by the impact is the value added. An example is to change the sourcing methods used to hire diverse workforce talent (activities/process), which shortens the time to fill jobs (outcome).

As jobs are filled faster (see impact 1), there is less need to use temporary or contract workers (see impact 2). The cost avoidance can be calculated and a dollar savings computed (see value added 1). If, through the

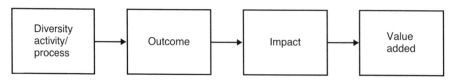

Figure 14-2. Four basic components of the value chain for implementing change. (Source: Hubbard, Edward E. Measuring Diversity Results. Petaluma, CA: Global Insights Publishing, 1997.)

Table 14-1. Typical Value Chain Examples

Activity/Process	Outcome	Impact	Value-Added
☐ Increase diverse talent recruitment sources	☐ Shorter time-to-fill rates ☐ Lower agency rates	☐ Jobs filled faster ☐ Lower hiring costs	☐ Reduced operating expense
☐ Improve diverse work team problem-solving processes	☐ Reduced time to solve	☐ Increase in reason given in survey for long service by diverse member	☐ Retention savings as compared to rolling average of previous years
☐ Install succession planning for diverse workforce	☐ Fewer emergency minority hires	☐ Less recruitment expense	☐ Lower operating expense

Source: Edward E. Hubbard, *Measuring Diversity Results*. Petaluma, CA: Global Insights, 1997.

diversity department's effort to change sourcing methods, jobs are filled faster, not only does the organization reduce operating expense, but the cost of the human resource product is also lowered and moved to market faster (value added 2). Lower human resource (product) acquisition cost and shorter human resource asset delivery time to the organization can create a competitive advantage (value added 3), especially in light of less successful competitors (based on benchmarking analysis comparisons).

Thus, scorecard measures of diversity activities and/or processes are vital in order to gain feedback on staff accountability for generating solutions to address such key business issues as inadequate diverse talent acquisition. Without these activities or processes, we could not produce the accompanying outcomes, impacts, and results. Even if these activities or processes produced poor results, the diversity organization can gain by knowing what else does not work and then shift its efforts to more productive outcomes.

Success is achieved through performance. Performance is more than activity. Each activity must be turned toward adding value. Most of those values must be measurable. In order to measure, it is vital to learn how to use simple arithmetic data to illustrate the value of the workforce diversity effort.

To define the value-creation process in your organization, the diversity organization should develop a strategy map to represent the organization's value chain. To begin the mapping process in your own organization, look closely at your organization's strategic objectives and its vision for diversity and ask yourself the following questions:

- ☐ Which strategic goals/objectives/outcomes are critical rather than nice to have?
- ☐ What are the performance drivers for each goal?
- ☐ How would we measure progress toward these goals?
- ☐ What are the barriers to the achievement of each goal?
- ☐ How would employees need to behave to ensure that the organization or the agency achieves these goals?
- ☐ Is the diversity function providing the organization with diversity management competencies and behaviors necessary to achieve these objectives? If not, what needs to change?

These simple questions can generate a wealth of information about how well an organization's diversity function has been contributing to the organization's success and its ability to create and enhance the pool of strategic capability.

A strategy map of the value-creation process contains hypotheses, or predictions, about which organizational processes drive organization performance. Normally, an organization validates these hypotheses only after achieving targets on performance drivers and observing the impact of these results on firm performance; however, if the organization can graphically depict the relationships among performance drivers while mapping the firm's value chain, it can have that much more confidence in its strategy implementation plan.

Action Step 4: Conduct Strategic Data-Gathering Interviews

It is important that the diversity scorecard project team takes time to meet with key stakeholders and executives to gather critical information. During these interviews, the architect obtains their input on the organization's strategic objectives and discusses tentative proposals for diversity scorecard measures across the particular diversity perspectives that make sense for the organization. These perspectives would have been chosen with the help of a qualified diversity measurement consulting professional to ensure they meet key requirements for performance and causality, especially if the diversity scorecard outcomes are to be linked to show compelling evidence of demonstrated ROI.

For simplicity's sake, we have referred to the architect as a single person, but in fact, the interview process and subsequent synthesis of information is best done by a group of two or three individuals. The architect, as the team leader, will typically conduct the actual interview, asking questions and probing after responses. The diversity measurement consultant may concentrate on the actual objectives and measures specified by the executive; another team member attempts to capture quotes that flesh out and give more meaning and context to the objectives and measures. The interviews can be free flowing and unstructured, but the interview process, as well as the aggregation of information supplied by the executives, should be facilitated such that the architect uses a common set of questions that generate a common set of potential responses.

The interviews accomplish several important objectives—some obvious, others less so. The explicit objectives are to introduce the concept of the diversity scorecard to senior managers, to respond to questions they have about the concept, and to get their initial input about the organization's strategy, and how this translates into objectives and measures for the scorecard. The implicit objectives include (1) beginning the process of having top management think about translating strategy and objectives into tangible, diversity operational measures, (2) learning about the concerns that key individuals may have about developing and implementing a diversity scorecard, and (3) identifying potential conflicts among the key participants either in their views of the strategy and objectives or their views of diversity or their conflicts at a personal or interfunctional level.

Action Step 5: Identify Diversity Deliverables within the Strategy Map

Diversity creates much of its value at the points of intersection between the people management system and the strategy implementation system. Maximizing that value requires an understanding of both sides of that intersection. Historically, diversity managers lacked the requisite knowledge of the business side of the intersection, and general managers did not fully appreciate the diversity side. Although this gap has narrowed in recent decades, diversity managers should take primary responsibility for depicting both the diversity performance drivers and diversity enablers on the strategy map.

This process can be difficult and does require the help of a diversity measurement expert or some strategic partner with that expertise. On the one hand, people management performance drivers such as employee competence, motivation, and availability are so fundamental that it may be virtually impossible to know where to locate them on the map. To perform this step, it is important to know which diversity deliverables (again, both performance drivers and enablers) support the firm-level performance drivers depicted in the strategy map. Try to focus on the kinds of strategic behaviors that are broadly a function of competencies, rewards, and work organization.

Misalignment between the diversity performance driver system and the strategy implementation system can actually destroy value. One example is the experience of a large money center. Like many other banks in their industry, the organization switched from full-time to part-time front-line tellers to offer flexible work time and to save payroll costs. In many of its locations, the company outsourced entire cadres of tellers and then leased the employees back from a contractor. In the short run, this strategy did lower labor costs; however, about a year later, the bank faced a shortage of candidates for the head teller and junior loan officer positions. Not only had the organization dismantled the training and development opportunities that had historically prepared tellers for promotion, but in its shift to part-time employment, it had attracted workers who were not particularly interested in full-time positions, as well as some individuals who were not necessarily promotable.

As an unintended consequence of the shift toward part-time employment, recruiting and compensation costs shot up for positions two to three levels above the entry-level teller positions. The bank was now forced to hire from the outside, but it no longer had the selection and training systems in place to do so. In the long run, total compensation costs thus increased significantly, including considerable time lost and discontent among other employees. The lesson is that the strategic diversity measurement system adopted by the firm (flexibility and short-term payroll costs) eventually harmed the business's overall performance and had exactly the opposite effect of what the problem fixers intended.

Action Step 6: Design the Strategic Diversity Measurement System

In Step 6, you actually design the diversity measurement system. This requires not only a new perspective on measuring diversity performance, but also the resolution of some technical issues that many diversity professionals may not be familiar with.

To measure the diversity firm performance relationship with precision, you need to develop valid measures of diversity deliverables. This task has two dimensions. First, you have to be confident that you have chosen the correct diversity performance drivers and enablers. This requires that you clearly comprehend the causal chain for effective strategy implementation in your organization. Second, you have to choose the correct measures for those deliverables. For example, in Figure 14-3, the diversity deliverable is senior staff employment stability, but there are several ways this concept could be measured.

Developing the actual measure would require that you precisely define who constitutes the senior staff (e.g., those with 5 to 15 years of professional experience) and what you mean by employment stability. Does the latter include all turnover or just voluntary? Does it include individuals who have been promoted to management responsibilities? Finally, you need to measure those variables accurately. This is why it is suggested that a qualified diversity measurement expert is hired as part of your team to help you accurately structure these scorecard elements and processes.

Sometimes diversity measures can be put forward with an aura of strategic import, but they do little to validate diversity's role as a strategic asset. Organizations may declare several people measures, such as diverse employee satisfaction, as having strategic value, and these metrics might even make their way into the reward system in some fashion. In such cases, there is a balance between financial ($$) and nonfinancial (NF)

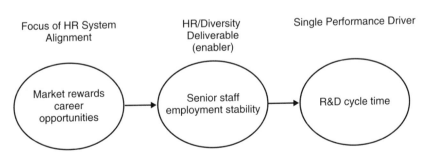

Figure 14-3. An example of a diversity deliverable. (Source: Adapted from Becker, B., M. Huselid, and D. Ulrich. The HR Scorecard. *Boston, MA: Harvard Business School Press, 2001.)*

measures, but there is no consensus about how these variables implement strategy; therefore, no strategic logic links these measures together.

SELECTING THE STRUCTURE FOR YOUR DIVERSITY SCORECARD

There are several different models on which to base the structure of your diversity scorecard. The one you select does not matter nearly as much as the metrics you end up including on your scorecard. In the chapter covering basic diversity scorecard components, the diversity scorecard was described as a balanced, carefully selected set of objectives and measures derived from an organization's strategy that link to the diversity strategy. And that the measures selected for the diversity scorecard represent a tool for diversity leaders to use in communicating to executives, managers, employees, and external stakeholders the diversity outcomes and performance drivers by which the organization will achieve its diversity mission and strategic diversity objectives. Because each organization's strategy is different, as determined by the specific industry and type of products and services it provides, its key diversity scorecard perspectives will also vary. Nonetheless, some basic objectives and measures to construct a sample diversity scorecard was highlighted using six perspectives:

1. Financial impact
2. Diverse customer/community partnership
3. Workforce profile
4. Workplace climate/culture
5. Diversity leadership commitment
6. Learning and growth

All of the measures that are selected to support each diversity scorecard perspective serve as translations of the organization's strategy and link them to the diversity strategy. Take a look at Figure 14-4.

The diversity scorecard is rooted in the organization's vision and strategy and driven by its leadership. To execute this vision and strategy, the final output from the diversity scorecard team should be, for each perspective:

☐ Identification of each perspective
☐ A list of the objectives for the perspective
☐ A list of the measures for each objective

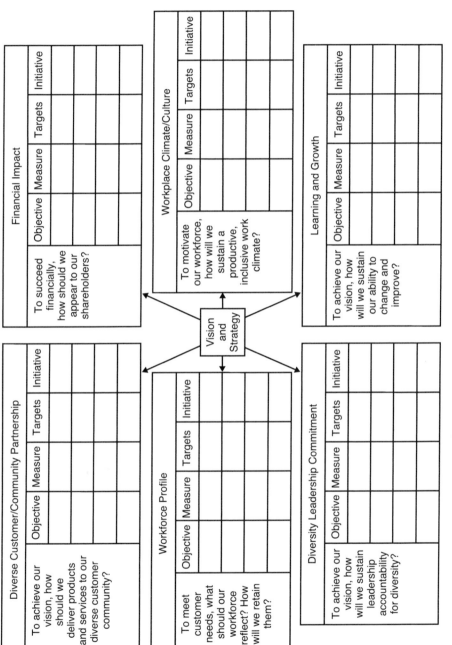

Figure 14-4. Basic objectives and measures for a sample diversity scorecard.

☐ A target(s) for each measure
☐ When available, the results for each measure listed

Sample diversity scorecard items might consist of the following representing perspectives (indices), objectives, and measures, such as those shown in Tables 14-2 through 14-7.

Table 14-2. Diversity Leadership Commitment Index

Objectives	Measures	Target	Results
Vision Formulation	☐ Diversity vision/mission written ☐ Number of times diversity mentioned as strategy in executive presentations		
Improved Diversity Climate	☐ Percentage favorable response on diversity climate survey – Leadership Dimension		
Career Development	☐ Number and percentage of IDPs achieved ☐ Internal promotion rate ☐ Percentage of promotion-ready minorities		

Table 14-3. Diverse Workforce Profile Index

Objectives	Measures	Target	Results
Recruitment	☐ Percentage new hires by demographic group ☐ Diversity hit rate ☐ Time-to-fill rate		
Workforce Representation	☐ Percentage people of color by demographic group ☐ Percentage minorities as officials and managers ☐ Percentage women as officials and managers		
Workforce Retention	☐ Percentage voluntary turnover: exempt and nonexempt ☐ Percentage diversity survival and loss rate ☐ Percentage diversity stability factor and instability factor		

Table 14-4. Workplace Culture/Climate Index

Objectives	Measures	Target	Results
Employee Satisfaction	☐ Percentage favorable ratings on climate surveys by demographic group ☐ "Employer of Choice" ratings versus top 5 to 10 competitors ☐ Perception of consistent and equitable treatment of all employees		
Grievances	☐ Cost per grievance ☐ Average time for dispute resolution ☐ Number of lawsuits by demographic group		
Work Life Balance	☐ Percentage work life benefits utilized ☐ Number and type of policies and procedures changed for diversity impact ☐ Workplace flexibility index ratings		

Table 14-5. Learning and Growth Index

Objectives	Measures	Target	Results
Diversity Training	☐ Number and percentage of diversity-competent employees ☐ Percentage employees with advanced degrees by demographic group ☐ Number of cross-trained employees by demographic group		
Productivity	☐ Project completion rate and quality index ☐ Innovation index ☐ Empowerment index		
Technology Access	☐ Percentage employees with computers ☐ Employee computer access by e-learning category		

Table 14-6. Diverse Customer/Community Partnership Index

Objectives	Measures	Target	Results
Ethnic Group Market Share	☐ Percentage ethnic market share penetration ☐ Number and percentage of new ethnic group customers ☐ Total annual dollar loss due to poor diverse customer management by group		
Diverse Customer Satisfaction	☐ Percentage diverse customer satisfaction ☐ Percentage customer retention by group ☐ Percentage customer loyalty		
Supplier Diversity	☐ Percentage subcontracting dollars to minority businesses ☐ Percentage subcontracting dollars to women-owned businesses		
Philanthropy	☐ Dollars given to community by group ☐ Number of sponsored community events		

Action Step 7: Implement Management by Measurement

Once the diversity scorecard is developed using the principles described in this book, the result is a powerful new management tool. Actually implementing this tool is much more than just keeping score of diversity's impact on organizational performance. If the diversity scorecard is aligned with the imperatives of the firm's strategy, diversity professionals will have new insight into what it takes to actually manage diversity as a strategic asset.

For example, GTE had always measured the turnover rates in its businesses, but before the development of its HR Scorecard, there had been little effort to understand the underlying dimensions of the turnover rates and their consequences for organizational profitability. In other words, although GTE HR measured turnover in the past, it really did not manage it as a business problem in its respective business units. As the GTE HR Scorecard was implemented, these turnover rates were more closely

Table 14-7. Financial Impact Index

Objectives	Measures	Target	Results
Profitability	☐ Human capital value-added ☐ Dollars saved as a result of diversity initiatives ☐ Diversity return-on-investment (DROI) ☐ Dollar incremental increase generated from diverse market share penetration		
Expense reduction	☐ Turnover costs ☐ Cost reduction in troubled family caseload resulting from diversity improvement ☐ Benefits costs as a percentage of payroll or revenue		
Litigation costs	☐ Reduced litigation costs ☐ Brand image impact enhancement costs		

analyzed, indicating substantial increases among new hires and the most experienced employees. A further analysis by demographic group would reveal even more data that turnover could be adversely affecting different groups within each population. The result was new people management interventions for both groups that addressed these problems with associated benefits for the performance of the business units involved (Becker, Huselid, Ulrich, 2001).

Action Step 8: Develop an Implementation Plan

A newly formed team, often made up of the leaders of each perspective subgroup, formalizes the diversity scorecard stretch targets and develops an implementation plan. This plan should include how the measures are to be linked to database and information systems, communicating the diversity scorecard throughout the organization, and encouraging and facilitating the development of second-level metrics for other organizational units. As a result of this process, an entirely new executive information system is created using diversity to link top-level business unit metrics and diversity down through the organization to support the overall strategy (Kaplan and Norton, 1996).

Action Step 9: Finalize the Implementation Plan

For a diversity scorecard to create value, it must be integrated into the organization's management system. It is recommended that management begin using the diversity scorecard within 60 days. Obviously, a phase-in plan must be developed, but the best available information should be used to focus the management agenda, consistent with the priorities of the scorecard. Ultimately, the management information systems will catch up to the process.

FINAL THOUGHTS

Implementing a new management process based on the diversity scorecard work done requires considerable change and flexibility. Moreover, the process is not just a one-time event. Diversity professionals must regularly review the diversity deliverables they have defined in order to be sure that these drivers and enablers remain strategically significant. This is particularly true for diversity enablers that have direct links to specific business objectives. Skilled diversity managers understand when an enabler is no longer playing a strategic role and needs to be replaced.

In the next section, the final part of this book will focus on key implementation issues that arise and must be addressed. It offers advice for achieving a strategic diversity scorecard alignment and dealing with some of the pitfalls of managing strategic change.

REFERENCES

Becker, Brian E., Mark A. Huselid, and Dave Ulrich. *The HR Scorecard: Linking People, Strategy, and Performance.* Boston: Harvard Business School Press, 2001.

Brown, Mark Graham. *Keeping Score.* New York: Quality Resources, 1996.

Brown, Mark Graham. *Winning Score.* Portland, OR: Productivity, Inc., 2000.

Kaplan, Robert S., and David P. Norton. *The Balanced Scorecard.* Boston: Harvard Business School Press, 1996.

FURTHER READING

Hubbard, Edward E. *The Diversity Scorecard Fieldbook.* Petaluma, CA: Global Insights, 2003.

Hubbard, Edward E. *Diversity Scorecard Stat Pak Software Series.* Petaluma, CA: Global Insights, 2003.

PART IV

Implementation Issues

CHAPTER 15

Achieving Strategic Alignment from Top to Bottom

CREATING A STRATEGIC LINK

Linking and aligning the organization's strategic business objectives with the diversity process is critical to the success of the effort. Diversity and inclusion-building processes are not created for their own sake. These processes are built to support, and where appropriate, lead the organization to achieve its vision and strategy. This diversity alignment must be built in concert with the organization's vision and strategy such that the top and bottom of the organization recognizes its roles, responsibilities, and accountabilities for action. For example, senior management roles, responsibilities, and accountabilities might include the following (adapted from Baytos, 1995):

Overall Role

Provide diversity leadership and direction in establishing an environment where the full potential of all employees can be utilized, in support of organizational objectives, without regard to ethnic, gender, racial, and other characteristics.

Establishing Vision and Strategies

- ☐ Include diversity commentary as part of the organization's mission and strategy statements.
- ☐ Co-create the diversity scorecard and cascade its application to all business units.

☐ Be clear in articulating what needs to be changed; don't be a guardian of the status quo.

☐ Develop a sound business rationale for allocating resources to diversity initiatives, identifying with clarity the potential adverse consequences of inaction.

☐ Provide for linkage of diversity activities with other ongoing initiatives in the organization, such as market share improvement, restructuring, leadership development, operational process improvement, and so on.

Allocating Resources

☐ Allocate sufficient budgets to sustain needed activities during both good and weak years of fiscal performance.

☐ Provide for the appropriate staffing to move the diversity process forward to implemented programs.

☐ Appoint senior executives to participate in task forces and other high-visibility activities.

Establishing Accountability

☐ Work with senior managers to establish challenging but realistic goals for diversity interventions and measurable results using the diversity scorecard.

☐ Monitor the progress against objectives and include information on results in operational reports.

☐ Provide appropriate financial or non-financial recognition of diversity progress, or withhold recognition and rewards when progress is disappointing.

Modeling Diversity Leadership Behavior

☐ Participate in diversity education and planning.

☐ Complete a self-assessment of personal biases and preferences that might impede effectiveness in leading the diversity process.

☐ Demonstrate a firm commitment in the face of backlash that might be stirred up by the diversity process.

☐ Avoid becoming personally defensive about feedback identifying current problems, focusing energies instead on developing solutions.

Putting Principles into Practice

☐ Implement the diversity scorecard perspective initiatives and work to integrate their use in the organization's business processes.

☐ Create diverse work teams to address meaningful issues.

☐ Question homogeneity in any organizational activity or at any level of the organization.

☐ Set policy against organization-sponsored memberships for executives in discriminatory clubs.

☐ Reinforce the diversity message in communications of all types, making it a normal part of doing business.

☐ Incorporate diversity into succession planning processes.

☐ Develop a personal understanding of the issues, through reading, training and contacts; use the knowledge to support changes in culture, systems and policies.

These are just a few examples of the roles, responsibilities, and accountabilities that should be in place to forge organizational alignment.

Implementing the organization's vision and strategy begins with educating and involving the people who must execute it. Some organizations hold their strategy secret, shared only among the senior executive group. The group implements the strategy through central command and control. While this approach was widely used by senior executives for much of the twentieth century, most executives of today's global, technology- and customer-driven organizations realize that they cannot determine and communicate all of the local actions required to implement a successful strategy. Organizations that wish to have every employee contribute to the implementation of the strategy must share their long-term vision and strategy, which is embodied in the business unit's organizational and diversity scorecards, with their employees, and will actively encourage them to suggest ways by which the vision and strategy can be achieved. Such feedback and advice engages employees in the future of the organization and encourages them to be part of the formulation and implementation of its strategy (Kaplan and Norton, 1996).

In an ideal world, every person in the organization, from the boardroom to the back room, would understand the diversity strategy and how his or her individual actions support the big picture. The diversity scorecard creates this top-to-bottom alignment. Development of the diversity scorecard should begin with the executive team and the Chief Diversity Officer as part of that team. Executive team building and commitment are an essential part of gaining benefits from the diversity scorecard, but they are only the first step. To gain maximum benefit, the executive team should share its vision and strategy for diversity with the whole organization and with key outside constituents. By communicating the strategy and by linking it to personal goals, the diversity scorecard creates a shared understanding and commitment among all organizational participants. When everyone understands the business unit's long-term goals involving and integrating diversity, as well as the strategy for achieving these goals, all organizational efforts and initiatives can become aligned with the needed transformation processes. Individuals can see how their particular actions contribute to achieving business unit objectives (Kaplan and Norton, 1996).

The alignment of an organization to a shared diversity vision and common direction is an extended and complex process. Some organizations have eventually involved large numbers of their employees in the alignment process. No single program or event can align this many people. Instead, these large organizations use several interrelated mechanisms to translate the strategy and the diversity scorecard into local objectives and measures that will influence personal and team priorities. Kaplan and Norton cite three distinct mechanisms that can be used:

1. *Communication and Education Programs.* A prerequisite for implementing strategy is that all employees, senior corporate executives, and the board of directors understand the diversity strategy and the required behavior to achieve the strategic diversity objectives. A consistent and continuing program to educate the organization on the components of the strategy, as well as reinforcing this education with feedback on actual performance, is the foundation of organizational alignment.

2. *Goal-Setting Programs.* Once a base level of understanding exists, individuals and teams throughout the business unit must translate the higher-level strategic diversity objectives into personal and team objectives. The traditional management-by-objectives (MBO) programs used by most organizations should be linked to the objectives and measures articulated in the diversity scorecard.

3. *Reward System Linkage.* Alignment of the organization toward the diversity strategy must ultimately be motivated through the incentive and reward systems. Although this linkage should be approached carefully, and only after the education and communication programs are in place, many organizations are already benefiting from linking incentive compensation systems to their diversity scorecards. Typical objectives for linking the diversity

strategy to incentives include the following:

☐ Motivate outstanding performance to achieve the strategic, financial, diversity climate, and operational goals of the organization.

☐ Provide key managers an opportunity to directly share in the benefits of outstanding diversity climate, operating and financial performance.

☐ Provide focus on particular areas of organizational concern and reward performance in those areas.

Strategic alignment of an organization and its business unit must take place in multiple directions. The obvious need is to achieve downward alignment to the employee base. This process, frequently referred to as *cascading*, is the most complex because of the sheer numbers and logistics involved. Frequently overlooked is the need for upward alignment, to corporate boards and shareholders. Both types of alignment are critical.

COMMUNICATION AND EDUCATION PROGRAMS

Communication to employees about an organization's diversity vision and strategy should be viewed as an internal marketing campaign. The goals of such a campaign are identical to those of traditional marketing campaigns: to create awareness and to affect behavior. The communication of the diversity scorecard should increase each individual's understanding of the organization's diversity strategy and enhance motivation for acting to achieve strategic diversity objectives.

A business unit implementing a diversity scorecard can have thousands of employees. A communication program to this many people requires a sustained, comprehensive plan. Some organizations, however, treat the diversity scorecard as a one-time event. Having just spent several months developing the scorecard and achieving a shared consensus among the senior management group, they rush to share their new insight with all of their employees. But they never follow up the initial publicity splash, and the employees treat the announcement as just another program-of-the-month that can be safely shelved and eventually ignored.

The organizational communication and education program should be not only comprehensive but also periodic. Multiple communication devices can be used to launch the balanced diversity scorecard program: executive announcements, videos, town meetings, brochures, and newsletters. These initial announcements should then be followed up continually, by reporting scorecard measures and outcomes on bulletin boards, newsletters, groupware, and electronic networks.

Several vehicles can be used to communicate the organization's diversity vision and strategies. Using a brochure, for example, instead of a statement of broad, general themes, can describe the specific measures the executives will use to monitor the success of their strategy. The brochure should be updated periodically to report trends and current performance along each of the specific goals and to describe the initiatives the organization is using to accomplish its goals. In general, organizations are encouraged to communicate the objectives, measures, and targets embodied in the unit's diversity scorecard by distributing these brochures throughout the organization.

Many organizations use organizational newsletters to embed the diversity scorecard in their ongoing communication programs with employees. The newsletter may begin by devoting a section of each monthly newsletter to the diversity scorecard information. Initially, this section would be used to educate and motivate employees. After communicating the purpose and content of the scorecard in the first few issues, the section can be shifted from education to feedback. Each issue could report recent results on the measures for one perspective. Raw numbers and trends could be supplemented with stories on how a department or an individual was contributing to the reported performance. The vignettes would communicate to the workforce how individuals and teams were using local diversity initiatives to help the organization implement its business and diversity strategies (Kaplan and Norton, 1996).

Some organizations, however, have deliberately chosen not to communicate the diversity scorecard, as such, to their employees. These organizations believe that their employees have been bombarded, in recent times, with all manner of vision and change programs, and that the employees have become cynical and insulated to high-level pronouncements about the latest management focus that is sure to swiftly transform the organization to breakthrough performance. In order to overcome individual resistance to these types of programs, the diversity implementation team will use the newsletters to disseminate the broad themes of the diversity scorecard without specifically labeling or naming this new organizational initiative. That is, executives and the implementation team, for example, will talk about the attributes that the organization wishes to deliver to key ethnic customers, but do not label them as the "value propositions for targeted customers." Having stressed the importance of satisfying specific preferences of customers in key ethnic markets, the communication program then emphasizes the processes and metrics that are most important for the organization to excel.

Electronic networks and groupware, like Hubbard & Hubbard Inc.'s MetricLINK system (network version), provide additional opportunities for organizations to communicate and gain commitment to diversity scorecard objectives. Organizations can post a complete set of diversity scorecard objectives and measures using MetricLINK's electronic metrics relationship tree and provide key strategies, tactics, and action plans in its strategic planning subsystem. Using other media, the diversity scorecard presentation can be enhanced to create a comprehensive communications package. With MetricLINK, actual results and trends of past performance on each diversity scorecard measure can be updated and displayed monthly, quarterly, semi-annually, and so on. To be effective, all of these tools must be woven together into a comprehensive communication effort that is directed at achieving strategic alignment over the long term. The design of such a program should begin by answering several fundamental questions:

- ☐ What are the objectives of the communication strategy?
- ☐ Who are the target audiences?
- ☐ What is the key message for each audience?
- ☐ What are the appropriate media for each audience?
- ☐ What is the timeframe for each stage of the communication strategy?
- ☐ How will we know that the communication has been received?

COMMUNICATING WITH THE BOARD OF DIRECTORS AND EXTERNAL SHAREHOLDERS

The diversity scorecard should be communicated upward in an organization to the top and the organization's board of directors or top-level governance body (if it exist). Conventional rhetoric declares that a principal responsibility of the board or top-level governance body is to provide oversight of organizational, agency, and/or business unit strategy. In practice, however, organizational boards spend more time reviewing and analyzing quarterly financial results than engaging in detailed strategic reviews and analysis. When the primary communication between senior executives and its outside board of directors consists of short-term financial measures, it is not surprising that meetings focus more on short-term operational results than on long-term strategic vision. Several experts argue that boards of directors must play a more active role in monitoring organizational strategy and corporate performance, which includes diversity performance.

The diversity scorecard can and should be the mechanism by which senior executives present their organizational and business unit diversity strategies to the board of directors. This communication not only informs the board in specific terms that long-term diversity strategies designed for competitive success are in place, but it also provides the basis for feedback and accountability to the board.

REWARD SYSTEMS LINKAGE

A major question that is faced by all organizations is whether and how to link their formal compensation system to the diversity scorecard measures. Currently, organizations are following different strategies in how soon they link their compensation system to diversity measures. Ultimately, for the diversity scorecard to create cultural change, incentive compensation must be connected to achievement of scorecard objectives. The issue is not whether, but when and how, the connection should be made. Because financial compensation is such a powerful lever, some organizations want to tie their compensation policy for senior managers to the diversity scorecard measures as soon as possible.

As seen in Table 15-1, some organizations use an incentive system for diversity that supports its evolution from activity-based measures in its scorecard to results-based measures.

This transitional model illustrates how an executive, supervisory, and management accountability system can be created to transition the organization toward performance and incentive-based diversity metrics focused on results. It shows that as time passes, executives, managers, and supervisors gain increasing responsibility for diversity results rather than completing diversity activities.

This should not suggest that organizations focus only on results. It is also important to examine the process by which the results are attained. Activity-based and process-based measures help build awareness and strategies to accomplish diversity goals while the scorecard's results-based measures lay the foundation for accepting responsibility for performance. This process helps generate the guidelines for rewards and incentives.

One CEO expressed his pleasure with the results from this plan: "Our organization is aligned with its strategy. I know of no competitor

Table 15-1. Incentive System for Diversity

Year	Activity-Based Measures	Results-Based Measures
Bonus Percentages by Period:	Requires managers to attend courses on diversity and to be active in diverse and/or multicultural workforce activities and events	Involves meeting the qualitative and quantitative metrics, ratios, and goals for hiring rates, training, promotion, succession planning, ethnic market share, process improvement, innovation, etc.
	Requirements:	**Requirements:**
Year 1	100% of Bonus Percentage	0% of Bonus Percentage
Year 2	75%	25%
Year 3	50%	50%
Year 4	25%	75%
Year 5	0%	100%

Note: This accountability system is developmental. Rewards can be given through informal or formal channels (depending on the culture), resulting in higher visibility and more incentives for those who participate actively in the diversity process and achieve its scorecard target objectives.

Source: Edward E. Hubbard. *Measuring Diversity Results*. Petaluma, CA: Global Insights, 1997.

that has this degree of alignment. It is producing results for us." Obviously, tying incentive compensation to your diversity scorecard measures is attractive, but it has some risks. Are the right measures on the scorecard? Are the data for the selected measures reliable? Could there be unintended or unexpected consequences in how the targets for the measures are achieved? The disadvantages occur when the initial diversity scorecard measures are not perfect surrogates for the strategic objectives, and when the actions that improve the short-term measured results may be inconsistent with achieving the long-term objectives. This highlights the importance of having a diversity measurement professional available to help the implementation team make key metric selections to include in the scorecard. Specialized professional diversity measurement resources are available through Hubbard & Hubbard, Inc. and the HDM&P Institute to assist in these processes.

In several organizations, the clear articulation in a diversity scorecard of business unit strategic diversity objectives, with links to associated performance drivers, has enabled many individuals to see, often for the first time, the links between what they do and the organization's long-term diversity objectives. Rather than behaving on automatic pilot, with bonuses tied to achieving or exceeding targets in the performance of their local tasks without regard to their diversity implications, individuals can now identify the tasks they should be doing exceptionally well to help achieve the organization's diversity and other objectives. This articulation of how individual tasks align with overall business unit diversity objectives creates intrinsic motivation among employees. Their innovation and problem-solving energies can become unleashed, even without explicit ties to compensation incentives.

Of course, because extrinsic motivation remains important, and if the organization begins to achieve breakthrough performance by meeting or exceeding the stretch targets for its strategic diversity measures, the employees who made such performance happen should be recognized and rewarded. Experimenting and monitoring changes will provide additional evidence on the appropriate balance between explicit, objective formulas and subjective evaluation for linking incentive compensation to achievement of diversity scorecard objectives.

FINAL THOUGHTS

Formulating a diversity scorecard that links a business unit's mission and strategy to explicit diversity objectives and measures is only the start of using the diversity scorecard as a management system. The diversity scorecard must be communicated to a variety of organizational constituents, especially employees, corporate-level managers, and boards of directors. The goal of the communication process is to align all employees within the organization, as well as individuals to whom the business unit is accountable (corporate executives and the board), to the diversity and business strategy. The knowledge and alignment among these constituents will facilitate local goal setting, feedback, and accountability to the strategic business unit's strategic path in utilizing diversity.

Alignment and accountability will clearly be enhanced when individual contributions to achieving diversity scorecard objectives are linked to recognition, promotion, and compensation programs. It sends the appropriate message that utilization of diverse human and other resources is in alignment with exceptional business excellence and performance!

REFERENCES

Baytos, Lawrence M. *Designing & Implementing Successful Diversity Programs.* Englewood Cliffs, NJ: Prentice Hall, 1995.

Becker, Brian E., Mark A. Huselid, and Dave Ulrich. *The HR Scorecard: Linking People, Strategy, and Performance.* Boston: Harvard Business School Press, 2001.

Brown, Mark Graham. *Keeping Score.* New York: Quality Resources, 1996.

Brown, Mark Graham. *Winning Score.* Portland, OR: Productivity, Inc., 2000.

Hubbard, Edward E. *Measuring Diversity Results.* Petaluma, CA: Global Insights, 1997.

Kaplan, Robert S., and David P. Norton. *The Balanced Scorecard.* Boston: Harvard Business School Press, 1996.

FURTHER READING

Daniels, Aubrey. *Bringing Out the Best in People: How to Apply the Astonishing Power of Positive Reinforcement.* New York: McGraw-Hill, 1994.

Drucker, Peter F. "The Information Executives Truly Need." *Harvard Business Review,* January/February, pp 22-31, 1995.

Eccles, Robert G. "The Performance Measurement Manifesto." *Harvard Business Review,* January/February, pp 42-49, 1991.

Hubbard, Edward E. *How to Calculate Diversity Return on Investment.* Petaluma, CA: Global Insights, 1999.

Hubbard, Edward E. *The Diversity Scorecard Fieldbook.* Petaluma, CA: Global Insights, 2003.

Implementing the Diversity Scorecard Process

STRATEGIES FOR IMPLEMENTING YOUR DIVERSITY SCORECARD

Developing a diversity scorecard and actually implementing one are two different things. It requires a planned, strategic approach that involves all levels within the organization. This chapter explains how to build the acceptance element of your diversity scorecard (i.e., how to be disciplined in applying lessons of change management to the implementation of the diversity scorecard you develop). It serves less as a roadmap to what is on the scorecard and more as a guide to implementing the scorecard.

Diversity is not a program; it is a process of systemic organizational change. Nobody will ever be "finished with diversity." There will always be people with differences and situations in the workplace that require a polyocular view for resolution and performance. Because diversity process and the scorecard that drives its results involve change (both personal and organizational change), those implementing the diversity scorecard process must be change masters. Change involves exchange: In order to get something, you must give up something. In many cases, the diversity scorecard process requires that people in the organization give up old notions of what diversity is all about and begin to view it in the business and performance context that makes it a competitive advantage. Having a *high-quality* diversity scorecard is not enough to ensure success. Without *acceptance*, this diversity scorecard change effort might begin with enthusiasm and excitement but will quickly fizzle out.

PERMANENT WHITE WATER

Today, organizational change is so constant that Peter Vaill created the metaphor *permanent white water* to describe the state of change in organizational life. If you have ever gone white-water rafting, you know what it takes to handle the white-water environment competently. First, no one does it alone; you are always part of a team. Second, the team always has a leader, although leadership can shift. The leader's job is to keep his or her eye on the course, to look for obstacles, and to think strategically before giving directions. Cooperation is necessary in white water. Balance is critical. These same skills are essential in the white-water environment of diversity measurement and management. Fierce competition has forced organizations to rethink previously sacred approaches and to accept rapid, geometrically complex change as part and parcel of the everyday organizing process that is, ultimately, essential to survival (Hubbard, 1994).

Today, we face an increasingly pressing challenge to success: the need to manage organizational change and to improve organizational and product quality. In recent years, a great deal of literature has been written focusing on the need to plan for a changing environment. In fact, some organizations have created entire organizational units whose mission is to examine the process and quality of change and to plan effective responses for the future. The goal of these units is to create a systematic method for dealing with change through formalized procedures and processes that not only anticipate changes in the structure, technology, and personnel of the organization, but also implement them. Implementing a diversity scorecard is critical among these tasks.

Change is a universal aspect of doing business. No business enterprise is exempt, regardless of its structure. Nevertheless, although change often presents a threat to survival, it also frequently offers unprecedented opportunity for growth, expansion, and learning. Today's managers and employees face the challenge of creating an organizational structure that is capable of remaining current, flexible, and viable to meet the needs of a diverse workforce and customer base, while remaining focused to contribute to the efficient and effective achievement of the organization's objectives. Meeting this challenge requires an approach that addresses both the structural and psychological dynamics of change as you implement the diversity scorecard.

CHANGE AS A PARADOX

Organizational change is a process, not an event. Internal and external pressures exerted on the organization cause it. Paradoxically, a business's success depends on its ability to remain stable while managing a complex, evolving series of changes. Change without order and order without change can be equally crippling. To be effective, an organization must be anchored in the past, yet immediately responsive and adaptable to a paradigm-busting future in which success is written at its edge. Thus, new-generation employees are hired while older employees retire, move on, or come back again. Established products are discontinued while new diversity-friendly products are introduced. Old markets expire while new diverse customer markets emerge and are rapidly exploited.

The amount, direction, and speed of change may vary, but change over time is an inherent aspect of all businesses. Therefore, there is a clear need to understand change and know how to introduce the diversity change process in a manner consistent with a business's objectives and with the needs of its employees. What is known with certainty is that coping with and mastering change are acknowledged needs of the present and the future.

ANALYZING READINESS FOR CHANGE

In order to create an effective diversity scorecard change process, it is essential to analyze the need for this change and the organization's readiness for the change. A simple formula for examining the dynamics of employee resistance and the organization's readiness for the diversity process change is as follows:

$$C = P(SV)D > R$$

Where

C = Change
P = Practical first steps
SV = Shared vision for the diversity future state
D = Dissatisfaction with current state
R = Resistance

Translated, this formula suggests that in order to manage a diversity change effort successfully, a concrete plan to get to the diversity change state, a clear, shared vision of the diversity future state, and the level of dissatisfaction in the system of the current organizational state must combine to be greater than employee resistance to change in order for the diversity change effort to have a chance at success. It suggests that a shared diversity vision and practical first steps are key elements to build along with selling the need to change (a component of which includes developing a measurement-based diversity business case).

We must keep in mind that employee resistance to change is natural and common. It is unrealistic to think otherwise. In fact, some resistance is healthy for the organization. It allows the organization to challenge itself regarding the need for change by answering employee questions and responses. Employee resistance prompts the organization to take a good, hard look at the circumstances that make the change necessary and puts pressure on the agents of change to clearly inform employees and build commitment. Instead of balking at resistance, the diversity change agent should anticipate it and see it as a normal reaction to organizational change and not necessarily an affront on the diversity effort per se (unfortunately, some contingents in the organization be exceptions to this perspective) (Hubbard, 1994).

Many Change Efforts Miss the Mark

Most efforts at change fall short of their goals. As Peter Senge and his colleagues report, many of their efforts to create learning organizations did not accomplish the intended results! Ron Ashkenas writes that only 25 to 30 percent of change efforts actually succeed (Senge et al., 1999; Ashkenas, 1994). James Champy shares similar findings about his work on reengineering, reporting success rates of about 25 to 33 percent. Clearly, interventions—no matter how well intentioned and carefully thought out—are far more difficult to put into action than we may think. Likewise, many companies believe diversity measurement matters and genuinely want to create and use a diversity scorecard. These companies often express enormous initial interest in this approach, conduct a workshop or two about how to use diversity scorecards, begin to sort out which diversity measures matter most, and track them once or twice. Soon, however, they discover that the commitment to the diversity measurement work was more rhetoric and hope than reality and action. In most cases, the technical aspect of the diversity scorecard is manageable. Executives can identify the right measures and create indices to assess them. But high-quality *thinking* about the diversity scorecard as a change process never occurs. These companies fail to apply change management lessons to their implementation of the scorecard.

The trouble with implementing change comes not from misunderstanding *what* to do, but from a lack of discipline about *how* to do what needs doing. Becker, Huselid, and Ulrich (2001) found a set of seven keys and processes to make change happen that have convergent validity in that they are consistent with the research on other change models (see Table 16-1). They also have face validity in that managers in organizations have confirmed that these factors help make change happen. Finally, the factors also have deployment validity. They have been used in their present or adapted form for thousands of change projects at hundreds of companies.

The seven factors in the table have been applied in multiple settings and thus offer some general lessons for successful implementation of a diversity scorecard. First, the organization must attend to all seven factors in order for the diversity scorecard to succeed. The process of initiating and sustaining the diversity scorecard may be iterative (i.e., you may need to cycle back through some of the earlier steps several times), but, in general, the process unfolds in the sequence shown in the table.

Second, you can use these factors to create a profile of your organization's present capacity for change on any given project, not just the diversity scorecard. You can generate this profile by scoring the extent to which each of the seven factors exists, using a range of 0 through 100, and plotting those scores as shown in Figure 16-1.

It is recommend that diversity change leaders routinely assess the progress they are making on each of the dimensions of the change process using a simple profiling system such as the one illustrated in Figure 16-1. During the planning phase, the profile could be used to inventory the strengths and weaknesses of your organization's *current* change process. When you consider past change efforts, where has the company been particularly effective and where have those efforts fallen short? This will give you a chance to concentrate on those areas where support and development are required.

The experience reflected in Figure 16-1 is probably typical of many organizations. For example, there is a reasonably enthusiastic cadre of change leaders, but they are only modestly successful at creating a shared sense of urgency around the need for change and communicating a coherent diversity vision of the future if the change is successful. The change leaders understand the need for change and what the future might look like, but they have not been effective at articulating that diversity vision to the rest of the organization. Because the foundational elements are not as effective as they should be, the rest of the change process is undermined. It is difficult to mobilize commitment to a diversity change effort outside the

Table 16-1. Keys and Processes for Making Change Happen

Key Success Factors for Change	Questions for Assessing and Accomplishing Change
1. *Leading change* (who *is responsible*)	Do we have a leader … ☐ who owns and champions the change? ☐ who demonstrates public commitment to making it happen? ☐ who will garner resources to sustain it? ☐ who will invest personal time and attention to following it through?
2. *Creating a shared need* (why *do it*)	Do employees … ☐ see the reason for the change? ☐ understand why the change is important? ☐ see how it will help them and/or the business in the short and long term?
3. *Shaping a vision* (what *will it look like when we are done*)	Do employees … ☐ see the outcomes of the change in behavioral terms (i.e., what they will do differently as a result of the change)? ☐ get excited about these outcomes? ☐ understand how the change will benefit customers and other stakeholders?
4. *Mobilizing commitment* (who else *needs to be involved*)	Do the sponsors of the change … ☐ recognize who else needs to be committed to the change for it to happen? ☐ know how to build a coalition of support for the change? ☐ have the ability to enlist the support of key individuals in the organization? ☐ have the ability to build a responsibility matrix to make the change happen?
5. *Building enabling systems* (how *will it be institutionalized*)	Do the sponsors of the change … ☐ understand how to sustain the change through modifying HR systems (e.g., staffing, training, appraisal, rewards, structure, communication)? ☐ recognize the technology investment required to implement the change? ☐ have access to financial resources to sustain the change?
6. *Monitoring and demonstrating progress* (how *will it be measured*)	Do the sponsors of the change … ☐ have a means of measuring the success of the change? ☐ plan to benchmark progress on both the results of the change and the implementation process?
7. *Making it last* (how *will it be initiated and sustained*)	Do the sponsors of the change … ☐ recognize the first steps needed to get started? ☐ have a short- and long-term plan to keep attention focused on the change? ☐ have a plan for adapting the change over time to shifting circumstances?

Source: Brian E. Becker, Mark A. Huselid, and Dave Ulrich. *The HR Scorecard: Linking People, Strategy, and Performance.* Boston: Harvard Business School Press, 2001.

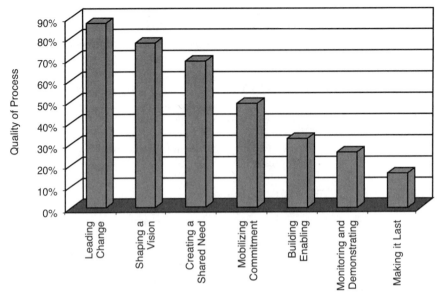

Figure 16-1. Quality of our change process by dimension.
(Source: Adapted from Becker, B., M. Huselid, and D. Ulrich. The HR
Scorecard. *Boston, MA: Harvard Business School Press, 2001.)*

core group because the message for the diversity change has not been persuasive (i.e., a measurable business case with compelling evidence has not
been presented). As a result, there is little support for changing other institutional levers, such as reward systems, that will reinforce and provide
momentum for the diversity change. Not surprisingly, there are no early
successes to demonstrate progress, especially since no diversity scorecard
is in place, and ultimately the diversity change effort never really takes
hold and it becomes just another "flavor of the month." Diversity change
sponsors should be prepared to answer the questions in Table 16-2.

As change becomes more complex, it requires holistic, systematic,
process-oriented approaches. Many who are affected by the varied faces
of the diversity change process feel that it is the one element that keeps the
organization in a constant state of flux because many people are still trying to grapple with the changes that are occurring on a global scale. This
is not accurate. It is not the changes themselves that disrupt organizations,
it is the transitions.

Change is not the same as transition. *Change* is situational. It may
involve a new selling location in another country, new boss of a gender

Table 16-2. Guidelines for Implementing a Diversity Scorecard

Change Checklist Items	Guiding Questions for Change Sponsors
1. *Leading change* (who *is responsible*)	Who is in charge of the effort? Who sponsors? Who champions?
2. *Creating a shared need* (why *do it*)	Why develop the diversity scorecard? How does it fit with our business?
3. *Shaping a vision* (what *will it look like when we are done*)	What is the desired outcome of the scorecard?
4. *Mobilizing commitment* (who else *needs to be involved*)	Who needs to support the project?
5. *Building enabling systems* (how *will it be institutionalized*)	How do we build systems to sustain the change?
6. *Monitoring and demonstrating progress* (how *will it be measured*)	What will we use to track the implementation process?
7. *Making it last* (how *will it be initiated and sustained*)	How will we sustain the effort?

different than the last, new diverse work team, new roles, or new policy such as domestic partner benefits. *Transition*, however, is the psychological process people go through to come to terms with the new situation. Change is external. Transition is internal. Unless an effective, systematic, psychological transition occurs, we can almost guarantee that the structural change to a new diversity scorecard measurement and management system will not work. Therefore, it is critical that we view the diversity scorecard implementation change in a holistic way.

What's the Difference?

According to the *American Heritage Dictionary*, the definition of the terms *change* and *transition* are as follows:

> change—l.a. To cause to be different; alter. b. To give or receive form or appearance to; transform. 2. To give and receive reciprocally; interchange. 3. To exchange for or replace

by another, usually of the same kind or category. 4. To lay aside, abandon, or leave for another; switch. 5. To go from one phase to another.
transition—l. The process of changing from one form, state, activity, or place to another.
2. The passage from one subject to another.

What becomes apparent immediately is that the definition of *change* implies an instant substitution of one thing for another; however, the definition of a *transition* suggests involvement in the journey, passage, or process of moving from one state, form, place, or activity to another. This difference is critical to our understanding of the diversity change process this move to the diversity scorecard may represent to others, and, more important, the process of transitioning they will need to undergo to achieve the change state of a diverse, inclusive environment driven by the diversity scorecard metrics.

It is essential to understand that it is not the changes that do you in, it is the transitions. If the transition is not effective, the change will not work. Transition is not a gradual or incomplete change. In change, focus is on the outcome the change will produce (i.e., the end result). Transition is different. The starting point for transition is not the outcome, but the ending you must make to leave behind the old situation (such as becoming aware or sensing the personal impact of a changed workplace after a workforce demographics shift). Using your own experience, think of any big change that may have occurred in your life: your marriage, your first managerial job, your first car, your first plane flight, or your first house. Perhaps each represented a good change, but as transitions, each began with an ending.

In your new managerial job, for example, you may have had to let go of the old peer group you used to hang out with. They were no longer your peers. Your new peer group may include people from races and backgrounds you have not had exposure to. The kind of work you really liked may have come to an end. Perhaps you had to give up the feeling of competence that came from doing the work. As manager, you now were required to get things done through others. You may have had to come to terms with your habit of leaving work at the office, when you began to take some of it home or work late to finish it. These represent endings that began your psychological transition. Given today's organizational requirements and changing marketplace, great demands have been placed on organizations to deal with the need for rapid and sometimes radically different changes. Unfortunately, many organizations have dealt only with the need for change and have neglected an effective transition to accompany that change.

This can be seen when organizations announce on Friday that a major organizational (structural) change will take place on Monday of the following week. This is often done with no general employee discussion or involvement in the decision. Yet, on Monday, it is expected that the new organization will be up and running in its new form without a hitch. Unfortunately, in many cases, it is believed that employees only need to be given a general reason for the change and they will comply.

This places a tremendous burden on the employees to transition over the weekend, to come to grips with the flood of behavioral ramifications this change may and will suggest, such as acceptance in a new work group, competence to handle new responsibilities, perceived personal value for contributions made in the past being reflected in their new role, and so on. For some, feelings that may have developed over a series of years must suddenly be reconciled because of the new mode of operation. Others may feel thrown for another loop and placed in turmoil because they still had not gotten over the last change the organization announced (which was implemented the same way).

Change handled without a psychological transition plan can cause havoc within an organization and destroy expected benefits. Change is often defined as setting something aside, abandoning or leaving something else for another. It can mean pulling a sudden switch on the employee without involvement regarding process or transition. This can build immediate resistance to the diversity scorecard change and could have been largely avoided.

Building transition processes offers the best opportunity for long-lasting, effective change. Handling the psychological aspect of an impending change through transition allows endings to take place, adjustments to be made, and commitment toward the new beginning to be built. Effective transition depends on letting go of the old reality and the old identity (e.g., having a workplace environment or customer base that is not diverse). Transitions must start with effective endings.

To some people, change is a defense-provoking word; to others it represents a panacea. Change is often presented as a zero-sum, all-or-nothing game that ceases to exist if employees do not immediately convert their behavior and make changes. None of these views, of course, is effective because organizations and individuals require a reasoned, commitment-inducing approach for their involvement.

Effective communication about the diversity scorecard can make or break a transition strategy. The greatest benefit of good communications is obtained if it is done early, when the change to a diversity scorecard is being considered. Therefore, the most important communication planning is done before implementation. It is critical to pay attention not only to what (and how much) is communicated, but how communication is carried out as a process. Timeliness and credibility go hand-in-hand at this stage. The first step is to build commitment.

Building commitment to the diversity vision of the future through the use of the diversity scorecard must be a shared process from the beginning, not at the middle or end of the change process. A simple formula for accomplishing this is:

$$C = G(P)$$

Where

C = Commitment
G = Goals
P = Possibilities

This formula suggests that the organization can build commitment by helping employees see a specific diversity goal and asking them to generate possibilities for themselves or giving them reasons why the diversity change will respond to the organization's and/or the customer's needs.

It is unproductive to institute a diversity scorecard process or any major change without foreseeing how many employees will experience this move for improvement as a loss of something they value. The result of this neglect is to waste valuable resources and to negatively affect internal and external customers at all levels. Every diversity sponsor or agent responsible for the diversity change process must be aware that either a hint or a full-blown announcement of the diversity scorecard change immediately affects an individual's value system internally. This impact must be thoughtfully and effectively handled.

BUILDING A RATIONALE FOR CHANGE

Change is more likely to happen when a clear reason for it exists. Moreover, the reason for the change has to carry more weight than any resistance to the change. The reason for a change may be related to danger ("we're in trouble if we don't change") or opportunity ("good things will happen if we do change"). Any change effort also offers both short- and long-term impact. It is important to share the reasons for change with those who will be affected.

Creating a shared need for a diversity scorecard requires understanding the importance of diversity measures and how these metrics support the business's strategy implementation. Investing in diversity measurement because other companies are doing it or because it is popular will not make the scorecard sustainable. This book supports a unifying theme that diversity measurement must be linked to business results. The diversity scorecard champion should thus be able to articulate the potential outcomes of investment in the initiative. These outcomes might include better allocation of time and money spent on diversity, a higher probability of implementing the organization's overall strategy, more productive and committed employees, a more competitive organization, and increased shareholder value (Becker, Huselid, and Ulrich, 2001).

Sometimes, pointing to the need for a diversity scorecard means asking, "How do we know if we've done a good job in diversity?" Without a scorecard, this question often prompts vague answers based on the respondents' personal experience and assumptions about what "good" means. A diversity scorecard gives context and concreteness to these assumptions and personal perceptions, and anchors them in hard data. In clarifying the need to invest in a diversity scorecard, champions should avoid some common pitfalls that will create resistance to it.

Scorecard champions may also face potential resistance from diversity professionals themselves. As in any other function, some of these individuals do not want their performance measured. Being in diversity without measurement can be a safe, nonthreatening career. With measurement comes accountability, and some of these employees may lack the confidence or competence to be accountable for the work they perform. A diversity scorecard champion can overcome these employees' resistance through extensive training and investment to ensure that they have the competencies to deliver against higher expectations (Becker, Huselid, and Ulrich, 2001).

For all of these reasons, diversity scorecard champions need to build a cogent business case for initiating and implementing the diversity scorecard. Skillfully crafted, this business rationale will inform line managers, help diversity executives make smart choices, and guide and inspire diversity professionals throughout the organization.

FINAL THOUGHTS

Diversity scorecards are not panaceas. They will not cure a poorly run diversity function. They do, however, provide a means by which you can collect rigorous, predictable, and regular data that will help direct your organization's attention to the most important elements of the diversity change process. Constructed thoughtfully, the diversity scorecard will

help your organization deliver increased value to its employees, customers, and investors. By applying the seven steps suggested in this
chapter, you can integrate the thinking behind the diversity scorecard
into every key aspect of your organization's management.

While much of the work of a diversity scorecard is technical, the
delivery of the scorecard is personal. It requires that diversity professionals desire to make a difference, *align* their work to business strategy,
apply the science of applied diversity measurement research to the art of
building diversity management capability, and *commit* to learning from
constant experimentation. When you create the diversity scorecard using
the approach described in this book, you are actually linking diversity to
the organization's strategic objectives for performance and results.

This book has laid out the theory and tools for crafting a diversity
scorecard. Clearly, no one can become a diversity measurement expert
after reading one book. Diversity measurement is a professional, applied
sciences discipline (like any other field) that requires intensive study,
professional training, application, and certification; however, by using
the ideas and tools presented here, along with the assistance of a certified diversity measurement professional, you can make informed choices
about the proper diversity metrics to use and help enhance diversity's
effectiveness and credibility as a strategic business partner. A business
partner that is clearly at the table, not on it!

REFERENCES

Ashkenas, Ron. "Beyond the Fads: How Leaders Drive Change with Results."
Human Resource Planning 17(2):1994, 25–44.

Becker, Brian E., Mark A. Huselid, and Dave Ulrich. *The HR Scorecard: Linking People, Strategy, and Performance.* Boston: Harvard Business School Press,
2001.

Champy, James. *Reengineering Management: The New Mandate for Leadership.*
New York: Harper Business, 1995.

Hubbard, Edward E. *The Hidden Side of Resistance to Change.* Petaluma, CA:
Global Insights, 1994.

Senge, P.M., A. Kleiner, C. Roberts, R. Ross, G. Rother, and B. Smith. *The Dance
of Change: The Challenges of Sustaining Momentum in Learning Organizations
Currency.* New York: Doubleday, 1999.

APPENDIX A

Hubbard Diversity Measurement and Productivity (DM&P) Institute

Creating Applied Sciences for Measuring Diversity Performance and Results

The Hubbard Diversity Measurement and Productivity Institute provides measurement skills, certification workshops, and applied learning conferences for assessing, measuring, applying, and evaluating diversity results in organizations.

This institute is dedicated to assisting diversity practitioners and other professionals with the tools and techniques to research and develop measurable business case examples for diversity, which clearly demonstrate their impact on bottom-line business objectives in financial terms. Our mission is to provide the most up-to-date measurement tools that diversity professionals need to make effective, timely decisions to create a measurable business impact.

Leading diversity practitioners find our workshops insightful because they transfer current tools and skills, drawn from real-world experiences, and share cutting-edge research. Each workshop complements each other and builds the foundation needed for participants to be an even more successful diversity professional.

PROFESSIONAL DIVERSITY MEASUREMENT SKILL-BUILDING WORKSHOPS

Workshops include topics such as:

- ☐ Diversity Facts, Figures, and Financials: An Executive Overview
- ☐ Measuring Diversity Results
- ☐ Building a Measurable Diversity Strategic Plan
- ☐ How to Calculate Diversity Return-on-Investment
- ☐ Building a Diversity Measurement Scorecard
- ☐ Creating and Implementing a Diversity Culture and Systems Audit
- ☐ How to Construct a Measurable Diversity Business Case
- ☐ Conducting a Cultural Due Diligence Audit
- ☐ Measuring Supplier Diversity Utilization
- ☐ Measuring Diversity Training Return-on-Investment
- ☐ Productivity Measurement for Diverse Work Teams

PROFESSIONAL CERTIFICATION WORKSHOPS

These workshops cover the following certifications and required courses with a diversity return-on-investment (DROI) focus:

Certified Internal Diversity Trainer

- ☐ **Level 1:** *Teaching diversity training, organizational impact skills, and measuring individual behavior*
- ☐ **Level 2:** *Teaching diversity management and leadership skills*

Certified Internal Diversity Advisor

- ☐ **Level 3:** *Developing effective diversity advisory board skills*
- ☐ **Level 4:** *Diversity culture and systems audit processes*

Each year the institute offers a full schedule of measurement skills training and a National Conference on Assessing, Measuring, and Evaluating Diversity Results.

DIVERSITY MEASUREMENT RESEARCH PUBLICATIONS

The institute also publishes research Casebooks and Performance Workbooks on Diversity Measurement and Diversity Management.

AUTOMATED DIVERSITY MEASUREMENT SOFTWARE SYSTEMS AND TOOLS

Sample diversity measurement tools are available from Hubbard & Hubbard, Inc. at www.hubbardNhubbardinc.com.

DIVERSITY SCORECARD AND SURVEY ASSESSMENT SOFTWARE SYSTEMS

- ☐ MetricLINK® Comprehensive Diversity Measurement and Scorecard Software System
- ☐ Diversity Survey Analysis System (SAS)^{tm}
- ☐ Web-based 360 Diversity Assessment Software Systems
- ☐ Diversity Training and Certification Workshops
- ☐ Diversity Metrics Consulting

DIVERSITY MEASUREMENT STAT PAKS^{TM}

- ☐ MDR Stat Pak^{tm}
- ☐ Combo Stat Pak
- ☐ Startup Metrics
- ☐ Diversity Measurement Scorecard Metrics
- ☐ Diversity Forecast & Trend Analysis
- ☐ Diversity Staffing and Retention Measures
- ☐ Supplier Diversity Metrics
- ☐ Calculating Diversity Initiative DROI
- ☐ and much more

Hubbard & Hubbard, Inc.
International Organization and Human Performance Consulting Corporation
World Headquarters
1302 Holm Road
Petaluma, CA 94954
Tel. 707-763-8380
Fax 707-763-3640

Index

About the Author

Edward E. Hubbard, Ph.D.

Edward E. Hubbard, Ph.D., is president and CEO of Hubbard & Hubbard, Inc., Petaluma, California, an international organization and human performance consulting corporation that specializes in techniques for applied business performance improvement, workforce diversity measurement, instructional design, and organizational development.

He is the founder of the Hubbard Diversity Measurement and Productivity Institute and is also author of the groundbreaking books *Measuring Diversity Results, How to Calculate Diversity Return-on-Investment, Pathways to Diversity Metrics for Corporate Legal and Law Firms*, and four soon-to-be-released books: *The Diversity Scorecard, The Diversity Performance Consultant's Fieldbook, Case Studies in Diversity Management and Measurement*, and the *Manager's Pocket Guide to Diversity Management*.

Dr. Hubbard is one of the first metrics authors in the field of diversity. As a result of his extensive research in the area of diversity measurement and expertise in computer programming, he is one of the first to develop automated software technologies for measuring diversity return-on-investment and performance improvements.

He has performed client work in organizational change and diverse workforce integration for private companies, the U.S. government, and corporate clients in the Far East, Europe, and Pacific Rim. His work includes assisting organizations with staff development, quality improvement, and performance improvement strategies, and restructuring work teams to utilize the strengths of a multiethnic workforce and handling diverse work group consolidations using self-directed work team and diversity return-on-investment measures and methods.

Hubbard is an internationally respected business consultant, trainer, former professor and director at Ohio State University, and has held professional positions at several Fortune 100 corporations, such as Computer Systems Analyst, Informatics Corporation; Computer Room Operations Manager, Battelle Memorial Institute; Internal Consultant, Mead Corporation; and Director, Training and Organization Development for the $17 billion McKesson Corporation.

The American Society for Training and Development (ASTD) inducted Hubbard into the prestigious ASTD New Guard for 2003. The New

Guard represents selected "members of the Training and Development profession who are taking themselves and the field in new directions." He is also a member of the ASTD ROI Advisory Board. In addition, Dr. Hubbard received double honors, being named to the prestigious Who's Who in Leading American Executives and Who's Who Worldwide of Global Business Leaders. Memberships are limited to those individuals who have demonstrated outstanding leadership and achievement in their occupation, industry, or profession.

Author of more than 37 books, some of Hubbard's other book titles include *The Hidden Side of Employee Resistance To Change, Managing Customer Service on the Frontline, Managing Your Business For Profitable Growth, Hiring Strategies For Long-Term Success, How To Start Your Own Business With Empty Pockets,* and *Managing Organizational Change: Strategies For Building Commitment.*

Articles by Dr. Hubbard have appeared in magazines and newspapers such as *Inc., Fortune, Cultural Diversity at Work, Next Step Magazine, Forbes, American Society for Training and Development Journal, Sonoma Business Magazine, Organization Development Network Journal, The Cleveland Plain Dealer, The Press Democrat, The Diversity Factor Magazine,* and many others. He has also been featured in several business films and management development videos, on radio programs, and is a regularly featured speaker and keynote for national and international conferences, teleconferences, seminars, and workshops.

Hubbard is an expert in Organizational Behavior, Organizational Analysis, Applied Performance Improvement and Measurement Strategies, Strategic Planning, Diversity Measurement, and Organizational Change Methodologies.

Hubbard earned bachelor's and master's degrees from Ohio State University and earned a Ph.D. with honors in business administration.

He can be reached at Hubbard & Hubbard, Inc., World Headquarters, 1302 Holm Road, Petaluma, CA 94954, Tel. 707-763-8380, Fax 707-763-3640, www.hubbardnhubbardinc.com